GENDERING EUROPEAN HISTORY
1780–1920

Barbara Caine and Glenda Sluga

LEICESTER UNIVERSITY PRESS
London and New York

Leicester University Press
A Cassell Imprint
Wellington House, 125 Strand, London WC2R 0BB
370 Lexington Avenue, New York, NY 10017–6550

First published 2000

British Library Cataloguing in Publication Data
A catalogue record for this book is available from the British Library.
ISBN 0–7185–0131–4 (hardback)
    0–7185–0132–2 (paperback)

Library of Congress Cataloging-in-Publication Data
Caine, Barbara.
    Gendering European history/Barbara Caine & Glenda Sluga.
        p. cm.
    Includes bibliographical references and index.
    ISBN 0–7185–0131–4 (alk. paper). – ISBN 0–7185–0132–2 (pbk. : alk. paper)
    1. Women—Europe—History. 2. Sex role—Europe—History. 3. Sex role—Political aspects—Europe—History. I. Sluga, Glenda, 1962– . II. Title.
HQ1154.C23 2000
305.3'094–dc21   99–28935
                                                                                                              CIP

Typeset by York House Typographic Ltd, London
Printed and bound in Great Britain by Redwood Books, Trowbridge, Wilts

Contents

Introduction

Recognition of the importance of gender as an historical category has begun to transform the writing of European history. Historians are paying increasing attention to the changing cultural meanings of masculinity and femininity, or gender, as central to the history of the formation of states and nations, citizenship and political participation, work and economic activity, home and family life. In the past few years, the French Revolution, industrialisation, the emergence of class-based society, 'new imperialism', the First World War, have all been radically rethought by European historians around the category of gender.

There are a number of excellent case studies of gender in late modern European history, but the overall importance of gender in the making of modern Europe still awaits analysis. This book is one contribution to this wider project. *Gendering European History* covers the period from the French Revolution to the end of the First World War. Rather than attempting a comprehensive social or political history, we have explored the articulation and development of key historical questions about identity, work, home, politics and citizenship generally and in specific national contexts, while providing the reader new to European history with general information about the social and political contexts in which those questions arose. Historians are increasingly emphasising that European history includes more than just events in Britain, France and Germany. We argue that, despite differences in economic, political and social developments across Europe in this period, a number of common themes and patterns pertaining to gender appeared across the metropolitan centres of East and West Europe, and that they became definitive of a 'European' experience. The influence of these themes and patterns operated at intellectual and cultural levels, affecting politics, economics, legislation and the everyday lives of men and women. Susan Bell and Karen Offen have put this view clearly in their introduction to a vast multi-volume collection of documents on nineteenth-century 'Western' women:

> Discussion on women's position, as on related sociopolitical issues such as freedom and slavery, never respected national boundaries. Social criticism originating in the urban centers of France or England crisscrossed the Channel, travelled north via the North

1

and Baltic Seas to the capital and port cities of Scandinavia, Poland, and Russia, and to the seaports of the old Hanseatic League, and quickly sailed west to the Americas. Thus, ideas elaborated in London or Edinburgh rapidly reached a reading public not only in the Low Countries and in New England but in Stockholm, Hamburg, Konigsberg, and St. Petersburg as well.

(Bell and Offen 1983: 7)

Our historical overview does not aim to homogenise the European history of ideas and experiences, but to trace the particular ways in which key questions about gender were raised in specific national contexts, and how they traversed national borders.

We have written these chapters as historical overviews which integrate the history of gender and analyses of the importance of gender into the mainstream history of Europe. Following other feminist historians, we argue that political, social and economic life is shaped by cultural concepts. Historians such as Joan Scott, Joan Landes, Genevieve Fraisse and Lyn Hunt, who have concentrated on the history of gender in the eighteenth and nineteenth centuries, have been able to show that culturally mediated conceptions of gender established the frameworks in which modern politics and modern society took shape. This book is a cultural history on the same model. We focus on the political and social importance of representations of sexual difference and of gender relations. We are particularly interested in gendered ideological and political discourses which shaped the political and social participation of men and women and which, in turn, gendered politics as a masculine domain, and the social as the province of the feminine. Overall, we try to show how changing conceptions of sexual difference and ideals of masculinity and femininity informed the gendered nature of work, public life and political activity throughout the nineteenth century and throughout Europe.

Rather than attempt a comprehensive coverage of social, political or economic developments, in this book we have focused on key episodes or developments in Europe and re-interpreted them by examining the importance of gender. This approach has allowed us to bring together the extensive but often fragmented existing literature on gender in European history in different European nations, and to introduce the key findings of this work within a general comparative framework. In many cases we have tried to compare the conclusions reached by historians dealing with particular national histories. We have also tried to introduce new questions, and new sources, particularly in relation to the growing historical interest in the

overlapping history of gender and nation-building. In the process, we hope
also to have provided a history of gender itself, and of the ways in which
conceptions of masculinity and femininity affected and were changed by
particular political and social developments. We emphasise that this history
does not fit into a simple linear and progressive model of change. Historians
have been able to show that the extent of discussion about gender across
nineteenth-century Europe is itself evidence that conceptions of masculinity
and femininity were changing and subject to continual disagreement. Then
as now, there was no consensus about the implications of sexual difference,
and political and social trends often had contradictory or paradoxical
outcomes. Feminist historians and philosophers have argued that the
Enlightenment produced both the promise of universal rights, and the
redefinition of those rights in gendered and raced terms. The French Revolution is associated with the definition of a new and exclusively masculine
political sphere on the one hand, and the rise of modern feminism with its
emphasis on women's rights and entitlement to full citizenship on the other.
Just as the French Revolution both excluded women from citizenship and
raised the possibility of it, so too liberalism and socialism offered women
new opportunities for participation, and devised ways to exclude them. The
subordination of women is a major theme in nineteenth-century European
history, but we are concerned also to show women's claims to political rights
and the anxieties these provoked. Thus while the growing sense of the
importance of motherhood in defining the nature of women was widely
accepted in France and Britain in the 1790s, and the French Jacobins drew on
conceptions of maternity to reinforce the view that women had no place in
the public sphere, women like Olympe de Gouges and Mary Wollstonecraft
drew on these conceptions of motherhood to articulate a new ideal of female
citizenship. The nineteenth-century political imaginary cannot be understood without recognising the potency of images of female rebellion as well
as male authority and conquest. The examples of the French market women
of 1789, the Vesuviennes of 1848, the *petroleuses* of 1870, had counterparts
in other parts of Europe, in the Belgian revolutionaries of the 1790s, in the
European women who fought campaigns for 'national liberation', in the
German Amazons, and in the life of Mary Wollstonecraft and the campaigns
of the British militant suffragettes.

    The chapters in *Gendering European History* follow a broadly chrono-
logical development, but they also unavoidably cut across each other
thematically. Each chapter begins with a general introduction to the themes
which will be developed, and in some cases provides an overview of ideas or

events that are important for the discussion which follows. The themes of citizenship and sexual difference are traced throughout the book, but Chapter 1 introduces them in the context of the Enlightenment and the French Revolution. Enlightenment ideals of sexual difference and conceptions of the rational and reasoning man and citizen provided the general intellectual backdrop to the political events of the 1790s. During the French Revolution, the category of citizen was closely identified with the attributes of the sexed male body; at the moment which most historians associate with the emergence of the modern state, the idea of female citizenship was constituted as fundamentally problematic. The French Revolution provoked a lasting hostility to women's direct involvement in social and political activity which made it difficult for women to exercise political rights, and which explained and legitimated their economic, legal and sexual subordination and their confinement to the world of family and home under the supervision of a male household head. Chapter 3 surveys the different ideological contexts which framed discussion of the gendered political identities and modes of political agency that emerged out of the Enlightenment and the experiences of the French Revolution – liberalism, socialism, nationalism and feminism – and their culmination in the revolutions of 1848.

Historical disagreement about the general situation of women in the nineteenth century has focused quite intensively on the ideology of separate spheres, which was a manifestation of prevailing ideas of sexual difference. The masculine public sphere incorporated political activity, paid employment and control over public institutions. Its feminine corollary, the private sphere, centred on domestic life and familial responsibilities. But the dimensions of the female sphere kept shifting in the nineteenth century. Some historians argue that the ideology of separate spheres, far from reducing women's public participation, made it both more extensive and more visible. Others have argued that there was a separate 'female' public sphere in which women undertook philanthropy, social work and cultural activities. In Chapter 2 we examine specifically how sexual difference, and the related notion of separate spheres, was an organising principle of industrialisation from the late eighteenth century until the late nineteenth century in different parts of Europe. Industrialisation was accompanied by the new discourse of political economy, which insisted that all unpaid work, including women's household production, was 'unproductive'. The gendering of work had a significant class dimension, and we explore the relationship between masculinity and various forms of manual, industrial and professional work. The emergence of the industrial male worker problematised the notion of women's work. The association of men with paid work and women with the private or domestic domain also had an impact on the possibilities open to working-class women and on their treatment in the now masculinised 'public' sphere. In Chapter 5 we look at how the rise of consumer capitalism in the late nineteenth century further reshaped the ways in which women had access to the public sphere. Urbanisation and the growth of cities provided a new material landscape for public activities and raised new questions about the separation of spheres and the gendering of material spaces.

Work on the history of nation building and on the expansion of the state has been particularly important to the historical revaluation of men's and women's political and public roles in the nineteenth century and the separation of spheres. In *Britons: Forging the Nation, 1707–1837*, Linda Colley has looked at the ways in which during the Napoleonic wars middle-class English women took up the opportunities provided by patriotic duty for limited entry into the public sphere. Women embraced nationalism as a cause which afforded them a form of political participation and new political identities. Men and women alike saw the nation as an ideal and eventually 'natural' form of association where social duty triumphed over individual self-interest. Nationalism and imperialism reinforced conventional associations of women with 'motherhood' and men with 'soldiering', and also challenged assumptions about gender inequality.

Alongside the discussion of gender and nationalism we also examine imperialism, its effects on gender relations and the extent of women's participation in imperial ventures. Feminist movements across Europe embraced both nationalism and imperialism while decrying assumptions about the masculine nature of the political. Yet feminist historians of Britain, the Netherlands, Germany and France have shown that patriotism and national identity were often important in allowing politically active women to organise and articulate political demands as 'women', which often meant an emphasis on their maternal role and responsibilities. By the late nineteenth century, the state had come to rely on 'maternalism' both in its demands on women and in its representation of its relationship to its citizens. The gendered nature of national citizenship, national identification, maternalism and patriotism is the key focus of Chapters 4 and 5. In these chapters we also explore the correspondence between imperial expansion, social Darwinism and racial ideologies, and the urgency they gave to surrounding debates on sexual difference and sexuality. The increasing concern about questions of sexuality and sexual difference in much of Europe in the 1880s and after, was evident in the developments of sexology and psychoanalysis, in new legislation concerning homosexuality, in the growing concern about venereal disease and the health or survival of the 'European races' and in widespread literary debate about sexual relations, marriage and family life. In Chapter 5 we look at how, by the end of the nineteenth century, debates about sexual difference had changed, permeating the organisation of culture, science and cities, as well as political life. In Chapter 6 we discuss the consequences of the themes of imperialism, nationalism, militarism and sexuality for understanding the outbreak of the First World War, the gendered experiences of war, and the impact of the war on gender relations, and the emergence of new national and international political identities that shaped the political identity of twentieth-century Europe.

Gendering European History began as a course that we taught together at the University of Sydney in 1994. It is the result of a sustained collaboration in teaching and research between both authors, and both of us are responsible for all of the text. Inevitably however, we divided the research and writing tasks between us: Barbara Caine was primarily responsible for Chapters 1, 2 and 5; Glenda Sluga for Chapters 3, 4 and 6. We have included suggestions for further reading in English-language secondary sources and brief lists of key primary sources at the end of each chapter. A more comprehensive listing of the primary and secondary source material that we explored and drew upon is provided in the general bibliography. Our thanks to a number of research assistants for help in bringing together this diverse bibliography, including Pat Fenech, Claire Salinas, Liza Stewart and Jane McAdams. We would like to acknowledge the generous financial assistance provided by the Australian Research Council. A final special thanks is due to Janet Joyce for her enthusiastic support of this project.

ONE

Citizenship and Difference: The Age of Revolution

In the century and a half prior to the French Revolution, intellectuals and philosophers across Europe had discussed a number of social questions which became the focus of political activity during the Revolution. The nature and merits of monarchy, the importance of equality before the law, the possibility or desirability of a republic, the basis of political participation and the meaning of the nation had been of central concern in the Enlightenment and were debated in Britain, in some of the German and Italian states, and in the Habsburg Empire as well as in France. In a similar way, questions about the meaning and implications of the physical and mental differences between men and women were discussed in a range of different fields: in educational thought, in medical and scientific debates, in the writings of jurists and political philosophers, as well as in literature and in social thought. Much of this discussion centred on the relationship between women's bodies and their conventional social roles, and between masculinity, military capacity and citizenship.

What had been largely an intellectual matter until 1789 became a major political issue from the start of the French Revolution. Women participated in some of the most dramatic events of the French Revolution from 1789 onwards. Some women insisted that they be allowed the right of citizens to bear arms in defence of the Republic which the revolution had brought into being. However, the new ideas about sexual difference which emerged in the course of the eighteenth century were linked directly to the question of citizenship. In the eyes of the revolutionary governments, it was clear that the rights of citizens to participate in political debate, to vote and to bear arms were intended only for men. As Lynn Hunt and Joan Landes have shown, the political symbols and the new political language which emerged in the French Revolution emphasised the close connection between masculinity and citizenship by designating the political sphere as masculine and insisting that women devote themselves to the private sphere of family and home

(Hunt 1984; Landes 1988). For the men who led the Revolution, as for their conservative opponents, the very idea of women participating in political activity and demanding new legal and political rights brought with it the threat of sexual promiscuity and the undermining of family life. Thus while the French Revolution of 1789 brought the birth of modern politics and introduced the modern European idea of the political individual and the citizen, it emphatically designated the masculinity of that citizen.

The precise impact of the French Revolution on women has long been the source of historical discussion and debate. The unprecedented level of activity and involvement of the women of Paris in revolutionary events, accompanied by the first formal demands for political rights and citizenship for women, have made the French Revolution into the central event of the emergence of modern feminism. Those women who protested angrily at their exclusion from the political realm and who demanded rights for women brought into being modern feminism with its central demand that women be granted their full recognition as citizens (Landes 1988; Caine 1997).

The participation of women in the early stages of the French Revolution had to some extent been anticipated by the involvement of women in the intellectual life of the eighteenth century. Enlightenment debates took place in salons organised by women. Moreover, increasing numbers of women were also beginning to write and to publish their work – albeit often under male pseudonyms. The novel, which was becoming increasingly popular in Britain and France in the eighteenth and early nineteenth centuries, provided a literary genre suited to urban experience and domestic life and in which women could excel. But women were also becoming prominent as poets, historians, essayists, and as literary and cultural theorists and critics. The phenomenon of the woman writer was itself the subject of social comment, and women's literary pretensions sometimes aroused the same hostility as their political involvement. By the end of the French Revolution, and the beginning of the nineteenth century, a new literary and cultural movement, Romanticism, emphasised the close connection between masculinity and creative power with its insistence that the genius was always a man – albeit a man with feminine sensibilities.

In this chapter we will begin by examining the Enlightenment debate about sexual difference and the ways in which some philosophers argued that the possession of reason, which naturally entitled people to certain rights, was a quality only applicable to men. We will then look at the role and participation of women in the French Revolution, at the attempts made by women to demand political rights and citizenship and at the reasons why those rights were denied to them. In the process we will explore the ways in which the idea of citizenship was connected with masculinity. We will also look at the impact on women of the legal codes established by Napoleon in France and adopted in many other European countries. Finally we will look at the emergence of women writers, at the ways in which women demanded the right to participate in literary debates and through literature in political and social issues. We will also explore the ways in which the questions about gender and sexual difference which were central to the political arena in the late eighteenth and early nineteenth centuries also shaped contemporary literature and culture.

Sexual difference and the Enlightenment

Many historians have commented on the discrepancy between the critical and questioning approach which the Enlightenment philosophers of the eighteenth century took to questions of government, religion and social institutions, on the one hand, and their acceptance and even endorsement of the prevailing inferior status of women, on the other. In France, in particular, there was much play with the idea of 'light', especially the light of natural reason, which alone could lead man to the perfection of knowledge and human wisdom. But this light rarely shone on either the situation of women or on prevailing beliefs about them. On the contrary, women, like the benighted savages to be found outside Western Europe, tended to be seen as lacking in that innate reason which was the basis of natural rights. Lacking the qualities which made social reform possible, women were regarded as obstacles to progress and reform rather than as requiring reform or assistance in their own process of enlightenment.

While some see this omission of women from the Enlightenment reform agenda as essentially an oversight, others see it as fundamental to the Enlightenment understanding and idealisation of reason. The philosopher Genevieve Lloyd, for example, has argued strongly that the idea of a 'man of reason' points to the conceptual link that was being made between masculinity and reason both in the eighteenth century and before (Lloyd 1984). From the earliest writings in Western philosophy, reason, masculinity, truth and intellect have been contrasted to sensuality, femininity, error and emotion. This contrast had particular importance in the Enlightenment when reason came to be seen as the highest human quality which brought with it an entitlement to legal and political rights. Thus the 'man of reason' became the central focus for discussion of political rights and of citizenship.

Lloyd's argument has been extended and endorsed by a number of recent historians who have pointed to the extensive interest in elaborating the differences between the sexes throughout the eighteenth century. Medical and scientific texts addressed in great detail questions about the precise anatomical and physiological differences between the sexes (Jordanova 1990). This medical literature complemented the discussion of sexual difference evident in works concerned with education and morality. Looking at a range of these medical and scientific texts, Thomas Laqueur has argued that the seventeenth and eighteenth centuries saw the development of a new model of sexual difference. Ideas about sexual difference up until this time had been dominated by the views of Classical Greek writers for whom women lacked any essential elements of their own, but were seen as smaller and lesser versions of men. In accordance with the ideas of the fifth-century Greek philosopher Galen – ideas which were reformulated during the Renaissance – women were imperfect men who lacked the heat and the energy which produced men's perfect form and their physical strength. In this model of sexual difference, the similarities between men and women extended even to their reproductive structures. Thus, as Galen put it, 'all parts that men have, women have too … the difference between them lies in one thing … that in women the parts are within the body whereas in men they are outside' (Laqueur 1990). Galen drew up careful diagrams of the male and female body with identical organs showing one as the analogue of the other. Female ovaries were equivalent to the testicles; the womb was the penis turned inside out. This is a model, Laqueur insists, in which there was really only one sex – the male. Women were lesser men rather than constituting a distinct or different sex.

By contrast, in the course of the seventeenth and eighteenth centuries, a new model of sexual difference came to the fore. Men and women came to be seen as completely different from, and even opposite to, each other. For the first time, medical texts began to include a female skeleton as well as a male one. They emphasised the broader pelvis, the narrower shoulders, and the smaller head, of the female, rather than assuming that a male skeleton served equally well for both men and women (Scheibinger 1989). The distinctive nature of male and female bodies was emphasised through the introduction of new sexual terms, including 'vagina' and 'vulva', to label the various parts of the female reproductive system. This need for a new language to describe bodily differences was accompanied by an increasing interest in bodies and an emphasis on their importance in the making of sexual difference. Scientific and medical texts devoted much attention to demonstrating the extent of this difference in every element of the human body, including the emotions, the hair and the finger nails. As Laqueur points out, this new model placed much greater emphasis on bodies and bodily difference than had been the case in earlier centuries.

For much of the eighteenth century, both models of sexual difference co-existed, but increasingly the new model which stressed difference predominated. It meshed neatly with a range of arguments about the importance of the nuclear family and the home and of the need to differentiate the activities of men and women and to locate them socially in different places. Perhaps the most influential and widely read text which spelled out the social and political implications of this new approach to sexual difference was Rousseau's *Émile* (first published in 1762). Although prohibited by the censors because of its religious comments, *Émile* was an immensely popular book in France and also in England and the German states. The popularity of Rousseau's text undoubtedly owed much to the way in which it laid out a new and child-centred approach to education in which the child's curiosity was the main driving force, while its physical and mental development determined the educational programme. At a time when increasing attention was being paid to children and to the need for them to be nurtured and cared for within a nuclear family, this educational ideal, which centred on an individual tutor taking complete charge of a child and working to ensure that its education encompassed physical, moral and intellectual development, harmonised well with the ideals and aims of a growing middle class. The education Rousseau laid out for his eponymous hero, Émile, seemed designed to ensure that Émile was not only able and competent, but also a model son, husband, father and citizen.

- Émile's education, as Rousseau made absolutely clear, was entirely sex-specific. The education Rousseau described for Émile emphasised the development of reason, and was completely different from the education he prescribed for 'Sophie', Émile's mate and the subject of the final chapter of *Émile*. Over hundreds of pages Rousseau detailed how the development of reason and judgement in a boy needed to be stimulated. Émile would learn to endure hardship, to explore the natural world, to develop physical strength and control, to exercise his own judgement and independence and to live according to his own values and beliefs. Sophie's education was dealt with much more briefly in a separate chapter in which Rousseau explained how every aspect of her education was to be the opposite of Émile's. Where Émile was to be free, Sophie was to be confined – even tied to a chair and forced to play with dolls. Where he was to develop intellectual independence, she was to be taught to submit her judgement to others and to follow the dictates of the world around her. Where he was encouraged to think highly of himself and to display his talents, she had to learn that modesty was the most important quality a woman could possess.

In his discussion of sexual difference, Rousseau made a complex play on the idea of 'nature'. Émile's education was to be 'natural', geared to allowing him to develop reasoning powers, undertaken as much as possible in the open air and the countryside, organised around his own nature, and helping him to understand and even master the natural world. Sophie, too, was to be educated according to 'nature'. But in her case, Rousseau shifted the emphasis of education, so that rather than her own desires, it is the nature of the world she will inhabit and the roles she will have to play as wife and mother that come to the fore.

Rousseau's ideas about the different education needed by Sophie and Émile were closely integrated into his ideas about the nature of society and of the political order. The establishment of an orderly domestic and familial life was, in his view, not only important in itself but integral to the establishment and maintenance of civic order and virtue. Looking towards a new political order in which men would participate as active citizens, exercising political rights and carrying out a range of civic tasks, Rousseau stressed that Émile's education had to prepare him for the interrelated roles of husband, citizen and father. Sophie, by contrast, required training in submission and domesticity to make her into a dutiful and obedient wife and mother. Women, in Rousseau's view, lacked any ethical sense and hence could not be guided by their own reason. They had rather to be guided by public opinion and the dictates of men.

Rousseau's ideas were extremely influential not only in France and Britain, but elsewhere in Europe. His insistence on the importance of women's confinement to the home, and his argument that this was both natural and conducive to morality and to civic order, provided a new form of validation of the legal situation, which prevailed in a number of countries, whereby women were completely subordinated to the rule of their husbands. In Britain, for example, in marriage husband and wife became one person in law. 'That is', as Sir William Blackstone explained in his *Commentaries on the Laws of England*, 'the very being, or legal existence of the woman is suspended during the marriage, or at least is incorporated and consolidated into that of her husband: under whose wing, protection and cover, she performs everything' (Blackstone 1753 cited in Hill 1987: 112). This meant that married women could hold no property – on the contrary, they were themselves the property of their husbands. The husband owned his wife's body and was entitled to any sexual or domestic services he desired. He also owned any children they might have. Married women could not inherit property, which, like any money they might earn, belonged to their husbands. Similarly they could not enter into contracts or sue or be sued without their husband also being involved. Blackstone, sharing Rousseau's sense that this legal status suited women's nature, saw this institution of 'coverture' as ensuring the protection of women and indeed as making them especially favoured. In a similar way, the German philosopher Immanuel Kant depicted women and men as having completely opposite characteristics, arguing that these differences provided the basis for marital laws which gave men the power to rule women (Hull 1996).

The increasing emphasis on sexual difference in the eighteenth century was accompanied by a growing sense of the importance of male sexual energy and activity as a central feature of the male political subject. For Kant (as for his influential student and fellow philosopher, Johannes Gottlieb Fichte in the early nineteenth century) the male sexual drive was closely associated with the impulse to independence, autonomy and freedom. Hence ideas about women's sexual passivity underlay the view that they were unsuited to political rights and full citizenship. Some historians have argued that this insistence on the connection between sexual and political activity was the consequence of an apparent increase in sexual activity, both within and outside marriage, and with a new sense of the importance and imperative nature of sexual desire in the eighteenth century (Abelove 1989; Laqueur 1992). This in turn brought a belief that the freedom to indulge sexual desire was a male prerogative, not available to women or children. For Rousseau, it was the power of male sexual desire which necessitated the domestic seclusion of women. Male sexuality, in his view, was a potentially subversive and destructive force that needed to be contained within marriage and in the home. Seeing this issue only in heterosexual terms, Rousseau argued that the only possible way to ensure political and social order was to completely exclude women from the public realm. The presence of women in the public world would, he argued, distract men and lead to promiscuity. By contrast, the confinement of women to the home would withdraw them from the promiscuous gaze of men, and thereby keep women chaste, and by confining male sexual activity to monogamous family life, masculine behaviour would be reformed.

In recent years, historical writing on the Enlightenment has extended beyond discussions of the ideas of prominent philosophers and interest in political, legal and social reform to explore the institutional frameworks in which the new ideas associated with the Enlightenment were expressed and debated. The development of public opinion and public debates through salons and coffee houses and through the extension of publishing and of the press have thus been widely explored. Much of this new work has pointed to the role of women in the Enlightenment. Although French salon women have been most extensively researched, it was not only in France that salon women were prominent (Goodman 1994). In many European cities in the late eighteenth and early nineteenth centuries, salons were a central feature of intellectual and literary debate. In Berlin and Moscow, as much as in London, women played a prominent role in them. The specific form and purpose of salons differed quite markedly from one country to another: thus in Berlin, salons run by prominent Jewish women provided a way for Jewish and gentile intellectuals and businessmen to meet. In Moscow and St Petersburg, salons played an integral part in the development of Russian as a literary language. As Joan Scott has argued, salons and the women who ran them fostered the growth of critical and dissenting opinion in France, particularly the growth of opposition to absolutism (Scott 1996). Activist and reformist women became involved in journals, such as *Le Journal des Dames* (*The Ladies Journal*), which anticipated the political demands made by women during the French Revolution.

As Rousseau's ideas gained European currency in the second half of the eighteenth century, and his belief in the complementarity and the differences between men and women became widely accepted, the participation of women in salons in France became the subject of debate and controversy. Rousseau himself was deeply hostile to the participation of women in any sphere of life outside the home and wrote at length of the evils attending women's involvement in salons. Intellectual life and the capacity to explore and debate scientific and social ideas were, in his view, compromised by the presence of women. If women were excluded from salons, men would be 'exempted from having to lower their ideas to the range of women and to clothe reason in gallantry' and could 'devote themselves to grave and serious discourse without fear of ridicule' (Wertheim 1995: 46–50). While some intellectuals and writers associated with the Enlightenment in France, like Diderot, rejected this view and insisted that the presence of women made it necessary to discuss the driest subjects with clarity and charm, others sided with Rousseau in accepting that masculine debate was necessary, especially for the development of scientific ideas and approaches. And indeed in the second half of the eighteenth century, more and more men's discussion groups and circles excluded women. In the process, the ideas that rational thought and science were specifically masculine pursuits and that femininity was more closely connected to stories and to poetry were also coming to be accepted.

Opposition to the participation of women in salons had a moral as well as an intellectual basis. A number of prominent salon women had sexual liaisons with the intellectual leaders who regularly attended their weekly 'evenings at home'. These women became particular targets of Rousseau's hostility and he attacked them for neglecting their family duties, for their sexual and moral corruption, and for their polluting of masculine intellectual debate. Rousseau was not isolated in these views. Increasingly in the second half of the eighteenth century, the charge of sexual promiscuity was levelled against any women who participated in political life. This hostility reached a peak in France in the years leading up to the revolution of 1789 in attacks on the Queen, Marie Antoinette. A host of pornographic pamphlets and cartoons suggested that she was not only dishonest and corrupt, but sexually voracious, indulging both in lesbian affairs and in incest with her son (Hunt 1992). These caricatures circulated widely in Britain as well as in France. Thus by the late 1780s, there was widespread agreement with Rousseau that women's involvement or even appearance in the public world of politics or political debate was immoral and indecent.

The French Revolution

Historians have found many different ways of setting out a chronology of the French Revolution. Questions of gender have become an increasingly important means of distinguishing between the early optimism and sense of new opportunities evident in the Revolution between 1789 and 1793, and the more radical republican phase of the Revolution instigated after that time. From 1793, women's claims were increasingly questioned, and their activities restricted until finally, with the assumption of power by Napoleon, women were definitively denied political rights, adult status or any recognition as citizens.

For many contemporary commentators, one of the most unsettling aspects of the early stages of the French Revolution was the very public participation of women. The English writer and political theorist, Edmund Burke, for example, viewed the march to Versailles to bring the King back to Paris, led by the market women of Paris in October 1789, as an appalling episode. He was indignant at the way the royal family was forced to return to Paris, 'moved along, amidst the horrid yells, and shrilling screams, and frantic dances and infamous contumelies, and all the unutterable abominations of the furies of hell, in the abused shape of the vilest of women' (Burke 1965 [1790]: 85). Burke's depiction of working women points to his support for monarchy and his belief that political activity ought to be the prerogative of educated men. His vision of the market women as harridans illustrates his worst fears about the consequences of drastic social and political change provoked by the challenge to the King's authority. As Joan Landes has shown, even in the more positive depiction of the women of Paris, in the many cartoons and drawings in which they carry liberty trees, or heads on pikes and walk beside, or ride with soldiers, it is implied that women have 'strong sexual and martial appetites' (Landes 1992: 20). Some of the women are depicted as engaging in sexual activities with soldiers and all of them appear disordered in their dress.

Direct involvement in local and community activities by Parisian working women was not new. Women had always played a major role in managing the family budget and hence in monitoring food prices. Throughout the eighteenth century, working women all over France had been very active in riots and protests over rising prices. Their responsibility for the well-being of their families had also meant that they had to become aware of and adept at dealing with the growing centralised administration which had emerged in the eighteenth century. Women had dealt with taxes, police and courts, and with public works. Parisian women also had a long-standing involvement in other local and community concerns: many women had been closely involved with the Church and had participated in the debates and disputes between Jansenists and Jesuits which had preceded the expulsion of the Jesuits in 1773.

In the years before 1789, there had been no conflict or opposition between working women's home, community and economic roles. Throughout the eighteenth century, it was generally recognised that women's responsibility for their families and for the well-being of their community automatically made the question of prices and the need to find a way to resolve the food crisis their concern. In the course of 1789, particularly in Paris, even questions about food and prices began to take on a more explicitly political cast. When the growing financial crisis of the late 1780s made it necessary for the King to summon the Estates General, the group whose assent he had to have in order to raise new taxes, this event generated a vast amount of public discussion. The meeting of the Estates General in 1789, the insistence by the Third Estate (the commoners, and all those not included within the estates of the nobility and the clergy) that it embodied the Nation, and the publication of the Declaration of the Rights of Man and the Citizen in July 1789, brought a widespread new interest in politics and a new sense of the connection between the struggles of daily life and the need for the Third Estate to be heard on the political stage. This combination of political issues and immediate economic concerns was very clear in the march of Parisian women on Versailles: the marchers were spurred on by the high price of bread in the capital. They intended to bring the King back to ensure that he did his duty as a ruler by regulating prices and overseeing conditions within Paris. Thus the march connected demands for food with a sense of the political obligations of the ruler, and of justice and moral order.

The women of Paris followed up the march to Versailles by participating in a number of other political activities, often alongside men. From 1789 onwards, women began to join radical and republican clubs, and participated in their debates. Women made up the crowds demanding a referendum on the King's fate in July 1791. By 1791 too, working women in Paris were involved in their own separate activities. They continued to engage in direct action. When in 1792 the price of sugar had risen beyond what they could afford to pay, working women seized sugar supplies from merchants. At the same time, women protested to the Jacobin clubs about food hoarders and those who artificially caused the price of food to rise, and sought the death penalty for speculators and hoarders. In 1793, the women who established the Society of Republican Revolutionary Women demanded a comprehensive programme of protective and repressive measures to ensure the safety of the people. And in seeking to demonstrate their support for the Republic, they urged that all women should be required to wear the tricolour cockade in public.

As many recent historians have shown, while the 1789 Declaration of the Rights of Man and the Citizen was apparently an inclusive document, it was imbued with a very particular idea of the meaning of the term 'man'. Women were not included in the rights being claimed any more than were black men or Jews. Rousseau's very influential ideas on sexual difference made it seem obvious to many that women should not be accorded the rights of men. But his views were not universally accepted. The first suggestion of women's entitlement to political rights and citizenship was made in 1790 in the *Journal of the Society of 1789*. In his essay 'On the Admission of Women to the Rights of Citizenship', the Marquis de Condorcet, a philosopher and a liberal aristocrat, argued that the rights of men 'result simply from the fact that they are sentient beings, capable of acquiring moral ideas and of reasoning concerning these ideas. Women, having these same qualities, must necessarily possess equal rights' (Landes 1988: 114–18). Condorcet's ideas were not taken up in any significant way by the influential Constituent Assembly which had promoted the Declaration of Rights, but the Assembly did nonetheless move immediately to deal with some questions about women's legal rights. In 1790 legislation was introduced which made divorce easier and removed earlier restrictions on women's inheritance rights. As Lyn Hunt has argued, this legislation did seek to bring a measure of greater equality into the family. Just as the king had been stripped of despotic powers, so many of those actively involved in the early stages of the Revolution sought to remove the immense powers of husbands and fathers. 'After having made man free and happy in public life', argued one Deputy in the Constituent Assembly in 1790, 'it remains for us to assure his liberty and his happiness in private life. You know that under the Old Regime the tyranny of parents was often as terrible as the despotism of ministers; often the prisons of state became family prisons. It is suitable therefore to draw up, after the declaration of rights of man and citizen, a declaration, so to speak of the rights of spouses, of father, of sons, of parents, and so on' (Hunt 1992: 17).

In the years 1790–93, a number of legislative changes were introduced in regard to family life which unquestionably benefited women. The attack on the power of the Catholic Church, the introduction of civil marriage and of divorce gave women considerably more rights within marriage as well as the right to end it. The establishment of a new Family Court in 1790, and the legislation in 1792 permitting divorce in the event of a complete breakdown in marriage made a very considerable shift away from the authoritarian family structure of the old regime and towards a new and more egalitarian one. The concern among revolutionary legislators to curb the powers of husbands and fathers also benefited women and girls in terms of inheritance. In March 1793, the National Convention declared equal inheritance of all in equal line of succession, and in November it also extended this equal right of inheritance to illegitimate children upon proof of paternity. The debates surrounding the Constitution of 1791 prompted a series of pamphlets and treatises on women's rights, the best known of which are Olympe de Gouges's *Declaration of the Rights of Woman and the Citizen* in France (1791) and Mary Wollstonecraft's *Vindication of the Rights of Woman* in England (1792). Olympe de Gouges was a playwright, pamphleteer and sometime courtesan who argued for the representation of women as citizens throughout the early stages of the French Revolution. Her *Declaration of the*

Rights of Woman and the Citizen paralleled the Declaration of the Rights of Man in its structure and form. It demanded all the rights and freedoms conferred on men for women, adding new demands which centred on women's need to be free of domestic tyranny. De Gouges put forward a new idea of the meaning of citizen, which included women as well as men, and insisted that the rights of the citizen needed to encompass not only the individual's political participation and activities, but also his or her personal and domestic lives and activities. She insisted that women needed some of these new rights in order to protect themselves against sexual exploitation. The right to 'the free communication of ideas and opinions' was important, she argued, because it would enable women to name the father of their child or children, and to demand shared responsibility in relation to those children. As Joan Scott has pointed out, by demanding the freedom for women to indicate the paternity of their children, de Gouges called attention to the fact that men were sexual as well as rational beings, and that women might need protection from men's sexual transgression (Scott 1996: 42–6).

The exclusion of women from many of the rights extended to men in France in the period 1789–92 also gave rise to feminist demands in other countries. Mary Wollstonecraft's *Vindication of the Rights of Woman*, still widely regarded as the founding text of Anglo-American feminism, was written in England in a few weeks of furious activity in 1792. Wollstonecraft had been a passionate supporter of the French Revolution, which she thought of as the harbinger of a liberal and democratic society. But when she saw that girls were excluded from the plan for compulsory schooling being laid down for boys in France, she was appalled. Wollstonecraft insisted that by denying women rights, and arguing that they were seeking to protect women and to secure their happiness, the men of the French Constituent Assembly were following the model of all the tyrants they ostensibly deplored. Like Condorcet and de Gouges, Wollstonecraft argued that women, like men, were rational creatures, and she set out at length the fundamental rights which ensued from this premise. Wollstonecraft did not deny the importance of sexual difference, indeed she accepted that men and women would exercise their rights in different ways and that they would have different duties. But in her view, bodily differences occurred alongside significant intellectual similarities and it was the fact that men and women shared the capacity for reason that was most important. Recognition of women as rational beings, she insisted, also required rethinking conventional ideas about women's conduct and moral qualities, taking as the first principle that there was only one standard of human virtue and that it must be the

same for men and women. Wollstonecraft particularly criticised the gendering of qualities, for example questioning the ways in which the term
'modesty' was used to refer in the case of men to 'that soberness of mind
which teaches a man not to think more highly of himself than he ought to
think' and, in the case of women, only to sexual demeanour.

Alongside her discussion of moral questions, Wollstonecraft also argued
for the institutional and legal changes which followed from the recognition
of women's rationality and moral autonomy: the need for an education
which was based on rational principles and which combined intellectual
training with useful skills; the need for an end to the sexual double standard;
the need for reform of marriage and for the admission of women to a range
of fields of study and of paid employment, which would allow them to be
economically independent. Wollstonecraft specified the study of medicine
and of business as possible professional pursuits, and politics and history for
their intellectual and moral improvement. For Wollstonecraft, as for de
Gouges, the question about women's precise rights and duties, and the actual
meaning of citizenship for women, were complex and sometimes confusing
issues. Both Wollstonecraft and de Gouges sought to demand rights for
women on the basis of their capacity for reason, and to establish the nature
of sexual difference and of the kind of sexed citizenship which accompanied
women's domestic and maternal duties. Hence, while protesting against the
ways in which women were seen to possess only a limited range of qualities
and were restricted to particular fields, they in turn emphasised maternity
and women's maternal duty as the basis of their claim to political rights, legal
independence and full citizenship.

During the early part of the 1790s, as women's organisations defended the
right of women to participate directly in political debates and in the defence
of France, women's rights were passionately demanded both in theory and
practice. In 1793 in Paris, these demands and debates were stifled. This was
a year of considerable economic hardship and suffering, and one in which
tensions among different women's groups came to the fore. There were
internal divisions within the Society of Republican Revolutionary Women,
as some turned against their former leader, Claire Lecombe, accusing her of
immoral conduct. There were also tensions between the Society, which
sought to insist that women wear the revolutionary cockade to emphasise
their patriotism, and many of the market women of Paris, who resented this
interference in their lives. The market women filed a protest against the
Republican Revolutionary Women. On 30 October 1793 (8 Brumaire in the
revolutionary calendar), the growing hostility of the National Convention to

women's political participation was manifested in its closure of the Society of Republican Revolutionary Women. Shortly after this, all women's clubs and societies were prohibited.

The prohibition of women's clubs was advocated by a prominent member of the Committee of General Security, André Amar, who echoed Rousseau in his insistence that the harmony of society required the observance of the natural sexual division of labour. 'Each sex', he insisted, 'is called to the type of occupation that is proper for it; its action is circumscribed within this circle from which it cannot escape' (Procter 1990: 162). The functions of women are 'to prepare children's minds and hearts for public virtue, to direct them early in life towards the good, to elevate their souls, to educate them in the political cult of liberty ... to make virtue loved'. Morality, nature and even the fate of the Republic, he argued, all depended upon women fulfilling these duties. Making quite explicit his view that citizens were men, Amar insisted that citizens were entitled to go about their business and their political activities secure in the knowledge that their homes and families were being looked after by their wives. Women's groups continued sporadic activity after this, but by the end of 1793 all agitation by women had ceased.

As women's political participation was brought to an end and their family roles were officially cultivated, citizenship became inextricably connected not only with masculinity, but with the prerogatives and privileges of being a husband and a father. In the course of these developments, the idea that citizenship was a masculine prerogative was extensively argued and demonstrated. The gendering of citizenship involved the very explicit and extensive reworking of images and ideals of masculinity. As both Lynn Hunt (1984) and Dorinda Outram (1989) have shown, in the early stages of the French Revolution new images of masculinity were developed and officially promoted. The figure of Hercules became more and more prominent in revolutionary iconography. Stoicism and self-control – both accepted as attributes of masculinity – came to be seen as important in new models of political behaviour.

As successive governments became more conservative on questions of social policy in the mid and later 1790s, there was some concern about whether the family legislation of the early 1790s allowing divorce and limiting paternal control was too liberal and might contribute to the breakdown in social order. This legislation remained in force until the early nineteenth century, when the new Civil Code introduced by Napoleon in 1804 eradicated the legislative gains for women. The Napoleonic Civil Code re-established and possibly strengthened patriarchal power within family life. It set up a framework for marriage which echoed the *ancien régime* requirement for parental consent for marriage. Women under the age of 21 and men under 25 could not legally marry without parental consent, and if parents disagreed, it was the father's view that counted. Parental control was also extended in duration. The age of majority was set at 30 and those under this age were deemed to be children subject to the authority of their parents. Under the Napoleonic Code, a father was given the right to have a child imprisoned for up to six months if he deemed it disobedient, another echo of the *ancien régime*. Just as the Code reasserted the power of parents, so too it re-established the authority of husbands over wives. A husband was charged with the protection of his wife, while she in turn owed him obedience. Women were designated as legally incompetent: unfit to witness certificates of marriage, birth or death; unable to sue in a court of law without their husband's consent; unable even to make or receive a gift or inheritance or succession without their husband's consent. So complete was the disregard of and distrust for women under the Code that a husband was required even to witness the birth of his children and to declare a child his own before it could be recognised as legitimate. Husbands were given unconditional control over family property and over the wages or earnings of their wives. Husbands were also given the power to determine all aspects of marital life: the nature and location of a residence, the schooling of children. Some historians have interpreted the provisions of the Code which prohibited paternity suits as the corollary of Napoleon's military background and his concern for soldiers. By prohibiting paternity suits, the Code prevented women from taking action against men whom they claimed to have seduced them. The Code also introduced the sexual double standard into marital law. Adultery was seen as a criminal offence for women, rendering an erring wife liable to imprisonment for a period of between three months and two years. By contrast, an adulterous husband would at most receive a fine. Moreover, adultery was a different crime for men and women: a wife could be charged with adultery on suspicion of any form of illicit sexual conduct. But a husband could be charged with adultery only if he brought his mistress into the home.

In the aftermath of the French Revolution, then, women were rendered completely subordinate to husbands. Regarded primarily as home-makers, married women needed their husband's permission to engage in paid work. The Napoleonic Code set the legal framework for women in France, in the German and Italian states, and in all the countries conquered by Napoleonic armies or which chose to adopt the Code in the course of the nineteenth century as a symbol of national progress. The introduction of the Napoleonic Code in some of the German-speaking states brought a slight deterioration in the legal position of women there. Independently of Napoleon, and before he came to power, there were moves in Germany to reinforce the centrality of maternity and to regulate women's maternal conduct. In the German-speaking regions governed by Prussia, the Allgemeines Landrecht laid down a framework for marriage in 1794, stressing the importance of procreation, and underlining the nature of women's conjugal duties and their subordination to their husbands. Following Rousseau's advice, mothers were enjoined by the law to breast-feed their children, and fathers were given the responsibility of determining how long the breast-feeding should continue. Women were, however, entitled to expect protection from their husbands and were given some legal control over their own property. A decade later, when the Napoleonic Code was accepted by the German states west of the Rhine, married women lost any control of their property and were in effect reduced to the legal status of minors. The Code gave men greater control over common matrimonial property and easier access to divorce than had previously been the case. Similarly in Eastern Europe, including parts of the Hapsburg Empire which borrowed from the Code, women were deprived of some traditional rights of inheritance and of power within family life. Similar conditions entailed in Britain, where a married woman legally owned nothing. Her husband owned all her earnings and anything she might inherit. He was entitled to exact sexual and domestic services, even to imprison her to enforce them. And she had almost no legal rights in regard to her children.

All of these developments have led to intense historical discussion about the overall impact of the French Revolution on women. Olwen Hufton argues that only small numbers of women were actively concerned about political citizenship or engaged in the Revolution which resulted in their political annihilation. The majority of women – poor, rural women – had few concerns about citizenship, and the Revolution brought them immense physical, financial and emotional hardship which made them long nostalgically for the re-establishment of the Church and the communal solidarity it had symbolised (Hufton 1992). Taking a longer perspective, but an equally bleak view, Madelyn Gutwirth has argued that 'the enforcement of a regime of separate sexual spheres institutionalised under Jacobinism, with the women retired from all public participation, was to prove to be perhaps the single most unalterable measure effected by Revolution, surviving all the

Separate spheres for women

nineteenth century's changes of regime' (Gutwirth 1992). But other historians put forward a rather different view, pointing to the importance of the idea of political participation for women that the Revolution inspired, and insisting on the importance of the Revolution for the emergence of modern feminism. While acknowledging the ultimate defeat of women's political aspirations, Darlene Levy and Harriet Applewhite argue that in the years from 1789 to 1795, the Revolution provided women with the opportunity to evolve from subjects, sometimes passive and sometimes protesting, but always leaving decision-making to those in power, into participating citizens demanding a say in government (Levy and Applewhite 1992: 97–8). This participation dramatically affected the nature of the Revolution and made it genuinely democratic. For historians interested in intellectual and cultural history and in the history of feminism, the French Revolution brought women few lasting gains, especially in terms of new political and legal rights; nonetheless, the claims women made during the Revolution fundamentally altered traditional ways of seeing and understanding sexual difference and citizenship, and raised women's emancipation as a major political issue throughout Europe for the rest of the nineteenth century. Women's activity during the French Revolution made it possible to articulate the ideal of women as active citizens participating fully in the political and social activities of the nation. In a similar way, though citizenship was explicitly made a masculine right and prerogative at this time, the questions of the gendering of rights and of the rights of women were never laid to rest. Indeed modern feminism was organised around the recognition that women were now subject to new forms of legal and political discrimination.

Women's voices

Women's demands for political rights and a public role were emphatically rejected in the course of the 1790s. But this did not mean that women retired submissively to the silent world of the home, as demanded by Rousseau. If anything, the participation of some women in public debate and the audibility of their voices increased. Salons declined in number in France and England, as their functions were taken over by learned societies, professional bodies and political parties. But in other countries, particularly Germany, Russia and Spain, salon woman only emerged in the early nineteenth century and were at the peak of their influence by about 1820. Where salons declined, women became increasingly prominent as writers. The expansion in publishing, particularly the increasing number of journals and magazines, provided an outlet for women writers. Writing offered many middle-class women from a humbler social class than the *salonières* a voice and the chance to earn a living. Despite Rousseau's strictures on the importance of marriage, domesticity and financial dependence for women, there were significant numbers of unmarried women in Western Europe. Moreover, many married women were deserted by their husbands, or found themselves married to men who were unable or unwilling to support them and who made it necessary for the women themselves to work for their support and that of their children. Some 400 women writers were published in England in the last two decades of the eighteenth century. For many of them, literature was a profession and a way of supporting not only themselves, but their families. While no other European country replicated entirely English developments, by the late eighteenth and early nineteenth centuries, there were increasing numbers of prominent women writers in France, the German and Italian states, and in Central Europe.

In England in particular, it is clear that the popularity of fiction played an important part in the rise of the woman writer. The novel allowed great scope for women because of its concern with the domestic world of family and private relationships and because it did not require the classical education or the knowledge of classical literature still deemed essential for poetry and drama. Thus the late eighteenth century saw the emergence of best-selling novelists like Fanny Burney or Ann Radcliffe, and the early nineteenth century of writers such as Maria Edgeworth and Jane Austen. Women did not only write novels. In Britain, Catherine Macaulay become a historian who was widely read. Her countrywoman Hannah More published plays, poetry, biblical dialogues and moral and religious tracts as well as her immensely successful *Strictures on the Modern System of Education* (1799). Though the French Revolution ultimately silenced women's political voice, like the wars which followed, it led to an outpouring of historical reflections, personal reminiscences and memoirs from French women, from English women like Mary Wollstonecraft and Helen Maria Williams, and from women in the German states and as far away as Greece. Indeed, women writers became involved in all the literary fields evident in their own countries. Thus Italian women were prominent in the writing of opera librettos, while their English and French counterparts were actively engaged in journalism.

The increasing number of women writers was made possible by economic change and developments within the world of publishing. The decline of patronage from wealthy and titled individuals, and the expansion of a literary market with more commercial publishers, more journals and a growing number of local lending libraries, all helped to provide women writers with ways to publish their work. There were specific magazines and journals written for and by women, like the *Lady's Magazine* in England or the *Journal des Dames* in France. Other women were able to make a living through editorial work or contributions to journals. Thus in England, Mary Wollstonecraft worked as editorial assistant on a radical monthly journal, the *Analytical Review*. Although women were able to make use of the commercial world of publishing, nonetheless, as Carla Hesse has recently pointed out, they faced considerable problems when it came to legal questions about who actually owned their work and what their rights within it were (Hesse 1989: 469–87). In France it was not until 1793 that the law recognised an author's claim to property rights in a text. Prior to that, ideas were thought of as a gift of God, revealed in a text, but not created by an author. Both male and female writers had been protesting against this, and finally in 1793 the national Convention passed what has been seen as 'the declaration of the rights of genius', giving male authors claims to their work. These rights were not extended to women. Although married women in France were given some new legal rights – the right to inherit and to sign contracts – they were still subject to their husband's authority and could not appear in a court without his support and consent. This in turn meant that in any legal dispute about publication rights, a woman required her husband to fight for what was, after all, his name. Married women were generally unable to publish work without the consent of their husband. In Britain too, married women had no legal standing and both their literary work and any money they might earn from it belonged legally to their husbands. Hence while women's voices could increasingly be heard in this period, women could still not participate in the literary world on the same terms as men.

Within the literary world, moreover, women were still confined in what they could write about and more particularly by prevailing perceptions of their literary abilities. This gendering of art was made very clear in the dominant aesthetic values and critical language of the late eighteenth century, which set the masculine 'sublime' against the feminine 'beautiful'. Mary Wollstonecraft's feminist anger was directed as much against the aesthetic and critical approaches which denied women true literary stature as it was against the legal and political structures which denied them rights. Just as she had attacked Edmund Burke for his political views, so too in her *Vindication*, Wollstonecraft attacked his influential *Philosophical Inquiry into the Origin of the Sublime and the Beautiful*. For Burke, as for his contemporaries, the highest art dealt with the sublime. He contrasted the sublime with the beautiful, but in ways which made the former masculine, while the latter was feminine. The sublime, for Burke, was exemplified by the awesome grandeur of rugged natural land and rock forms, especially the Alps. But it was also evident in the spectacle of powerful men gazing on or overcoming nature, in images of the kinship between gifted men and God as the creator of nature, or of men exercising their terrible strength and overcoming any natural obstacles which prevented them from gaining a particular goal. Burke contrasted the sublime with the beautiful, which he regarded as more graceful, but less overwhelming or significant. He applied the term beautiful to that which was small, delicate and graceful either in art or in nature, including women and the works they created. While the sublime was masculine, the beautiful embodied those qualities that men found desirable, especially in women. Wollstonecraft charged Burke with having convinced women, 'that *littleness* and *weakness* are the very essence of beauty and that the Supreme Being, in giving women beauty in the most supereminent degree, seemed to command them, by the powerful voice of Nature, not to cultivate the moral virtues that chance to excite respect, and interfere with the pleasing sensations they were created to inspire'. Thus eighteenth- and early nineteenth-century women writers or artists had to contend with a set of aesthetic values which immediately diminished the value of what they produced.

The advent of the woman writer coincided also with the rise of Romanticism towards the end of the eighteenth century. While disputes about the nature of Romanticism and the place of gender and of women within it continue, several recent writers have argued that Romanticism served to privilege and empower men, largely because it incorporated a new and very explicitly masculine idea of creative genius. One of the key features of Romanticism was its emphasis on the importance of feelings and emotions as defining human characteristics and as the source of creativity, knowledge and moral insight. Romanticism stressed the importance of feeling in opposition to the Enlightenment idealisation of reason. The hero of Goethe's novel *Wilhelm Meister's Apprenticeship* in 1824 (originally published in German in 1795) exemplified a masculinity untethered by the materialist concerns of business, work or domesticity. Wilhelm Meister personified the liberal tenets of autonomy, and brought together feeling and reason, combining 'the brightest and most capricious fancy, the most piercing and inquisitive intellect, the wildest and deepest imagination . . . his faculties and feelings are not fettered or prostrated under the iron sway of Passion, but led and guided in kindly union under the mild sway of Reason' (Carlyle 1874: 23). This form of 'intellectual manhood' was characteristic of Romanticism, and of the desire for an alternative to the mediocrity of bourgeois norms, of a 'new Poet for the world in our own time, of a new Instructor and Preacher of Truth to all men'. For Romantics, intuition, sensation and feeling, rather than reason, were the key to knowledge and truth. While this stress on feeling linked Romanticism to femininity, it did not lead to the idea that women, who were generally seen as more emotional than men, had any superiority in terms of their imaginative or creative capacities. It was rather the case that exceptional men, and particularly men of genius, combined these feminine characteristics with masculine physical and intellectual strength. Romanticism thus developed a particular ideal of androgyny, in which the highest creative power was associated with a person who combined masculine and feminine characteristics, but always within a male body. For the Romantics, creative power or genius was the quality of greatest worth and, as Christine Battersby has argued, a genius was always a man who combined his masculine attributes (especially his bodily strength and sexuality) with feminine intuition and sensitivity (Battersby 1990: 103). By contrast, a woman with a masculine mind was seen as unnatural or monstrous. The Romantic idea of a genius also involved a sense of a man, battling alone, alienated from the surrounding culture, seeking solace in the natural world where he could find spiritual peace and a sense of the immense power of God, as the creator of nature. But this image, too, drew on ideas about men as the explorers of unknown continents, or as solitary beings who devoted their time to discovering the wonders of nature. Within the Romantic world view, as was made so clear by Rousseau in *Émile*, women were identified with society, with the world of triviality, everyday life, and with corruption. The figure who stood alone, seeking an authentic life and a close connection with the natural world, was always a man.

Romanticism gave a high place to feminine characteristics, although this did not mean that there was any marked empathy between romantic writers and women. On the contrary, women were depicted as exotic and strange in the writings of most Romantics, and were the supreme and mysterious objects of male desire. In some cases, as Anne Mellor has argued, the Romantic ideal of love did involve a sense of man and woman as spiritual soul mates. In these cases, however, the woman had no separate identity as she came to mirror or to be absorbed into her male lover. Describing his love of Mary Godwin (the daughter of Mary Wollstonecraft), the English poet

Percy Shelley explained, 'so intimately are our natures now united, that I feel while I describe her excellencies as if I were an egoist expatiating upon his own perfections' (Mellor 1993: 25). For Mellor, Romanticism is characterised by its extreme tendency to deny, obliterate or efface women, and to absorb feminine qualities into men. This effacement and absorption are seen most clearly in the way Romantic poets and writers attempt to appropriate the reproductive powers of women. Shelley in his *Defence of Poetry*, for example, described the poet as a mother bringing forth a work of art as if it were a child. By usurping the mother's womb, the poet becomes like God, sole ruler of the world. Mary Shelley's novel *Frankenstein* critiques this assumption about women's reproductive powers. The novel depicts a monster which is created – and then rejected and ignored – by the young scientist, Frankenstein. Frankenstein seeks the creative power of women, but feels none of the care or concern for his progeny that women feel for their babies. Shelley's novel has been read as an allegory of the ways in which the creative capacity of women was denied in Romanticism, much as it was in politics during the French Revolution.

The intensity of attempts to silence and erase the voices of women in the late eighteenth and early nineteenth century in Europe points to anxieties about the place and potential power of women and about the stability of the gender order. For much of the nineteenth century, this gender order was debated and renegotiated as women's participation in home, in the workforce and in the political arena became more and more pronounced.

References and further reading

Primary sources

Burke, Edmund (1965 [1790]) *Reflections on the Revolution in France*, New York.

De Gouges, Olympe (1986 [1791]) '*Declaration of the Rights of Woman and the Citizen*', in B. Groult (ed.) *Oeuvres*, Paris.

More, Hannah (1799) *Strictures on the Modern System of Female Education*, London.

Rousseau, Jean Jacques (1911 [1762]) *Émile*, trans. Barbara Foxley, New York.

Wollstonecraft, Mary (1988 [1792]) *A Vindication of the Rights of Woman*, New York.

Wollstonecraft, Mary (1975 [1796]) *Maria or the Wrongs of Woman*, New York.

Sexual difference and the Enlightenment

Abelove, H. (1989) 'Some speculations on the history of sexual intercourse during the long eighteenth century in England', *Gender* 6: 125–30.

Goodman, D. (1994) *The Republic of Letters: A Cultural History of the French Enlightenment*, Ithaca, New York.

Hill, B. (1987) *Eighteenth Century Women*, London.

Hull, I. (1996) *Sexuality, State, and Civil Society in Germany 1700–1815*, Ithaca.

Jordanova, L. (1990) *Sexual Visions: Images of Gender in Science and Medicine Between the Eighteenth and Twentieth Centuries*, London.

Laqueur, T. (1990) *Making Sex: Body and Gender from the Greeks to Freud*, Cambridge, Mass.

Lloyd, G. (1984) *The 'Man of Reason': Male and Female in Western Philosophy*, Sydney.

Scheibinger, L. (1989) *The Mind Has No Sex? Women in the Origins of Modern Science*, Cambridge, Mass.

Spencer, S. (ed.) (1984) *French Women and the Age of Enlightenment*, Bloomington.

Steinbrugge, L. (1995) *The Moral Sex: Women's Nature in the French Enlightenment*, trans. P. Selwyn, New York.

Wertheim, M. (1995) *Pythagoras' Trousers: God, Physics and the Gender Wars*, New York.

French Revolution and the origins of feminism

Caine, B. (1997) *English Feminism, 1780–1980*, Oxford.

Godineau, D. (1990) 'Masculine and feminine political practice during the French Revolution, 1793–Year III', in H. B. Applewhite and D. G. Levy (eds) *Women and Politics in the Age of the Democratic Revolution*, Ann Arbor.

Gutwirth, M. (1992) *The Twilight of the Goddesses: Women and Representation in the French Revolutionary Era*, New Brunswick.

Hufton, O. (1992) *Women and the Limits of Citizenship in the French Revolution*, Toronto.

Hunt, L. (1984) *Politics, Culture and Class in the French Revolution*, Berkeley.

Hunt, L. (1992) *The Family Romance of the French Revolution*, Berkeley.

Landes, J. (1988) *Women and the Public Sphere in the Age of the French Revolution*, Ithaca.

Landes, J. (1992) 'Representing the body politic: the paradox of gender in the graphic politics of the French Revolution', in S. E. Melzer and L. W. Rabine (eds) *Rebel Daughters: Women and the French Revolution*, New York and Oxford.

Levy, D. G. and Applewhite, H. B. (1992) 'Women and militant citizenship in Revolutionary Paris', in S. E. Melzer and L. W. Rabine (eds) *Rebel Daughters: Women and the French Revolution*, New York and Oxford.

Melzer, S. E. and Rabine, L. W. (eds) (1992) *Rebel Daughters: Women and the French Revolution*, New York and Oxford.

Outram, D. (1989) *The Body and the French Revolution*, New Haven.

Proctor, C. E. (1990) *Women, Equality, and the French Revolution*, New York.

Scott, J. W. (1996) *Only Paradoxes to Offer: French Feminists and the Rights of Man*, Cambridge, Mass.

Taylor, B. (1992) 'Mary Wollstonecraft and the wild wish of early feminism', *History Workshop Journal* **33**: 197–219.

Women writers and the age of Romanticism

Battersby, C. (1990) *Gender and Genius: Towards a Feminist Aesthetic*, London.

Butler, M. (1981) *Romantics, Rebels, Reactionaries: English Literature and its Background, 1760–1830*, Oxford.

Carlyle, T. (1874) 'Introduction', Goethe, *Wilhelm Meister's Lehrjahre*, trans. T. Carlyle, London.

Hesse, C. (1989) 'Female authorship and revolutionary law', *Eighteenth Century Studies* **3**: 469–87.

Kirkham, M. (1983) *Jane Austen: Feminism and Fiction*, Brighton.

Mellor, A. (ed.) (1988) *Romanticism and Feminism*, Bloomington.

Mellor, A. (1993) *Romanticism and Gender*, New York and London.

Yaeger, P. S. and Kowalski-Wallace, B. (eds) (1990) *Refiguring the Father. New Feminist Readings of Patriarchy*, Carbondale, Illinois.

TWO

Spaces and Places: Changing Patterns of Domesticity and Work

The impact of industrial capitalism on European economies and societies in the period from 1780 to 1920 brought about a transformation of work and the workplace, and of home and the meaning of domesticity. Industrialisation also produced new understandings and representations of gender. The advent of new sources of power, new workplaces and new technologies brought major changes in the sexual division of labour, and a new image of men as industrial workers. The complementary development for women centred on the image of the housewife, located in the home or the private sphere, which was designated as a specifically feminine space and location.

Patterns of industrialisation differed significantly from one country to another. In Britain, new methods of agriculture, the establishment of textile factories and the application of steam to manufacture brought what continues to be defined as an industrial revolution in the period 1780–1830. By contrast, France industrialised much more slowly, with substantial development in railway construction and factories getting underway only in the mid nineteenth century. In Germany and Russia, industrial expansion occurred still later in the century: after 1870 in Germany and in the 1890s in Russia. Despite the different pace of industrialisation, however, there were some common patterns throughout Europe concerning women's work, wages and general conditions in relation to those of men. For the most part, industrialisation served to emphasise and to make more rigid the sexual division of labour. The emergence of the industrial work that was introduced in the nineteenth century was undertaken by men. In factories and mines, on railways, roads and ships, for example, the vast majority of workers were men, and these new kinds of work brought in turn a new idea of the 'worker' as one engaged on a full-time basis in industrial labour. This industrial worker, alongside the traditional male artisan, on the one hand, and the middle-class professional or businessman, on the other, served to underline the idea that work itself was a masculine activity and indeed was central to the idea of masculinity. While the range of occupations available to men expanded with industrialisation, finding work became ever more difficult for women. The introduction of factories and larger workshops, which served to separate home from workplace, and the long working days which came with them produced immense problems for women who had to combine paid labour with familial responsibilities. Increasingly, married women sought home-based work or part-time and casual work which allowed them to supervise families. Trade unions, socialist groups and the many professional associations emerged in the mid nineteenth century that served to constrain the prospects for women workers. These work organisations were all concerned to improve working conditions for men. They were dominated by men in terms of their membership, and often sought the exclusion of women from particular occupations, or indeed from any kind of paid work.

The conception of the masculinity of work and the workplace had as its counterpart the idea of the home as a private and feminine sphere. The notion of 'separate spheres' for men and women developed first through a middle-class pattern in which a male household head engaged in the public sphere of work and political activity, working to support his family while his wife and daughters remained at home. The notion of separate spheres fitted very neatly into prevailing ideas of sexual difference. Work was clearly the necessary activity of strong, energetic, rational and independent man. By contrast, immersion in the home and dedication to husband and children suited the temperament and emotions of women. Throughout Europe, separate spheres were regarded as integral to the social, civic and moral order. In Britain, in the late eighteenth and early nineteenth centuries, the growing influence of evangelical religion brought a new emphasis on home and family as the basic unit in religious observance and moral order. By contrast, in France, from the 1790s onwards, the new Republic demanded close family ties and maternal duty in order that children would learn civic virtue and their duties as citizens at their mother's breast. In the German states and the Habsburg empire, the new emphasis on family life and on the home emerged in the early decades of the nineteenth century, and was associated closely with the post-Napoleonic Restoration, political conservatism and the reassertion of the importance of hierarchy in the state. Thus for all their political and social differences, evangelicals, republicans and conservatives held common views about the nature of the public sphere, about sexual difference, women's activities and the importance of family life.

The sense of home promulgated by the middle classes at the beginning of the century also became an ideal among skilled artisans and even socialists in the mid and later nineteenth century. As a result, the question of women's work and indeed the very idea of the 'woman worker' became extremely problematic (Scott 1993). While the vast majority of women had to engage in paid work to support themselves and their families, the range of employment opportunities available to women and their wages were all set in a framework that viewed them as supplementary or casual income-earners, whose major commitment and responsibility was to marriage and family life. Moreover, since in this ideological framework women were suited only to domestic life, certain forms of paid employment, for example many kinds of industrial or agricultural work, were almost unthinkable for women, and others, especially any form of domestic service, seemed 'natural' or suitable. It was by no means the case, however, that domestic labour was any less arduous for women than other forms of employment. Many women protested against the confinement they faced in their conventional work and domestic roles. Some demanded greater opportunities to work in order to support families or to develop financial independence. Others sought rather to gain access to a wider public world through an emphasis on the tasks they undertook at home.

In this chapter we explore the ideal of family and home that developed in the nineteenth century alongside industrialisation and urbanisation. We begin by looking at the development of the new style of domestic life evident in the middle class, with a male breadwinner and a family and a home concerned with consumption rather than production. We then look at the impact of this model of family life on the working class, focusing on the gendering of work and on the difficulties this entailed for working-class women.

Family life and home

For many historians, the economic, political and social developments of the nineteenth century produced a new class society in which the values and beliefs of the middle class came to dominate all others (see Chapter 3). Hence the nineteenth century is often referred to as the 'bourgeois century' and it was among the bourgeoisie, or the middle class, that the importance of the home was first extolled and that the new model of family life first appeared. From the late eighteenth century onwards, in both Britain and France, the close-knit family was one of the prominent features of bourgeois urban life. The meaning of the term 'family' changed over the second half of the eighteenth century, as it increasingly referred to the unit composed of parents and children, in contrast to earlier meanings which had stressed either lineage groups or households with apprentices. This new meaning of family derived from the middle-class pattern in contrast to an aristocratic one. Family life in turn played a major part in establishing a distinctive middle-class life-style in which domestic affection, intimacy and a sense of domestic duty were extolled and seen to provide the basis for a superior social and moral order. In the late eighteenth and nineteenth centuries, love between husband and wife began to replace financial or social interest as the proper basis of marriage, while parental love, especially that of a mother for her children, was regarded as essential for harmonious family life. Maternal devotion was also seen as an integral part of a woman's nature, and as something which differentiated civilised women from their 'savage' female counterparts.

This distinctive and morally superior middle-class family and its new domestic life-style also became the basis of the middle-class demand for a new social and political status. As Catherine Hall and Leonore Davidoff have shown, in Britain during the first half of the nineteenth century, the capacity to provide a comfortable home to maintain a wife and children was regarded as a primary indication of a man's independence, of his status as a gentleman and of his entitlement to political rights and recognition (Davidoff and Hall 1987). In France too, the middle-class family had a particular role to play, and the middle-class family man was given a special political status. As Isabel Hull has argued, the Napoleonic Civil Code served to protect the married, propertied male citizen and 'his private social status as presumptive family father and producer of wealth became the basis for his greater, state-guaranteed rights' (Hull 1996). Before 1848 the claims for political rights made by the middle class in the German states were not recognised and, consequently, men retreated to the domestic world and shared with women a deep involvement in family life. Ute Frevert argues that a certain amount of mockery was directed towards middle-class men who devoted themselves to domestic life rather than seeking a wider use for their abilities (Frevert 1989). Later in the century, however, the unified German nation recognised the political importance of the middle-class male household head (see Chapter 4).

In the eyes of some historians, the emergence of a more affectionate family and the enhancement of women's maternal role lessened the patriarchal nature of family life and improved the status of women. The ideal wife as depicted by Hannah More or Jane Austen in England at the turn of the nineteenth century was a genuine 'helpmeet' to her husband, valued and beloved in accordance with her dutifulness and devotion. In this view marriage was a companionate relationship, husbands and wives were domestic and social companions as well as sexual partners. Yet, as middle-class women became immersed in domestic and family life, they withdrew from some of their economic activities, and became economically dependent on their husbands or fathers. Though many women in the middle ranks participated in family businesses in the eighteenth century, from the 1780s onwards, middle- and upper-middle-class women withdrew from paid labour so they could devote themselves fully to family life. In both England and Germany, this process was completed by about 1850, after which time, middle-class women were expected to devote themselves to the home. Unpaid philanthropy or charity work was their main activity beyond the domestic hearth. In France, the prevalence of small family firms rather than larger businesses which could employ paid labour meant that some middle-class women continued to be economically active well into and beyond this period. Bonnie Smith has shown that despite the existence of maternal societies and a literature extolling maternity, the bourgeois women of the Nord worked alongside their husbands for long hours each day well into the 1840s, putting children out to wet nurse or sending them to boarding school so they would not interfere with their labours. By the 1850s and 1860s, however, these women, too, were devoting themselves to domestic activity and religious observance. Where once female virtue had included the capacity to work hard for a family business, it was now defined in terms of managing a family and maternal devotion. Bourgeois men made very clear their sense that business was no place for women. It is worth pointing out that women who had once prided themselves on their robust health were now being described as delicate and in need of special care (Smith 1981: 53–90).

The middle-class emphasis on the moral basis of family life had its material counterpart in the expansion of the home, which became a focus for new middle-class patterns of consumption. Middle-class homes grew considerably in size and grandeur during this period. Indeed, the home provided a significant market for textiles, furniture and artefacts, the manufacture of which supplied middle-class incomes. From the 1860s and 1870s, electricity was harnessed to the home, bringing light and more efficient heating. In a similar way, the design and building of comfortable homes and villas located in suburbs away from the centre of towns and cities, increased the demand for architects, builders, painters and decorators, as well as credit services, banks and lawyers. It also involved the expansion of new industries which supplied furniture and ornaments, garden implements and plants. Thus the middle-class home provided the basis for new professions and for an expansion of commercial services and enterprises.

Care of home and family and a constant concern with maternity were ostensibly regarded as integral to women's 'nature'. But the immense number of works in every language which set out to instruct women in their natural role and to explain exactly what wifedom, mothering and domestic care involved, seem rather to question the extent to which, even in the nineteenth century, family life and domesticity were seen as 'natural' for women. During the Napoleonic era, dozens of French manuals on home economics and family welfare were published, seeking to instruct the women about their bodies, sexual identities and roles, and about all aspects of child-rearing including infant cuisine. The predominant German-language literature for women in the later eighteenth century still depicted women as *Hausmutters* (literally 'house-mothers'), assuming they would preside over agricultural estates with their husbands. By the 1830s, however, the *Hausmutter* had been replaced by the *Hausfrau* ('housewife'), whose concerns centred on domestic life. Some of the qualities expected of the *Hausmutter* were evident also in the *Hausfrau*. Frugality, orderliness and the notion that the household was the prescribed sphere of woman's existence lost their specific economic focus, but they remained as foundations for bourgeois social ideas of womanhood, shoring up the notion that women should be the guardians of the private sphere of life while men gained new roles in the market-place and the workforce (Gray 1987). The period 1780–1830 saw an absolute explosion in English-language publications explaining to women their duties and roles as wives, daughters and mothers. All of these works contained a range of discussions, extending from direct information about child care and domestic activities to moral and religious exhortation. Manuals on motherhood and women's duties were not only remarkably similar across Europe, but were translated from one country to another. Thus, the preface of an extremely popular English book of the 1840s, Sarah Lewis's *Woman's Mission* (London, 1839) made clear that the work was largely derived from a French work by M. Aimé-Martin, *De l'Education des mères de famille, ou de la civilisation du genre humain par les femmes* (Paris, 1834).

Some of the impetus behind this early and mid-nineteenth-century outpouring of works on women's duty may have lain in the belief that women's domestic role was closely connected to the wider social, political and moral world. The 'home' over which women presided was not simply a physical space, but was constituted also in moral terms. The best known and fullest English exposition of this ideal of home was set out by John Ruskin in his essay 'Of Queen's Gardens', in *Sesame and Lilies* published in 1865. Home for Ruskin had a powerful metaphorical meaning. It was 'a place of Peace; the shelter not only from all injury, but from all terror, doubt and division'. Unless it functioned in this way, Ruskin insisted, a house could not truly be a home. It was the duty of women to shut out the external world of work, toil, strife and moral delinquency, and to utilise their moral and emotional qualities to ensure that the house became truly a home. Ironically, in his insistence on the need to separate the home from the outside world, Ruskin demanded that they be connected. A properly constituted home would protect its inmates from external dangers and exercise a benign influence on the external world. If the home was properly run and organised, Ruskin argued, and if women carried out fully their domestic and moral duties, there would be a diminution of social and political disorder, sexual promiscuity and war (Ruskin 1865: 77–9). Ruskin was clearly following Rousseau from a century before, but only up to a point. While Rousseau argued against any activity of women outside the home, Ruskin believed that modest and chaste wives and mothers had a responsibility to engage in philanthropic and charitable work, and especially to attempt to reform other women who had fallen from virtue. Rousseau, in his great fear of women's sexuality, saw the very presence of women outside the home as an invitation to vice. By the time that Ruskin was writing, the ideal of women's virtue was rather more widely accepted, especially in regard to middle-class married women. It was believed that the virtue of these women could be utilised to assist their weaker sisters.

A number of paradoxes and contradictions were evident in the relations within the domestic sphere. In the first place, while the ideal home was presided over by a woman and seen as her 'natural' sphere, she did not own it. Women, like the children they bore and the house in which they lived, all belonged to their husbands. Indeed, in Ruskin's view, 'a true wife, in her husband's house, is his servant; it is in his heart that she is queen' (Ruskin 1865: 75). As we have already seen, the precise powers of husbands and fathers varied from one country to another, but they were always extensive, throughout the nineteenth century. Maternity was deemed the highest moral, religious and social duty for women. But women's care of children was under the control of their husbands. Fathers had extensive rights in regard to their children (see Chapter 1). While designated a 'female sphere', the home and the family were legally and conventionally under male control and authority.

The ideal of home as a place of leisure and contentment was derived from the viewpoint of the men who returned to it at the end of the day, rather than from the women who lived constantly within it. Home was certainly not a place of leisure for women. Wealthy women may simply have presided over an army of servants, but the majority of middle- and even upper-middle-class women had a range of domestic tasks which could include either supervising or providing lessons for children, making clothes, shopping, cooking, arranging social events. Moreover, whether or not the lady of the house was directly engaged in these activities, the vast majority of servants who carried them out were women. It was no secret that maintaining homes required extensive labour, and indeed many manuals for women stressed the need to make sure that all housework was done while the lord and master was out at work so that he could enjoy not only peace, but harmony and domestic order on his return.

The paradoxes underlying family life extend also to the idea of it as a 'private sphere'. The idea of 'privacy', of the home as a secluded haven, safe from prying eyes, was basic to the middle-class ideal of home. At the same time, throughout the nineteenth century, the home was increasingly subject to public debate and to intervention and regulation by governments and intellectuals. Much of the intervention in homelife was a result of a growing scientific interest in the question of maternity. As we saw in Chapter 1, medical thought throughout the eighteenth century paid particular attention to defining and classifying women's reproductive systems. This was accompanied by an emphasis in medical manuals on the importance of reproduction and of motherhood as the centre of women's lives. In the process, the physiological details of motherhood, of pregnancy, birth and breast-feeding became matters of widespread scientific and general discussion. Ruth Perry argues strongly that the new emphasis on motherhood in the late eighteenth century involved a 'colonisation of the female body for domestic life', with a consequent denial to women of their sexuality (Perry 1991: 167). The significance of motherhood and the responsibilities of mothers for the care and education of their children were also widely discussed. Medical treatises, sermons, moral and educational literature of many kinds stressed the importance of breast-feeding as something which was good for women, essential for the health of their children and beneficial for the nation as a whole. The vogue for breast-feeding was accompanied by a new language and a series of images which depicted the maternal breast as the fountain of both physical and moral nourishment. During the French Revolution, public ceremonies and pamphlets insisted that children were to drink in republican values at the breast (Jacobus 1992). Later in the nine-teenth century, British medical manuals showed children drinking in moral virtue and physical health at the breast.

The most significant change in ideas of motherhood across the nineteenth century was the shift from the earlier concern with the moral and religious importance of motherhood, to the later emphasis on questions of physical health and well-being. The rise of the medical profession in the mid nine-teenth century was accompanied by the establishment of new specialist disciplines including gynaecology and obstetrics, which dealt specifically with women's reproductive systems. But the development of these female branches of medicine was accompanied by a new stress on the extent to which women deviated from the norm set by the healthy male body, and a view of women as fundamentally weak, fragile and in need of constant medical attention. In the eyes of many nineteenth-century doctors, and influential intellectuals like Jules Michelet, every feature of the reproductive development of women, from the onset of menstruation through pregnancy to menopause, was a form of illness and had to be guided and controlled by a medical specialist (Jalland and Hooper 1986). The medical, educational and political concern about motherhood and child care, about family life and education, about the relationship between domestic order on the one hand, and social and political order on the other, served to make women's private activities a source of public debate and discussion. This is evidence of the practical impossibility of creating any absolute distinctions between the public and the private sphere. The new emphasis on the private world of home served at least as much to make women's activities visible as to restrict their scope.

These paradoxes about gender are evident also in regard to the moral connotations of home and the place of family life in ideas of social and civic order. As both Rousseau and Ruskin make clear, women and their domestic government determined the tenor of social and political life. Many nineteenth-century authors were far more explicit in their demand that women 'regenerate society' and that they ensure that their families have the right religious and moral or political values. But through all of this, women were expected to be the religious and moral guides and leaders of men to whom they were in every way subordinate. They were expected to raise the moral and religious tone of their family, household and local community – and through that of the wider economic and political world – a world to which they were denied any direct access.

The tensions between this new sense of women's virtuous domesticity with its religious underpinning, and the secular nature of the masculine political world were evident in much of Europe, but they were particularly marked in Catholic France. Women's greater religiosity, their close ties with local priests and their dependence on parish churches and religious charities had made many of them antagonistic to the disestablishment of the Church carried out by the Revolution. When the Church was re-established, the support it gained from women reinforced a belief already held by some secular-minded liberals that it was through women that the priests attempted to exert control not only over the domestic life, but also over the social life and the political behaviour of men. The secularism and anti-clericalism of many French radicals and republicans led to a powerful attack on the alliance between women and the Church and their presumed conspiracy to limit the freedom of independent men.

The world of work

In nineteenth-century Europe, the corollary of representations of the domestic sphere as feminine was the conception of the new world of work as masculine. The vast majority of the new forms of work which came with industrialisation were undertaken by men. Although some women worked in factories, particularly in textile and clothing factories, most factory workers were men. The mining and metallurgical industries, like the chemical and electrical industries, were almost exclusively male. Men monopolised the senior and the skilled positions even in textile factories. Employers who were installing new machinery in nineteenth-century factories automatically assumed that only men would have the strength and the skill to manage this complicated new equipment. In some cases, this reflected the fact that men had worked as mechanics or had overseen domestic machinery before moving into factories. It also reflected the ways in which masculine traits, and manliness itself, were deemed to be essential to the notion of 'skill', making men into superior workers (Rose 1992: 23–35; Phillips and Taylor 1980). Moreover, men's work was very visible in the nineteenth-century towns and cities which were being transformed by new methods of transport. While some women were certainly street sellers, most women worked indoors. By contrast, rail and road laying, building and dock work were exclusively masculine. Thus men were closely associated with the work which was bringing into being new industrial cities.

The association of work with masculinity became a central feature of radical politics and of labour organisation in the nineteenth century. The new emphasis on work and the separation of home and workplace meant that for very large numbers of working-class men, work served to define their identity. To be employed as a skilled worker gave a man economic and social status. In Britain, the skilled male worker could aspire to independence: to be free to sell his labour power; to support himself without the aid of charity; to have some freedom in regard to the regulation of his trade. Independence for male workers carried with it also the connotation which was central to the ideal of middle-class male independence: namely the capacity to maintain dependents within the home, to have a wife and possibly daughters who did not have to engage in paid work. The ideal of manly independence led to strong support from many working men for legislation which would exclude women from particular forms of paid labour, or would limit drastically their working hours. In many cases, hostility to women's paid work reflected fears from working men that the lower wages paid to women would reduce their wages too. As Anna Clark and Sally Alexander have recently shown, the need to reassert and to maintain their patriarchal privileges so strongly felt by male working-class radicals in Britain led to considerable domestic, familial and social tension (Clark 1995; Alexander 1994). Few male radicals, social-ists or trade unionists were prepared to listen to the claims and demands of women. Rather they insisted that women remain under the protection of their menfolk. Radical political groups, like the British Chartists of the 1830s and 1840s, indicated that they shared this sense that women did not belong in the public sphere by campaigning for manhood rather than universal suffrage, and by ignoring the demands of their womenfolk for political rights.

The insistence that work was a masculine prerogative is evident elsewhere in nineteenth-century Europe. In Germany, workingmen's associations established during the revolutions of 1848 were generally open only to men (see Chapter 3). Moreover, in those industries employing women such as printing and cigar-making, for example, the General German Workers Association set up by the socialist Ferdinand Lasalle in 1863, and other new men's associations, joined male tailors in demanding an end to women's industrial labour. Other socialist and trade union organisations in Germany, and especially the workers educational association, rejected this view and insisted on women's right to work, but little was done to attract women to trade union or socialist organisations or to push demands for better pay and conditions for them (Frevert 1989).

The close identification of work with men, alongside the ideal of a family wage earned by men, made the 'woman worker' seem an oddity and an anomaly. From about 1820 onwards, the 'woman worker' was the centre of considerable debate among social and political reformers and in literature. This was not, as Scott and Alexander have argued, because there was any significant change in the quantity of women's work in this period compared with the preceding one. Rather, concern about the 'woman worker' arose because contemporary ideas about sexual difference and about the importance of domesticity made the idea of women working, and especially of women working outside the home, a disturbing one. It is undoubtedly the case that new industrialised forms of work outside the home posed serious problems for women because they could not combine paid work outside the home with the supervision of children. Further, the image of factories, mines and workshops as male spaces increased moral concerns about their suitability for women. The novelist Elizabeth Gaskell, writing in the 1840s, was concerned about how women who worked full-time in factories would learn the appropriate skills for domestic life (Gaskell 1848). Other critics feared the impropriety, sexual promiscuity and disorder that women might bring if they worked in inadequately supervised places. In the view of the socialist writer Friedrich Engels, the employment of women in preference to men in some tasks or industries because they were cheaper to employ, threatened an inversion of the family order by making women breadwinners while men were unemployed. For Engels, as for the widely read French novelist Emile Zola, heavy and dirty labour for women raised the issue of sexual difference; in this new industrial order both men and women seemed 'unsexed' (Engels 1892) as women lose their feminine qualities and men their manliness.

Regardless of these strictures, women continued to work throughout the nineteenth century. Although many trade unions and socialist groups advocated a 'family wage' which would enable men to support their families, only a very small number of skilled workers were able to provide for their families. Throughout the nineteenth century, most urban workers were in the same situation as peasants and other rural workers, requiring that every member of the family contribute labour or earnings if the family was to get by. The traditional rural family economy in which members of a family all worked together in an agricultural or craft-based enterprise changed its form in urban centres. For the most part, families no longer worked as a unit; instead they were wage earners who pooled their earnings. But the family economy continued to underlie the survival of both rural and urban workers.

In Europe, work by women followed a traditional pattern. Agricultural change occurred irregularly across Europe and brought with it a range of different situations. The slow pace of industrial development in France and Italy and its late advent in Germany and Russia, meant that for many women agricultural work continued to be the norm. In Germany and in France, about half of the female labour force continued to be employed in agriculture until after the First World War. Women were accustomed to extremely heavy agricultural work. In peasant communities throughout the nineteenth and early twentieth centuries, for example, women were expected to provide food and clothing for the family and to engage in a variety of different forms of agricultural labour: dairy work, feeding and supervising poultry, growing vegetables or working in the fields when planting or harvesting were under-way. In France, women augmented their income with lace-making. In western Prussia, small holdings continued as they did in France. However, new and labour intensive crops like potatoes and beets meant that many women were engaged in very heavy field work.

In countries where capitalism had been applied to agriculture, creating enclosures and new large-scale farms, women's work underwent the most dramatic change. Large farms which employed agricultural labourers introduced patterns of work which resembled those in factories, in that they required full-time work on particular tasks and made it impossible for women to combine farm work with family duties (Frader 1987). This was the case in England where enclosures had removed common land and thereby made it impossible for women to engage in independent agricultural production. Many women were forced off the land. Some became wage labourers, often working in agricultural 'gangs' on other farms. Similarly in eastern Prussia, where the emancipation of serfs brought land enclosures and large capitalist farms, women worked as full-time agricultural wage labourers. While there were very different patterns for the sexual division of labour in different countries and different peasant communities, it is clear that rural women worked for as many hours as men and in jobs that were as heavy. Early twentieth-century studies suggest that in Russia and in Ireland, peasant women were engaged in considerably more hours of arduous labour than were men, and that they were excluded from many of the masculine recreational activities.

The advent of factories certainly brought some new work for women. Textiles factories provided work for quite large numbers of women spinners and weavers in Britain and France in the early and mid nineteenth century, and in Germany, Austria and Russia in the later part of the century. Women were also employed in the clothing, food, tobacco and paper industries. The numbers and percentages of women engaged in factory work varied from one country to another. Britain had the highest percentage of women engaged in factory work. From 1841 to 1911, the percentage of female factory workers rose from 35 to 45 per cent of the female labour force. By contrast, in both France and Germany it remained at about 25 per cent of the female labour force (Frader 1987: 318). National figures tend to be somewhat misleading, however, as industrial work for women, as for men, was heavily concentrated in particular areas. In Germany, for example, women made up about 60 per cent of workers in the Bielefield linen industry, while in Britain, women were engaged in textile factories largely in the north of England, in Lancashire and Yorkshire.

Factories demonstrated in the most stark way the incompatibility between the demands of paid work and family responsibilities which came with industrialisation. Factory conditions were fairly similar across Europe and in all cases involved workers in extremely long hours of work during which it was impossible to leave the factory. In many places, factories were locked and workers could not get out. Factory working days were generally between 12 and 15 hours, and were regulated strictly by the clock. Workers were fined for being late and were given only very short breaks for meals. Hence the women who undertook factory work were generally young and single. They were expected to leave once they married. Factory work was poorly paid and working conditions were harsh and difficult for men as well as women, but young women were also vulnerable both to sexual exploitation and to harsh discipline from male factory overseers (Glickman 1984; Frevert 1989). Many men shared with women the harsh life of the factory worker, but no women were in positions of power within factories. Commissions of inquiry in Britain, and the memoirs of articulate working women like Jeanne Bouvier in France or Adelheid Popp in Germany illustrate the harshness of factory conditions: the fines for late work, the beatings of those whose work was seen as inadequate, the dangers of machinery which was poorly maintained and not protected, the constant sexual harassment (Frader 1987: 320).

The advent of the factory did not bring out-work or home-based work to an end. Grey Osterud has shown how the hosiery industry in Britain provided work for women at home, seaming and finishing off the stockings which were woven in factories. There was also an expansion in unskilled 'slop work', centring on the making of basic clothing like shirts, or furniture making, box-making, book-binding, flower-making, which often employed people in workshops (Osterud 1986). Workshop wages were usually lower than those of factories, and their conditions resembled those of factories in terms of their long hours and strict regulation. Low rates of pay meant that women who worked at home might have even longer hours than those who worked in factories and workshops, but this option was often the only possible one for women who had both to work and to care for children.

Ironically, while middle-class ideals of home and family life made work seem aberrant for women, it was middle-class homes which provided the largest amount of paid work for women. Seeking work as a servant was a traditional part of rural life, where the daughters of tenant farmers had long worked on neighbouring farms or in towns as servants to earn a dowry. In the nineteenth century, however, domestic service expanded its scope and changed its form dramatically. Until the late eighteenth century, employing servants was largely an aristocratic privilege. In the course of the nineteenth century, domestic service, as Joan Scott says, 'became more democratic'. Increasing numbers of middle- and upper-middle-class families came to need servants (Scott 1993: 399–405). As service was less and less associated with agrarian life and farm work, and more and more concentrated on middle-class urban homes, it also became a feminised occupation. Domestic servants throughout the nineteenth century were overwhelmingly female and, conversely, domestic service was often the largest category of women's employment. In both London and Berlin in the 1860s, approximately one-third of all women aged between 15 and 24 were domestic servants. In St Petersburg, the number of men and women domestic servants were more or less the same, but by 1890, the number of women had almost doubled, and the percentage of women in domestic service was almost one-third, the same as in London (Glickman 1984: 60).

Factory work was frowned upon for women, but domestic service did not attract criticism from those many middle-class commentators concerned about working-class family life and morality. Middle-class observers and authorities regarded factories and mines as undesirable because they were often dirty and dangerous, allowed girls or women to work alongside men without any supervision, and encouraged, it was thought, promiscuous sexual contact. Industrial work also deprived women of any training in domestic life. Domestic service, by contrast, was seen as unexceptionable, and indeed as a desirable way to educate working-class girls in the domestic arts and customs of the middle class. Most nineteenth-century commentators applauded domestic service as beneficial, but later historians have questioned this evaluation, pointing out that domestic servants were vulnerable to excessive work loads, to sexual exploitation and to cruel treatment in unregulated settings. The lives of domestic servants were extremely hard and often unrewarding. Servants were most often employed alone, as 'maids of all work', or at most with one or two fellows. Their conditions, their hours and their rates of pay were completely unregulated. Sometimes servants were paid annually, or even at the end of a number of years. Most servants lived in and thus could be on constant call. Many were not provided with adequate sleeping or living accommodation. Fortunate servants might sleep in an unheated attic. Others might be required to sleep in closets or in a corner of the kitchen. They were under constant scrutiny, could be called on at any time and were vulnerable to the sexual demands of employers. Because they lived in, servants lacked the control of their non-working hours available to other workers. Their capacity to carry on any form of social or sexual life was minimal. Any suggestion that a servant girl was engaging in a sexual relationship would almost guarantee her dismissal and the women who remained servants throughout their lives were generally unmarried and celibate. In many cases, girls worked as full-time or live-in servants only until they married, but substantial numbers of older domestic servants lived permanently as celibate dependents in the homes of employers.

For those seeking to explore the world of women's work in the nineteenth century, census figures and surveys are always problematic because they seem to under-represent women's work. Writing about London in the 1830s and 1840s, Sally Alexander points to the discrepancy between statistics which show only some 60 per cent of working-class women as being employed at a time when it is clear from other evidence that among the working class it was assumed that all family members, including married women, should contribute to the family income. This discrepancy can be explained by looking at the very different patterns evident in women's work as compared with that of men (Alexander 1994: 3–12). While women's work in factories and workshops bore some resemblance to the full-time work sought by men, much work undertaken by women was casual and part-time, and therefore scarcely noticed. In the nineteenth century, as in the twentieth, many women managed to combine their economic needs and their family responsibilities by doing part-time work, which was never included in formal census data or statistics, including cleaning and charring, sewing, washing and laundry work.

The idea that men were the major family income earners and that women worked only in a supplementary character served to define women as unskilled and provided the framework for wages differentials. Inevitably this meant that women always earned considerably less than men. The sexual basis of wages is most evident in the very low rates of pay available to those women engaged in specifically female activities: domestic service, sewing, millinery, cleaning and laundry work. Wages in these areas lagged significantly behind those available to women engaged in factory work. In Berlin by the late nineteenth century, as Ute Frevert has shown, a full-time domestic maid of all work earned only about one-third of the wages of a woman employed in the linen industry and considerably less than half the wages of a female factory worker (Frevert 1989). Female factory workers earned between half and two-thirds of the wages of male factory workers. Women earned only a fraction of men's wages regardless of the industry: in factories manufacturing textiles and clothing, pottery and china, and processing wood, paper, minerals and metals. Validations of this situation included claims that women were less literate and less efficient than men, or that they worked at lighter and easier tasks. Recent research in Britain, Germany, France and Russia challenges these claims, and shows that women earned lower wages because of normative assumptions about the masculine nature of work. Rose Glickman argues that in Russian factories women did work which was as difficult, as heavy and as dangerous as men's tasks, but accepted lower wages because they saw no alternative and because they tended to share the assumption that their primary duty was to their family (Glickman 1984). Moreover, Kathleen Canning and Sonia Rose point also to the fact that women earned less than men even when they were engaged in exactly the same tasks (Canning 1992; Rose 1992). Wages were set in accordance with sexual assumptions about the needs and entitlements of the wage earners rather than in accordance with any precise measure of output.

Low wages were also a marked feature of the lives of the many women who were engaged in non-industrial labour, mainly as outworkers or in workshops. In cities like London, there was a vast amount of work in clothing, hat making, food preparation, furniture making, box making and in the manufacture of other household necessities. Most of the skilled trades as bespoke tailors, or cabinet-makers or chefs, for example, were undertaken by men. The concern among tailors and other skilled workers that women's competition lowered wages generally was clearly combined with a new sense of the proper location of women within family life and with a demand for a family wage which would enable men to support their families. A few women counted as highly skilled dress-makers or milliners, but the vast majority of women were regarded as semi- or unskilled and worked for very low wages. In many of these areas, especially those connected with fashion or with food, work was seasonal with immensely long hours during the fashion 'season' and periods of little or no work before and after. All of this meant that a very large proportion of women workers received an income which was inadequate to their needs. Seasonal slumps or ill-health could deprive them of any income at all.

In view of the extreme moral concern expressed about women's work throughout the nineteenth century, and most particularly the fear that it would lead to sexual promiscuity, it is ironic that the generally low level of wages, and the intermittent periods of unemployment, often meant that women, especially young women, had no way to earn a living at all unless they resorted to prostitution. While some women clearly chose prostitution, seeing it as offering better pay and conditions than what was available in any of the other avenues open to them, others were driven to it through the sexual inequalities which they confronted at work. In many cases, working women were expected or required to provide sexual services to their employers or overseers. This was so for domestic servants, for shop assistants and for women employed in industry and agriculture. In other areas of employment, casual or intermittent prostitution was taken for granted. The urbanisation which accompanied industrialisation and the development of leisure as an industry with shopping precincts, dance halls, theatres, promenades, hotels and bars increased the opportunities for prostitution and by the mid nineteenth century, prostitution was rife in all European cities. Every city in England had at least one area notorious for prostitution and in London, prostitutes were thought to number at least 100,000 by mid century. Other major cities had similar figures: contemporary estimates suggest that Berlin had about 16,000 prostitutes in 1870, rising to 40,000 by 1909; St Petersburg, which had a population of 1.5 million by the turn of the twentieth century, was estimated to have between 30,000 and 50,000 prostitutes.

In her final work, *Maria or the Wrongs of Woman* (published after her death in 1796), Mary Wollstonecraft pointed in a very graphic way to the immense difficulties women faced in supporting themselves, and to the ways in which this drove them into prostitution, or into relationships based solely on their need for economic support and their agreement to engage in sexual intercourse to provide it. The needs of working-class women for paid employment was a matter of discussion among feminists within the utopian socialist movements of the early nineteenth century. In Britain, socialist feminists wrote and spoke at length on the double difficulties they faced as a result of the sexual division of labour and low wages, on the one hand, and from the hostility of their own menfolk to the very idea that they should engage in paid work, on the other (see Chapter 3). This was less of an issue in France, where the participation rates of married women in paid labour were higher than they were in Britain throughout the nineteenth century. Nonetheless, most of the women who became involved in the Saint-Simonian movement identified themselves clearly as workers and insisted on their right and their ability to combine paid with family responsibilities.

The need for paid work for women was a central concern to all the feminist and philanthropic organisations which began to emerge in the mid nineteenth century. In Britain, the extreme hardships of middle-class women who did not have husbands, fathers or brothers to support them had been of concern to feminists from the 1840s. Harriet Martineau, a very well known writer and journalist, published an influential article in 1859 in which she sought to show 'the full breadth of the area of female labour in Great Britain', and to demand recognition of the varieties of work done by women and of the huge numbers of working-class women forced to be self-supporting. The census results and various major surveys, she argued, now revealed that, contrary to popular beliefs, 'a very large proportion of the women of England earn their own bread'. The census of 1851, she argued, showed the increase in the numbers of women involved in paid employment: 'While the female population has increased (between 1841 and 1851) in the ratio of 7 to 8, the number of women returned as engaged in independent industry has increased in the far greater ratio of 3 to 4' (Martineau 1859: 277–30). Women were now employed in many forms of agriculture; in mining and extractive industries; in many industries concerned with 'the produce of the waters', including catching, curing and selling fish; in a wide variety of crafts and trades; and in domestic service. New occupations for women included manufacturing, especially the textile, lace and ribbon industries, as well as telegraphy and clerical. Increasing numbers of women were also engaged in the keeping of lodging houses.

Martineau's article provided the stimulus for the establishment of a number of British campaigns to expand the range of paid employment available to women, including the creation of the Society for Promoting the Employment of Women in 1859, which established employment bureaus, training schemes and particular forms of work like printing. In a similar way, in the 1860s and 1870s, in Germany, Russia and the Habsburg empire, middle-class feminists and philanthropists began to organise ways to extend paid employment for women, sometimes through the setting up of co-operative workshops or training schemes. The St Petersburg Society for Women's Work was established in the 1860s. The Viennese Women's

Employment Association, founded in November 1866, initiated what is referred to as the 'era of the organised woman' in Austria (Good, Gradner and Maynes 1996). Its immediate impetus was the widespread economic distress which followed the defeat of Austria by Prussia earlier that year, and which had made many women, both married and single, destitute and in need of employment. This organisation was followed by a series of other associations dedicated to the improvement of women's education and to the support of lower-middle-class girls by assisting them in obtaining appropriate training. While essentially philanthropic, the Viennese Women's Employment Association recognised the need for financial independence for women.

The capacity of philanthropic groups or of middle-class feminists to address the needs of working-class women was challenged in the 1880s and 1890s and in the early twentieth century by a number of women associated with the labour movement or with socialist organisations. In Britain, women like Barbara Hutchins and Beatrice Webb associated with trade unions and the Fabian Society, in Germany, Klara Zetkin as the leader of the women's organisation set up by the German SPD, in Russia, Alexander Kollontai, the leader of the Bolshevik women's group – all insisted that the needs of working women could only be addressed from within the framework of socialism. The specific issues over which there was major disagreement between these women and middle-class feminists and philanthropists were industrial legislation and trade union membership for women. For the most part, middle-class feminists opposed any form of industrial legislation that applied to women and not to men and they also opposed trade unions as interfering with the freedom of individuals.

The whole question of work for women, and the related issues of family responsibilities on the one hand, and special industrial legislation on the other, is a complex one. Many middle-class feminists demanded the right of women to work on the same terms as men. In Britain, this involved a direct conflict of views between the old-style economic liberalism of the women's movement and the much more interventionist ideas of socialists and members of the labour movement. In the 1880s and 1890s members of women's movements continued to oppose any industrial legislation which was applied to women and not to men. Such legislation, in their view, denied that women were rational adults capable of ascertaining or following their own interests. It served also to reduce the employment opportunities and the income-earning capacity of women. Many women associated with the labour movement attacked this approach. They opposed the political and economic

framework on which it was based, arguing that feminists lacked any understanding of the problems of industrial labour. Beatrice Webb, for example,
insisted that protective legislation, far from restricting the freedom of
women, was essential to that freedom since it offered the only way to
improve their pay and conditions of work.

While it is clearly the case that working women needed protection,
throughout Europe the labour codes and legislation of the late nineteenth
century were more concerned to ensure the pre-eminence of men as household heads and primary income earners, and to ensure that women's
maternal role was recognised, than to ensure women's rights as workers
(Canning 1996; Stone 1995). This issue was a dilemma within the rapidly
expanding socialist and labour organisations, many of which were com-
mitted to the idea that a man should earn a family wage sufficient to support
his wife and children. The question whether women should be treated as
equal to men as workers, and entitled to equal pay and conditions, or
whether they needed special protection, was debated across Europe by
socialist and labour organisations, along with the question whether, and on
what terms, women could join socialist organisations. The 1893 conference
of the Socialist International passed a resolution demanding equal pay for
men and women, but also spelled out particular conditions which should
apply to women's work, including the eight-hour day, a prohibition of night
work and of work in jobs which might be detrimental to their health
(Sowerwine 1987). Of all nineteenth-century questions about gender, wom-
en's needs as workers and how women's work can best be combined with
their family responsibilities have remained the hardest to resolve.

References and further reading

Primary sources

Aimé-Martin, Louis (1834) *De l'Education des mères de famille, ou de la civilisation du genre humain par les femmes*, Paris.
Engels, Friedrich (1976 [1892]) *The Condition of the Working Class in England*, New York.
Gaskell, Elizabeth (1985 [1848]) *Mary Barton: A Tale of Manchester Life*, London.
Lewis, Sarah (1839) *Woman's Mission*, London.
Martineau, Harriet (1859) 'Female industry', *Edinburgh Review* 109, 222 (April): 293–336.
Michelet, Jules (1854) *Oeuvres Complètes* (ed. P. Viallaneix), vol. 16, Paris.
Ruskin, John (1865) 'Sesame and Lilies', republished in *The Complete Works of John Ruskin* (1897), Boston.

Zola, Emile (1956 [1887]) *Germinal*, London.

Family life and home

Angerer, M. (1996) 'The discourse on female sexuality in nineteenth-century Austria', in D. F. Good, M. Gardner and M. J. Maynes (eds) *Austrian Women in the Nineteenth and Twentieth Centuries*, Oxford and Providence.

Davidoff, L. and Hall, C. (1987) *Family Fortunes, Men and Women of the English Middle Class 1780–1850*, London.

Delamont, S. and Duffin, L. (1978) *The Nineteenth Century Woman: Her Cultural and Physical World*, London.

Donzelot, J. (1980) *The Policing of Families*, trans. R. Hurley, London.

Frevert, U. (1989) *Women in German History: From Bourgeois Emancipation to Sexual Liberation*, trans. S. McKinnon Evans with T. Bond and B. Norden, Oxford and New York.

Gray, M. (1987) 'Prescriptions for productive female domesticity in a transitional era: Germany's Hausmutterliteratur 1780–1840', *History of European Ideas* 8, 4/5: 413—26.

Hull, I. (1996) *Sexuality, State, and Civil Society in Germany, 1700–1815*, Ithaca.

Jacobus, M. I. (1992) 'Incorruptible milk: breast-feeding and the French Revolution', in S. E. Melzer and L. W. Rabine (eds) *Rebel Daughters: Women and the French Revolution*, New York.

Jalland, P. and Hooper, J. (eds) (1986) *Women from Life to Death*, Brighton.

Perry, R. (1991) 'Colonizing the breast: sexuality and maternity in eighteenth-century England', *Journal of the History of Sexuality* 2, 2: 204–34.

Ross, E. (1993) *Love and Toil: Motherhood in Outcast London, 1870–1918*, New York.

Smith, B. G. (1981) *Ladies of the Leisure Class: The Bourgeoises of Northern France in the Nineteenth Century*, Princeton.

The world of work

Alexander, S. (1994) *Becoming a Woman and Other Essays in the 19th and 20th Century*, London.

Canning, K. (1992) 'Gender and the politics of class formation: rethinking German labor history', *American Historical Review* 97, 3: 736–68.

Clark, A. (1995) *Struggle for the Breeches*, Berkeley and London.

Frader, L. L. (1987) 'Women in the industrial economy', in R. Bridenthal, C. Koonz and S. Stuard (eds) *Becoming Visible: Women in European History*, Boston.

Frader, L. L. and Rose, S. O. (eds) (1996) *Gender and Class in Modern Europe*, Ithaca, New York and London.

Glickman, R. (1984) *Russian Factory Women: Workplace and Society, 1880–1914*, Berkeley.

Good, D. F., Gradner, M. and Maynes, M. J. (eds) (1996) *Austrian Women in the Nineteenth and Twentieth Centuries*, Providence.

John, A. V. (1986) *Unequal Opportunities: Women's Employment in England 1800–1918*, Oxford.

Lown, J. (1990) *Women and Industrialization: Gender at Work in Nineteenth-Century England*, Cambridge.

McCelland, K. (1989) 'Some thoughts on masculinity and the "representative artisan" in Britain, 1850–1880', *Gender and History* 1: 164–77.

Osterud, N. G. (1986) 'Gender division and the organization of work in the Leicester hosiery industry', in A. John (ed.) *Unequal Opportunities*, Oxford.

Phillips, A. and Taylor, B. (1980) 'Sex and skill: notes towards feminist economies', *Feminist Review* 6.

Pinchbeck, I. (1981[1930]) *Women Workers and the Industrial Revolution*, London.

Rose, S. (1992) *Limited Livelihoods, Gender and Class in Nineteenth Century England*, Berkeley.

Scott, J. W. (1993) 'The woman worker', in M. Perrot (ed.) *History of Women in the West*, Cambridge, Mass.

Scott, J. and Tilly, L. (1975) 'Women's work and the family in nineteenth-century Europe', *Comparative Studies in Society and History* 17: 36–64.

Sowerwine, C. (1987) 'The socialist women's movement from 1850 to 1940', in R. Briderthal, C. Koonz and S. Stuard (eds) *Becoming Visible: Women in European History*, Boston.

Stone, J. F. (1995) 'The Republican brotherhood: gender and ideology', in E. A. Accampo, R. G. Fuchs and M. L. Stewart (eds) *Gender and the Politics of Social Reform in France*, Baltimore.

Walkowitz, J. R. (1980) *Prostitution and Victorian Society: Women, Class and the State*, Cambridge.

THREE

Gendering Politics and the Political

The distinguishing feature of the so-called 'Restoration period' after Napoleon's defeat in 1814 was social and political uncertainty. The post-1814 political order restored divine right to its privileged place over the notion of 'popular sovereignty', and gave preference to the rights associated with birth rather than merit or talent. But the French Revolution had exposed absolute monarchy as fallible, enabling a new form of political participation for middle-class men. It had also enabled groups usually considered irrelevant to political developments (such as women, peasants and the working classes) to engage in political action, inspiring enthusiasm for and faith in the possibility of social and political change. Particular ideas of political and social change became the central focus for new ideologies, among which liberalism, feminism, socialism and nationalism were the most prominent. These ideologies promised new political frameworks and expanded political representation for groups that traditional dynastic states had excluded from political power. For the most part, conservatives associated these alternative political approaches with the threat of revolution.

This new approach to political participation in the late eighteenth and early nineteenth centuries was accompanied (and made possible) by the emergence of the public sphere. Jurgen Habermas has argued that the public sphere encompassed a variety of activities and associations where public opinions could be formed outside the official space of the courts, or of state institutions. The concept of a public sphere was closely associated with the development of 'public opinion', expressed through the press and other forms of publication.

As we have seen, in pre-revolutionary France salons organised in an intellectually prominent or economically powerful woman's private residence had provided the opportunity for intellectual debate, and for the consolidation of alternative sites of political power to the royal court. In eighteenth-century England, reading clubs, coffee houses and the expansion of the press had played a similar role. In the nineteenth century, across Europe, the growth of the bureaucratic modern state occurred alongside the emergence of a range of non-governmental forms of public activity, which allowed many individuals otherwise excluded from direct political power to wield political and social influence. These organisations took many different forms: professional groups, civic and municipal organisations, chambers of commerce, Masonic lodges, political groups and clubs, learned societies, dining clubs. Although ostensibly non-political, all of these groups provided new arenas for political debate and sometimes for the exercise of political pressure among their mostly male membership. In her autobiography Harriet Martineau commented on the spread of the 'Economy of Association' and the growing importance of 'the London Clubs, our Model Lodging Houses, and dozens of new methods of Assurance' in Britain (Martineau 1875: 232). By the middle of the nineteenth century, there were over two thousand 'circles' or societies in France where bourgeois men engaged in political and economic debate. In many German-speaking states in the period the middle class did not exercise direct political power, and were deprived by press censorship from open expression of their opinions. Bourgeois men, however, were closely involved with 'business' and with associations which were concerned with a range of civic causes and concerns, including education, social welfare, culture, trade, religion, science and athletics. Dining groups, choral societies and gymnasiums (some boasting up to 100,000 members) became the focus of nationalist and patriotic associations in the German-speaking states. National identification and the fostering of patriotism was a significant aim of 'association' and a focus of publishing in this period. Jonathan Sperber has described how even in 'the eastern reaches of the Habsburg Empire' where there was no significant or politically powerful middle class, 'the decades of the 1820s through the 1840s saw the formation of literary societies and cultural foundations, the writing of national histories, grammars and historical philologies, and the publication of books, magazines, newspapers in languages long thought of as exclusively oral, peasant tongues' (Sperber 1994: 95). Reading clubs and libraries made the press a forceful site for the forging of public opinion, while the expansion in the publication of other materials including broadsheets, pamphlets, religious tracts and etiquette manuals fostered the creation of new collective identities among diverse social groups, including the working classes and women. In the industrialising areas of Europe, the working class employed the power of public 'association' by forming economic and cultural co-operatives, and by publishing their own news sheets.

The new societies and associations explicitly replaced the old salon in political and cultural significance, bringing together eligible men and giving them the collective power to form and influence 'public opinion', to express opposition to particular governments or politics, and to question monarchical authority. The public sphere – or 'publicity' – was an important means of expressing opinion, gaining political recognition and pressing for more direct political representation for men, but for women access to this sphere was very difficult. The public nature of these new forms of expanded political and social participation made them masculine domains. While a 'public man' was seen as deserving respect, the term 'public woman' was synonymous with 'prostitute'. Respectability required that women not be known or even mentioned in public. At the same time, male authority in the public sphere was linked to the individual man's independence from patronage or feudal ties, and to his own responsibility for dependants, namely women and children. Catherine Hall argues that in the 1830s and 1840s the search by middle-class British men for 'masculine independence, for a secure identity, was built on their assertion of their superiority over the decadent aristocracy, over dependent females, over children, servants and employees, over the peoples of the Empire, whether in Ireland, India or Jamaica, over all *others* who were not English, male and middle class' (Hall 1992: 207). For middle-class men seeking to establish a different basis for authority from that which had been used by the nobility, moral authority became the key issue, evident in the power exercised by a man over the nuclear or bourgeois family, and in his ability to regulate women's sexuality through her protection and containment in the domestic sphere. Consequently the assertion of independence by women, or the demand for access to the public sphere, contravened not only the belief that respectable femininity and publicity were incompatible, but undermined the authority of the husband or father on whom women were dependent.

In this chapter we will explore the major ideologies of the first half of the nineteenth century in the context of the gendered public sphere. The widespread acceptance in Europe of the idea that the private and public constituted separate and gendered realms provided the basis of the modern state and of modern politics, and was incorporated into the liberal, socialist and nationalist ideas that dominated this period. Mainstream or moderate liberalism rose on the wave of demands for 'popular sovereignty', but liberalism served to reinforce the middle-class values of domestic respectability and the separation of the public and private spheres. Patriots also proclaimed the universal inclusiveness of national 'liberation' or 'unification', but the new national forms of state organisation were exclusive in their conception of citizenship, and in the way they defined different roles for women and men within the national community. Liberalism, socialism and nationalism were ideologies associated with the political and intellectual public interventions of men, but they were also evoked by women who sought ways in which to participate in the public sphere. At the same time, the gendered character of the public sphere and of politics inspired the formation of a gender-specific ideology, feminism. But, as we will see, feminists had not only to negotiate a public space for women, but also to engage with the divisions and antipathies between socialist and liberal world-views. In 1848, revolutionary events gave a new edge to the liberal, socialist, nationalist and feminist demands voiced and debated in varied forms and intensity in the first half of the nineteenth century throughout Europe. They also led to the refinement of the distinct gender and class interests represented by each of these loose ideologies.

Liberalism

After 1815, the countries that were represented at the Congress of Vienna – England, Prussia, Austria and Russia – reordered the balance of state powers in Europe in favour of conservative and monarchical forces, and against the varying liberal and national ideas associated with the French Revolution and the Napoleonic era. Despite their eagerness to restrain French military capacity and to destroy the potency of French revolutionary ideas, they allowed France to maintain the legal and social basis of the state established by Napoleon, and repressed only the political institutions of the Revolution. An élite fraction of the propertied middle classes was given the right to vote (males aged over 30 who paid at least 300 francs in direct taxes each year) but the political rights of Jews and of Christian men without property were denied, as of course were those of women. Robert Nye argues that the Restoration involved on the one hand a 'libertarian transformation of public life', and on the other 'a conservative codification of inheritance, family and marriage law' (Nye 1993: 47). Despite the predominance in Restoration Europe of absolute monarchy and restricted suffrage (in the states of the Italian peninsula, Prussia and Habsburg Austria, for example), over the next few decades, a number of European states adopted liberal ideas of franchise and the rule of law as they became bureaucratic modern centralised states. In some cases, these developments occurred within constitutional monarchies (e.g. in Britain, France, the Netherlands, Belgium, parts of Scandinavia and the German-speaking states of Bavaria, Baden and Saxony); in others they occurred within republics (the Swiss cantons, the German city-states of Frankfurt, Hamburg, Bremen and Lubeck) (Sperber 1994: 55). Modernising states gave limited political representation to a male propertied élite, and in some cases to religious minorities. They also enshrined rights in new constitutions (but with limited meaning in practice). For the most part, these modern concessions have been attributed to the power of liberal ideas in the early nineteenth century. But for women, liberalism did not bring new rights. The codification of rights and representation always involved the systematic denial to women of legal rights. Another marked feature of the modern liberal state was the legal domestication of women. Where rights were not codified, as in some of the more traditional absolutist states such as Austria, a female élite retained property and other rights.

By the nineteenth century, liberal political views were closely linked to economic changes, and particularly to the idea of the market. The idea that society was made up of individuals, and that the activities of rational individuals pursuing their own interest were (as the leading eighteenth-century liberal economic theorist Adam Smith had argued) the basis of the 'wealth of nations', provided the framework for liberal economic and political thought. The close relationship between economic and political liberalism grew even more influential in the course of the nineteenth century against the backdrop of an expanding entrepreneurial middle class. Even in Germany, where political liberalism was often rejected, 'economic liberalism changed Germans' views of the ideal relationships between property and people, estate owners and workers, males and females, and humans and the market, leaving the economic landscape of German-speaking Europe transformed forever' (Gray 1990: 54). But in some cases there were limits even to the adherence to the rules of the market by liberals. In the central Italian-speaking states and southern German-speaking states, for example, some liberals were hostile to industrialisation in the early nineteenth century because they believed that it would reduce the possibility for adult males to become property owners.

Liberalism was often identified with the interests of the middle class, but in the early nineteenth century the numbers of individuals who could be identified by their economic status as middle-class were still small. Moreover the category of middle-class could include not only business men and entrepreneurs, but an educated élite: doctors and lawyers who were empowered by their new professional status; white-collar workers who included men aspiring to the economic security of the more privileged middle class; poorer teachers, tax collectors and clerks. Liberal ideals were also supported by a large number of notables and landowners, as well as bureaucrats, financiers and industrialists. In eastern and central Europe, noble land-owners, members of court society, men at the upper levels of government service and the armed forces, and businessmen who grew rich on government contracts, were most likely to be conservatives who feared liberalism (Sperber 1994: 68). Similarly, liberalism and conservatism were to some degree fluid, and not clearly linked to either economic or social status. For example, liberals did not completely reject the world of their aristocratic predecessors, or the aristocratic conventions of honour that had defined noble manhood. In France, the Habsburg empire, and the Prussian state, aspiring middle-class men adopted the aristocratic chivalric code and even took up the aristocratic practice of duelling. As Pamela Pilbeam has argued: 'Liberal sentiments cut across class lines, although they were the preserve of an educated minority, sometimes titled, sometimes bourgeois' (Pilbeam 1990: 253).

Although liberalism cannot be defined as any one single outlook, most forms of liberalism included a belief in free trade and a free market, a belief in the importance of law and of equality before the law, and a rejection of the conventions of dynastic rule. In the early nineteenth century, what dis-tinguished conservative from liberal expectations generally was the conception of the legitimate basis of the state and of political participation: Conservatives accepted sole rule of a monarch whose power rested on his right of birth; by contrast, sovereignty in a liberal society was to be based on a social contract between men, on the rule of law and on the rights of the property-owning individual enshrined in constitutions. These aspects of liberalism did not necessarily imply a belief in democracy. Liberals held a range of different views as to the best form of government, and liberal political conceptions of freedom did not remove racial, gender and class prejudices. The liberal conception of individual freedom inspired anti-slavery movements and the abolition in 1834 of slavery in the British colonies; but it was not effective until the twentieth century in justifying equal political or economic rights for women, men without property, mar-ginalised religious or cultural groups, or for non-Europeans.

For the propertied middle class or bourgeoisie, the class who had perhaps benefited most from the political and economic changes that revolutionary governments and then Napoleon established, the tenets of liberalism nat-uralised only their own right to political, legal and economic power. In formulating a new 'liberal' French constitution after Napoleon's defeat, Madame de Staël and Benjamin Constant argued that popular government was a form of tyranny. Since the majority of people were incapable of reasoning, they had to be ruled by a minority who could best make political and economic decisions on their behalf. Because of the significance accorded by liberals to property ownership as a basis for political participation and male dignity, liberals confined political rights to men, and often supported legal restrictions on women's control of property, particularly among married women.

Most liberals evoked the patriarchal household as the microcosm for the social, economic and political order. According to liberal assumptions in England, men had to own property to be properly masculine. Thus, the wealthy middle class aped the aristocracy by buying land in the country, and by building great country houses as soon as they could. But unlike the aristocracy, middle-class masculinity also required domestic respectability. Liberal criticism of the *ancien régime* state model, and of the corruption of the aristocratic classes, was translated into a preference for the gendered separation of private and public life. Isabel Hull (1996) maintains that, after 1814, in the German-speaking states the privacy of the family was protected by public law. This legitimated the private sphere as a space of complete male domination. What Hull argues in the case of Germany, Davidoff and Hall have confirmed in regard to Britain – that a middle-class ideal of male independence required the subordination and dependence of women (Davidoff and Hall 1987). According to Hull, 'man was emancipated from subjection (to his father and to state scrutiny) at the same moment that [the law] made him the subjugator of his wife. Her unfreedom created his freedom; his position as private dominator qualified him to participate in the wider, public sphere of equals, in civil society' (Hull 1996: 411). *[handwritten margin note: Most like Scott]*

Gender identities and relations in the private sphere were important to the public or civil status of men in other ways. As we saw in Chapter 1, during the Enlightenment liberals argued that the ability to reason was a primary masculine attribute which entitled men to participate in the social contract. In the nineteenth century, ownership of property and virility became equally important features of the politically self-determining and now economically 'self-made' middle-class man. Robert Nye has argued that in France 'male sexual capacity was a qualifying feature for full citizenship in the modern state, and only a man who was sexually potent could live in and through the heirs who received both his goods and the imprint of his person' (Nye 1993: 67). As Hull has shown, in Germany too, the sexually potent man was complemented by the woman who was his opposite, as wife and mother (Hull 1996: 411).

The attribution of masculinity enhanced an individual's public status and political power. In the nineteenth century norms of masculinity were redefined not only through the power the male exerted over female subordinates or through evidence of sexual potency in the private sphere, but through relations between men in the public sphere. In early nineteenth-century Europe, middle-class men attempted to exert their power by organising new male institutions. Chambers of commerce, charitable institutions and schemes, support for the arts and culture, all served to establish middle-class communities of shared male economic, political and social interests. The middle-class men who joined these clubs and societies sought political empowerment as individuals, and the social endorsement of their manliness. At the same time these forms of male association contributed to the redefinition of respectable forms of male sociability and, consequently, masculinity. In France as in England, etiquette books stressed the importance of politeness, of finding forms of civil behaviour between men to replace the use of physical force. Circles and societies often reinforced codes of manly behaviour by exacting fines for their infringement (Nye 1993: 131).

Intrinsic to liberal debates regarding the nature of society, religion and politics were the assumptions that women were different from men in their capacity for reason, that Jews differed from Christians in their civility and manliness, that working-class men were politically unequal to the middle classes because of their failure to own property or their incapacity to exercise authority over a wife and children in the home, and that non-Europeans were generally inferior to Europeans in all these ways. While masculinity was a requirement for participation in the public sphere, this participation was limited to some men on the basis of religion or nationality, wealth or their literacy. When the young Benjamin Disraeli (a future English Prime Minister) craved membership of any important London club in order to make his way in English society in the 1820s, he found most clubs were closed to him because he was a Jew. Catholics suffered similar discrimination in England until 1829 when they were awarded civic rights. The German dining clubs organised by the aristocrat Achim Von Arnim in the 1810s cultivated a Christian German-speaking membership, and explicitly excluded Jews as well as women.

Liberal views of the gender, class, religious or cultural basis of the political rights and social authority of non-aristocratic individuals (as male, middle-class and Christian European), and of the gendered separation of spheres, exerted influence through changing laws and new institutions and forms of association. They also affected public opinion and the forms of self-identification or even self-censorship. During the Restoration period in Europe, some women did engage in public activities, but never without criticism or without recognising the difficulties and limitations which they faced. Rahel Varnhagen, for example, established a reputation in the 1820s in Europe for her Berlin salons – intellectual centres attended by famous male philosophers and writers. However, despite the extent of her intellectual reputation, Varnhagen never published any of her writing, denying herself the right to 'publicity', first because she was a woman and secondly because she was a Jew (Goodman 1982).

The effects of changing representations of gender identities and relations and political norms on social behaviour are evident in examples of the decreasing political visibility of women in the first half of the nineteenth century. In the 1790s – when the Belgian provinces were still under absolutist Habsburg rule – Belgian women inspired by the French Revolution were important instigators of rebellion against absolutism. Female involvement in revolutionary activity was accepted by their male peers because of the power of female artisan guilds. However, when the revolution against Habsburg rule succeeded with French assistance in 1794, the French immediately obliterated the guilds that had been the basis of the corporate power of artisan women. In the early nineteenth century, the Belgian provinces were conquered by Napoleon's armies and the introduction of the Napoleonic Code made married women the dependants of their husbands, eradicating the Habsburg laws of community property that had given scope for some women to exercise legal and economic power. With the fall of Napoleon, the Belgian provinces came under the administration of the Netherlands. In 1829, there was renewed unrest with the demand for the creation of a Belgian state on the basis of a new liberal constitution which would include individual rights and democratic principles. By contrast with the 1790s however, in this national revolution there was little evidence of women's involvement. Janet Polansky suggests that the 'economic transformation of industrialisation together with the acceptance of the liberal theory of individual citizenship' and, more specifically, the proliferation of literature instructing young Belgian bourgeois girls in their domestic duties, had taken its toll (Polasky 1986: 97). The 1830 Belgian constitution consolidated these changing gender roles by making the individual property-owning male citizen the foundation of liberal government. Political progress in Belgium meant the legally codified and physical retreat of women from the public sphere, and the exclusive association of liberal citizenship with bourgeois masculinity and property.

The history of Queen Victoria's rule in England illustrates the difficult juxtaposition of femininity and political power in the century some historians have labelled 'bourgeois' to denote the success of middle-class and liberal ideals. As head of state from 1837 to 1901, Queen Victoria presided over England's industrial development and its conquest of much of the world's territories. But Victoria represented herself to her subjects as a wife and mother, as reliant on her husband's guidance, and after his death other male advisers. For much of her reign, she eschewed public appearances and remained within the domestic sphere. Although the Queen was a member of the aristocracy, it was the bourgeois or middle-class pattern that, even for her, represented the new standards of social respectability, of personal identity and of national status embedded in the gendered segregation of public and private spheres.

In practice, many women as well as men attempted to negotiate to their own advantage middle-class norms of masculinity and femininity. By the mid nineteenth century, middle-class women were encouraged to participate in public causes designated as philanthropic or 'social' work, or to influence public opinion. As we saw in Chapter 2, women were called into (and thrust themselves into) charitable social work on the basis of their feminine virtues, on the correspondence between them and an innate 'social' consciousness. Women's social work was intended to mirror men's individualist civic role in establishing community services and institutions. It also often provided individual women with an alternative way into a feminised public sphere. In some cases, women were slowly called into political action on the basis that the moral status associated with their private roles as wives and mothers was politically advantageous. In the 1830s and 1840s middle-class English women participated in major liberal campaigns by organising anti-slavery and anti-Corn Law activities. In 1846 the Anti-Corn Law League forced the British government to repeal the Corn Laws which had protected landed interests over those of free trade, and were harmful to the middle-class entrepreneur. Women thus contributed to the establishment of economic liberalism as national policy. These 'social' forms of public participation encouraged a greater awareness among women of their public power, their moral authority, and provided them in many cases with a social validation for demanding greater political participation and representation, as women.

The different ways in which individuals and groups interpreted the promise and possibilities of liberalism gave rise to different views of politics and versions of democracy. The revolutions that took place in 1830 in Europe made manifest the tensions between divergent liberal views of political organisation. As many historians have shown, these revolts resulted in a much clearer distinction between moderate liberals who generally believed in the franchise only for the propertied classes (and in some cases propertied women), and radical or democratic liberals who favoured more inclusive conceptions of citizenship rights for the different classes (only in some cases women). In France and Belgium the 1830 revolts resulted in the creation of constitutional monarchies and the expansion of political representation to the wealthy male bourgeoisie, and the legal disempowerment of women; but they also animated more radical ideals of republicanism and broader-based citizenship among certain groups across Europe. Although England did not experience revolution, fear of insurrection among conservatives there helped in the passing of the 1832 Reform Act, which increased the number of voters from just over 200,000 to nearly 700,000 in a population of 14 million. Later Reform Acts of 1867 and 1884 retained the principle of household suffrage which privileged fathers and husbands, but extended suffrage further to those who rented urban accommodation and to agricultural labourers. In each of these cases, most of the propertied and liberal men who agitated for the extension of suffrage to themselves saw any further extension to unpropertied men, let alone women, as a threat to their own political, social and economic authority. Those more radical ideals of democracy and citizenship were taken up in different ways by republicans, socialists and feminists.

Socialism and the social

The changes that capitalism and industrialisation had begun to stimulate in England and northern Europe by the early nineteenth century – the displacement of traditional communities, the creation of an exploited underclass of urban workers (male and female), massive social inequities – provoked liberal reforms, but also inspired more radical alternatives to liberalism, and led to the creation of new political and social movements. In the later nineteenth-century Engels described a distinctive group of early nineteenth century movements which shared a belief in the emancipation of all, and lacked a specific class identification or revolutionary agenda, as utopian socialists – even though this was not a term that those groups themselves had used (Engels 1880). Like liberals, utopian socialists exploited the political potential of association and of publicity. They were reformist rather than revolutionary, and concentrated on different ways of organising industrial and domestic work, rather than overthrowing existing political institutions.

The emergence of utopian socialism in the early nineteenth century was closely linked to the French Revolution which, after centuries of apparent political and social stagnation, had inspired the possibility of radical change. Utopian socialists aimed to bring harmony to the relationships between different classes that comprised the new industrial society – workers and industrialists, the poor and the wealthy – and between men and women. They focused on developing a science of society which could transform the character of individuals, the shape of society and the organisation of private and public life. Although the utopian socialist groups differed in their specific approach, and changed their aims over the course of the first half of the nineteenth century, several of them challenged the sexual subordination of women and the existing legal institutionalisation of marriage and the family.

One of the most important of the utopian socialists was the French Charles Fourier. Between 1808 and the 1830s Fourier published his ideas for reorganising labour and private relations as the key to a new kind of harmonious society, 'where every individual whim would be satisfied'. Fourier advanced what would become a widely held nineteenth-century idea that a society's progress could be judged by the status of its women. The 'progressive liberation of women', Fourier argued, was the fundamental cause of all social progress. He saw 'sexual passion' as 'an unconscious psycho-dynamic underlying all historical change' (cited in Taylor 1983: 29). Fourier argued that masculinity and femininity were elements found in various combinations in men and women: the feminine principle was more sensual and sedentary; the masculine was vigorous and lacking in sensuality. Fourier also argued more conventionally that women's physical weakness required that they should undertake less laborious tasks than men, and that men were naturally more productive because of their vigorous and stronger natures. In order to realise his vision he planned an ideal community, the *phalanstere* or Harmony, adapted to these distinct male and female characters (Fourier 1808). These communities of up to 1800 persons were to be organised around households. Ten per cent of the women in each household would have responsibility for domestic tasks, and the other women would be free to pursue more interesting work that would offer them economic independence. Like other utopian socialists, Fourier believed in the liberating potential of science, which would develop labour-saving devices for use in kitchens, laundries, for heating – all of which would result in more women being available for productive labour.

The reorganisation of domestic and industrial labour was central to utopian socialism. It implied a radical acceptance of women's place in the workforce even if it was still based on the gendered division of labour. At the same time, Fourier's alternative social model did not advocate the abolition of private property, and left fathers and husbands a key role in deciding at what pace social change, including any change in the status of women, could be brought about. His ideas spread across Europe, attracting feminists, radicals and even members of the wealthy upper classes who were reassured by the message of gradual change in which his utopianism was couched. Even the liberal John Stuart Mill was briefly attracted to Fourierism because he believed it engaged with the problem of sexual inequality without posing any threat of social upheaval.

The issues of sexuality, gender relations, property, labour organisation and domestic communality were also central to the most influential of the early nineteenth-century utopian socialist movements, Saint-Simonism. Named after the aristocratic social theorist, Comte Claude Henri de Saint-Simon, the movement followed the writings of Saint-Simon, which stressed the importance of 'association' and of developing a science of society. Saint-Simonism was influential in the 1820s and 1830s in France, England, Italy, Germany, America and Egypt. In the 1820s, the Saint-Simonian movement was based in Paris. It was led by middle-class 'managers' who recruited working-class members by organising teaching programmes and co-operative workshops for seamstresses and tailors in different districts of the larger French cities. For the former artisan class who were being displaced by the introduction of the factory system, whose families had been separated by the need to find work, and who lived mostly in poverty, Saint-Simonism offered security and solidarity. The Saint-Simonians set up collective apartments (*maisons de famille*) in Paris and other large towns where domestic tasks were organised on a collective rather than family basis (Moses 1982).

Within the Saint-Simonian movement the question of sexual equality was a constant subject of heated debate. For the Saint-Simonian leadership 'woman' tended to be a symbol, rather than an agent or beneficiary of change. In 1831 the Saint-Simonian leader, Prosper Enfantin, advocated the movement's concentration on *sensual appetites* and *intellectual appetites* and on how they could be controlled or 'directed, ordered, combined, and separated'. This concern to rehabilitate the flesh and to recognise the importance of sexuality alienated large numbers of the movement and left a distinct imprint on the characterisation of Saint-Simonism as an 'erotic' cult. Although an expression of a minority view among Saint-Simonians, for the critics of Saint-Simonism, Enfantin's emphasis on sexuality confirmed the close association between socialism and feminism, and socialism's threat to bourgeois norms of respectability.

In England the best-known form of utopian socialism was Owenism. As early as the 1790s the industrialist Robert Owen's cotton factory near Glasgow, 'New Lanark', was the centre of a new model of collective social and labour organisation – a factory system in which welfare, education and housing were provided for its workers. Owen believed that the liberal emphasis on private property and on family interests encouraged a disregard for anyone outside the family, and 'transformed all human relationships into competitive contests for individual gain' (Taylor 1983: 20). In contrast to the British marriage laws, which Owen argued transformed even women into the property of individual men, Owenites supported the companionate ideal of marriage and the extinguishing of patriarchal laws that bolstered the authority of men over women. They believed that human character could be changed if everyday life was reorganised so as to emancipate both sexes: men from their conventional selfishness and stupidity, and women from their learnt servility. Owen, like Fourier, imagined his ideal community as an extensive population in which women would share responsibility for child care and domestic needs. The Owenite ideal of marriage reform and their mixed social and discussion groups attracted lower middle-class women stymied by the bourgeois ideal of feminine domesticity. To their critics, Owenite support for the abolition of private property and for the reconfiguration of gender relations also symbolised the socialist threat of class and gender anarchy.

Utopian socialist organisations flourished in the 1820s but more or less came to an end in the 1830s. The demise of Owenism in Britain and the repression of Saint-Simonism in France coincided with successful middle-class challenges to aristocratic power – specifically the 1830 revolution in France and the 1832 Reform Act in England – and with the revival of religious conservatism. During the 1830s, the few remaining utopian socialist organisations began to reject their earlier radical ideas on the role of women, either by excluding women from the organisational structures (as occurred in the Owenist movement), or by elevating sexual difference into a principle of social order – whereby the political was masculine and the 'social' or moral feminine (as among Saint-Simonists). Barbara Taylor has shown very clearly the ways in which the women associated with the Owenite co-operative movement in Britain in the 1820s and 1830s struggled to assert their right to paid work in the face of fierce opposition from many groups of male workers, especially skilled artisans, who insisted on the primacy of women's domestic responsibilities and sought to end their access to various forms of paid work (Taylor 1983). After 1834 the central Saint-Simonian organisation remained the domain of men, but its members began to search for a female Messiah whose saint-like femininity would redeem the world of conflict. Socialists employed the moral power of symbolic 'woman' as the guiding principle of harmonious association between classes and the sexes. 'Woman's' difference, her maternal femininity, was invoked as the symbol of socialist and co-operative sentiments.

As these changes in the organisation and aims of Saint-Simonism took place, some of the women who had been prominent in the movement, like Suzanne Voilquin, became increasingly frustrated. Voilquin had originally been attracted to the movement because of its emphasis on the collective good (an ideal she associated with the French Revolution) and on 'social action' (Moses and Rabine 1993: 164). Once the status of women in the Saint-Simonian movement changed, Voilquin and other literate working-class Saint-Simonian women in Paris created a newspaper that only published the writing of women, regardless of their class or social interests. In 31 issues published from 1832 to 1833, the *Tribune* provided a forum for the discussion of women's equality in marriage, for the reform of the Civil Code (in particular the removal of the article which enforced women's submission to their husbands) and the reinstitution of civil divorce. By this time, too, socialist women, like some of their middle-class counterparts, had begun to invoke woman's moral superiority as a convenient basis for legitimating female agency in the public sphere and for articulating women's rights. In the pages of the *Tribune*, women's disabilities were only one aspect of a wider social struggle, and the remedy was 'association'. The *Tribune*'s editors called upon women to be moral guides rather than political leaders, and to exert a feminine social benevolence. Similarly, in the 1840s, Flora Tristan, who was influenced by the Saint-Simonians, utilised a conventional notion of gender difference in order to argue that social change required political action by women and a new feminine order. For her, progress meant the evolution of society from a masculine to a feminine model; from the rule of physical force to the rule of morality and socialism. If real change was to take place, men had to be feminised, and a 'universal union of workingmen and women' created (Grogan 1992: 177). For Tristan, the 'reign of women' was crucial to social change and to the elevation of workers, and she herself was the female Messiah predicted by the Saint-Simonians.

Utopian socialism impacted on European political life in the early decades of the nineteenth century by expanding the scope of the political and of the public spheres. Under the influence of utopian socialism women became symbolically important to politics. But ultimately even utopian socialists reinforced the identification of the political with masculinity and of the social with femininity. These gendered representations of the political and the social permeated other socialist and working-class organisations. In the 1830s, the radical English working-class political movement, Chartism, for example, depicted itself as more masculine, and therefore more politically credible than Owenism. By the mid nineteenth century, socialist-inspired trade unions in England questioned the political credibility of utopian socialists because of their 'feminine' ideals. This change occurred against the background of a contraction in employment opportunities, and the rapid decline in working conditions for women. By the latter half of the nineteenth century communists like Marx and Engels, who rejected the utopianism of the earlier socialists in favour of a more 'scientific' approach to social change, emphasised the masculinity of their socialism. The emancipation of women was discussed within the new scientific socialism, but gender took second place to the problem of class struggle. As a result, gender tensions were evident in the mass Marxist-inspired socialist organisations that emerged in the latter half of nineteenth century. Taylor argues that:

> As the utopian imagination faded, so also did the commitment to a new sexual order. As the older schemes for emancipating 'all humanity at once' were displaced by the economic struggles of a single class, so issues central to that earlier dream – marriage, reproduction, family life – were transformed from political questions into 'merely private' ones, while women who persisted in pressing such issues were frequently condemned as bourgeois 'women's rightsers'.

(Taylor 1983: xvi)

The state as nation

Socialists were not the only groups concerned in the nineteenth century with the increasing atomisation of society associated with the economic tenets of liberalism. Nor were conservatives alone in fearing the pluralism of opinions promoted in the expanding public sphere by the political premises of liberalism, and their divisive social effects. Liberals also shared these concerns. For liberals in particular, the idea of a shared national identity, and patriotic allegiance to that identity, promised a socially cohesive form of liberty. Liberal men and women alike, saw the nation as an ideal and 'natural' form of association in which social duty, defined as patriotism, triumphed over individual self-interest. The association of national liberation with liberalism underlay the insistence at the Congress of Vienna that the nations created by Napoleon should be dismantled, and their supporters suppressed. Yet, for liberals, especially those who lived in established nation-states like England and France, the national ideal of homogeneity struck a chord among those who feared the proliferation of public opinion and seeming social anarchy fostered by socialist and feminist agitation. At the other end of the political spectrum, some socialists who asserted the political and economic empowerment of the labouring classes regarded the nation as a direct obstacle to more radical social change.

In the nineteenth century, national patriotism vied with and overlapped with liberalism and socialism as one of the most important forms of political identification. For the middle classes who felt politically repressed by English, Habsburg, or Turkish rule, the nation-state represented political and economic freedom. After 1815 a number of battles against authoritarian regimes took place in Europe in the name of national liberation. The success of the revolt by Greek nationalists against the Ottoman Empire in 1830 fuelled expectations that the creation of nation-states would accompany liberal progress in the nineteenth century. Likewise, the 1830 revolution in the Belgian provinces which led to the creation of Belgium excited the promise of political change and of emancipation. In the 1830s and 1840s Romantics promoted the causes of Polish and Hungarian independence from the Russian and Habsburg empires, and the unifications of the German and Italian-speaking states in the name of progress, liberty and patriotism. They also expected that women and men would express their patriotism in distinct ways: women as wives and mothers, men as soldiers and fathers.

In the late eighteenth century Rousseau had argued that the virtue of patriotism resolved the competition between family and state loyalties. The state was defined as a fatherland, and the family as a microcosm of the state – duty to the fatherland mirrored duty to the father. The idea that the patriarchal family was the basis of the moral order and of the nation-state was also propagated by the major proponents of the creation of Polish, German and Italian nation-states. The philosopher Johannes Gottlieb Fichte gave the father a central role in the private cultivation of German patriotism among the various German-speaking states of central Europe. He conceived of his 'Germans' as masculine, aiming for perfect manhood through the development of their spiritual national identification. In his 1807 'Address to the German Nation', Fichte argued that it was through the example of the 'father' – preoccupied with public responsibilities – that 'Germans' would be educated to the strength of character and instinct for mutual respect which would bond them as 'men of one mind' (Fichte 1968: 148). In this same period, during the wars of liberation against Napoleon (1812–13), 'German' women's patriotic associations were formed under the auspices of the royal and princely houses in the anti-French German-speaking states. These associations eventually came under the control of the Protestant Church and were transformed into philanthropic societies encouraging women's patriotic participation in the civic sphere of local communities for the 'German' social good.

After 1830 a number of nationalist movements emerged in Europe, the best known of which are the writers labelled 'Young Germany', and Giuseppe Mazzini's political movements 'Young Italy' and 'Young Europe'. The men who belonged to Young Italy, Young Germany, and even Young Europe, were inspired by the literary and political tenets of Romanticism. Young Germany was not an organised group, but rather a group of writers who shared a concern with challenging aesthetic and moral norms that affected literary sensitivities and manners (Mosse 1980; Paulsell 1976). They promoted the idea of a masculine tradition of German aesthetics and literature, which celebrated the ideal Classical Greek male body as an object of national symbolism, in contrast with the desexualised woman who represented 'eternal forces', 'innocence and chastity' (Mosse 1985: 98). Despite their renowned advocacy of political, social and sexual liberation, in practice Heinrich Heine and Theodor Mundt, amongst others, exhibited both disdain for women and a fear of them (Goodman 1982).

Giuseppe Mazzini, the creator of Young Italy and Young Europe, had a reputation throughout Europe in the 1830s and 1840s as the advocate of the nation as the new basis for cultivating fraternity and a shared humanity. His specific political cause was the formation of an Italian nation out of the many states and principalities that made up the primarily Italian-speaking peninsula. Born in Genoa – a city-state under the administrative control of the Habsburgs – Mazzini's written contribution to the ideals of patriotic nationalism were his main source of fame. His more practical political ambition was to see the unification of Italy as a nation. Mazzini wanted Rome (ruled at this time by the Papacy) to be the capital of Italy. Italy would then represent an alternative social, political and moral order to that offered by the example of the French Revolution. Instead of natural rights and a focus on the individual, Italy would offer a new model, a new divine law, of social duties as well as individual rights, embodied in the nation.

In the early stages of his career, Mazzini was influenced by Saint-Simonism and Fourierism. He was particularly impressed with Fourier's conciliatory approach to social change and the elevation of woman's *social* role as an educator. However, he soon abandoned socialism and presented the idea of the republican nation as an alternative religion of humanity, and as the most fully evolved social form of human association. For Mazzini, individuals without a 'Country' were the 'bastards of Humanity', 'soldiers without a banner'. Country and family were 'like two circles drawn within a greater circle which contains them both'; just as the task of the Country was 'to educate *men*', the task of the family was 'to educate *citizens*' (Mazzini 1966: 61–2). Mazzini insisted that men and women had 'equal status' both in the family and in the nation, but because men and women were like two different 'peoples' (or different nations) they had 'distinct functions in humanity'. He claimed that women's domestic role suited her to promoting the 'social' good, rather than individual rights – this made her an important symbol of his conception of national duties. 'Woman' was to be man's equal in civil and political life, but her role in the nation's destiny, and in the education of its progeny, was as the 'Angel of the hearth' who guarded 'the Country of the heart', the Family. By contrast, the father influenced whether his sons 'turn out men or brutes' (Mazzini 1966: 65). As with Fichte's much earlier description of German national identity, Mazzini admonished fathers to provide their sons with a patriotic and political education in national duties:

> Speak to them of their Country, of what it was, of what it ought to be. When at evening the smiles of the mother, and the artless prattle of the children upon your knee, make you forget the toils of the day, tell them over again the great deeds of the common people in our ancient republics; teach them the names of the good men who loved Italy and her people, and endeavoured through suffering, calumny, and persecution to improve her destinies. . . . Let them learn from your lips, and from the tranquil approval of their mother, how beautiful it is to follow the paths of virtue, how great to stand up as apostles of the truth, how holy to sacrifice oneself, if needs be, for one's brothers.
>
> (Mazzini 1966: 65–6)

The father's important role in educating his children into patriotic citizenship was also advocated by the influential French historian Jules Michelet. In his reflections on *The People* (1845), Michelet portrayed national patriotism and love of country as the solution to the problems being created by industrialisation – the destruction of traditional peasant lifestyles and the division of French society. Mazzini and Michelet used images of the patriarchal family as a 'natural' unit, of the male citizen as the active and military patriot, and of women as reproducers of the nation's citizens and their nurturers, to shore up the legitimacy of the nation-state.

In the 1830s and 1840s Mazzini assumed the proportions of a Romantic hero, both on the Continent and in England. English women admired him for what they regarded as his expansive empathetic sensibility, and for the explicit (if limited) symbolic place he gave women in nations. In her late nineteenth-century history of 'the birth of modern Italy', Jessie White (an English woman who devoted her own life to the cause of Italian unification) described the effect of Mazzini on the wife of Peter Taylor, a middle-class anti-Corn Law League agitator: 'for Mrs Taylor there came to exist only one being in the world besides her husband whose words and deeds must never be questioned by common mortals, and that was Mazzini' (White Mario 1909: 90). But Mazzini was only one of a number of new 'national' heroes who gained popularity across Europe in this period. These included his rival in female adulation and national heroism, Giuseppe Garibaldi, the Hungarian liberal Lajos Kossuth, the Polish poet-revolutionary Adam Mickiewicz (a favourite of the French novelist George Sand), and the poet Lord Byron who died in the Greek national campaign.

By the mid nineteenth century, national patriotism could be respectably construed as a noble mission in any European bourgeois (or aristocratic) woman's life, whether as mothers of the nation's progeny, or as moral influences on the state. Just as national patriotism provided some women with a means of negotiating the social norms and gender hierarchies represented by these contrasting images of women, some nationalist women legitimated their public roles by emphasising their status as 'mothers' of the nation. Already in the 1820s, the successful Polish writer Katrina Tanska saw one of her literary roles as the inspiration of Polish patriotism (Lorence-Kot 1987). Tanska was brought up writing French, but she kept her diary in Polish in order to set an example, to establish the literary legitimacy of Polish and develop a Polish style, and perhaps even a Polish female identity. She believed that it was women's task to encourage the transmission of the Polish language and ideals of 'Polishness' as she understood it, primarily by being good mothers and wives. Ironically, while Tanska saw herself as creating something uniquely Polish, her effort to articulate a distinctive Polish national culture relied on notions of bourgeois morality and sexual difference that were becoming distinctive of European identity in general.

In the 1830s and 1840s the conservative German-speaking states invited women to be volunteers for a General Charity Organisation in the cause of a German patriotism that defended middle-class values and staved off working-class discontent. The 4,000 women who joined the organisation were given the task of dealing with the problems of welfare, of increasing poverty, displacement and desperation that were so widespread in these industrialising regions at this time. Their efforts were not successful in warding off a wave of revolts against economic conditions, which culminated in 1848, the so-called 'springtime of peoples'. The events of 1848 suggest that the utilisation of women to dissipate social tensions in the name of patriotism had assisted the spread across Europe of modern feminism, with its demand that women have a legitimate place in the national polity, as an integral part of the 'people'.

1848

Like 1789, the year 1848 represents a turning point in European history. Revolts against economic conditions in southern Europe, and then in Paris, climaxed in major challenges to the conservative political *status quo* that had been established by the Congress of Vienna after Napoleon's defeat in 1814. Events in Paris in February 1848 triggered off revolution after revolution across the major cities of Europe – in Berlin, Munich, Vienna, Budapest, Venice, Milan and Krakow. Revolt in the Prussian capital Berlin in March was sparked by news of events in Paris, and fuelled by long-term economic conditions and political agitation in the period known as the 'Vormarz' ('before March'). From Berlin, revolt spread to the other German-speaking states. As a consequence of the revolutions of 1848 all men in France were (temporarily) given the vote, Germany was for a short time 'unified', and revolts in central and southern Europe led to the temporary usurpation of Habsburg government by nationalist and bourgeois groups in Hungary, Poland and Italy, and, to some extent, the emancipation of peasantry and Jews. For a brief time too, some working-class, middle-class and aristocratic women joined in the political tumult. The uprisings of 1848, and the mood of liberation they inspired, provided radicals, feminists, liberals, socialists and patriots with the freedom to voice their demands and concerns, to participate in an expanded public sphere. But ultimately middle-class demands for authority and power predominated, and the aims of radicals, socialists and feminists were rejected, and the 'unified' German states disbanded. The restitution of conservative governments after 1848 brought some concessions to liberalism, but in most of the German states and in France, socialists and women (whether or not they were feminists) were branded subversive and outlawed from political participation for the rest of the century.

The outbreak of revolution in 1848 occurred in the context of the general economic discontent that followed a period of chronic unemployment and food shortages in newly industrialising European centres. In Autumn 1847, for example, 200 women were involved in an attack in Messina (Sicily) on the palace of King Ferdinand (King of the Two Sicilies). Similar economic conditions led to uprisings in Paris in February 1848, only there the middle-class joined in to express its disapproval of economic stagnation and of the reigning constitutional monarch, Louis Phillipe. In France, propertied but otherwise politically marginalised men took charge of the revolt and established a liberal-minded provisional government. Immediately after the February revolution the new provisional government removed existing censorship and political restraints. Political activity flourished in Paris just as it had after 1789. Clubs and committees were set up where workers' rights, women's rights, and the fraternal association of democrats of both sexes could be promoted. Placards and papers claimed the end of economic inequality and even, as described by Alexis de Tocqueville (an important member of the provisional liberal government), 'the oldest of inequalities' between man and woman (de Tocqueville 1893: 108).

In the early months of 1848 in Paris, some mainly young and unmarried women demanded mandatory military service and took up arms to defend the new provisional government. They became known as the 'Vesuviennes' (or volcanoes). Cartoonists derided their ambitions to carry arms and wear trousers, demanding in turn who would look after the children or make dinner if women were on night patrol? The humour in these attacks suggests that men were not as anxious about women's demands for civic rights in early 1848 as they had been in 1793 (McPhee 1997). Amid the revolutionary fervour of the post-February period, Vesuviennes and other feminists were free to defend their political and civic expectations. In March 1848 Jeanne Deroin and Suzanne Voilquin, former Saint-Simonians, assisted in the publication of a new feminist newspaper, *Voix des Femmes*, which proclaimed optimistically to its readership their expectations that women too would profit from the political changes that were occurring: 'When [the provisional government] abolish all privileges, they will not think of conserving the worst one of all and leaving one half of the nation under the domination of the other half' (Strumingher 1987: 451).

The creation of separate national workshops for unemployed men and women indicate the inclusive class and gender dimensions of the revolution in its initial stages. The women's workshops were set up on the invitation of the government and under the supervision of Desirée Gay, a former Saint-

Simonian and a contributor to *Voix des Femmes*. However, the journalists from *Voix des Femmes* were soon reporting on the desperate fate of women who could not get work in these establishments, or who had to work for lower wages than men (Strumingher 1989). Similarly, although the provisional government had discussed universal suffrage, which included women and workers, it extended the right to vote only to small landowners. The women's suffrage bill was introduced and defeated by 899 votes to 1. Within a few months, the provisional government followed its limited enfranchisement with the closure of the workshops, which they now portrayed as strongholds of working-class and female subversion. Government authorities began to harass women active in political clubs and involved in the production of newspapers. As in the 1790s, the 'public woman' became a symbol of the threat of social anarchy and of revolution. De Tocqueville, for example, commented in his memoirs of this period on the contrast between his own wife's model behaviour, her support 'so rare and so precious in times of revolution', and the women whom he feared had abandoned their homes and families for politics (de Tocqueville 1893: 126). For de Tocqueville, the antithesis to his wife was George Sand, a woman who sought publicity through her writing, and who championed the radical socialist cause of communism in this period.

Infuriated by the conservative turn of the provisional government, workers and socialists, men and women, took to the streets of Paris again in June 1848. For de Tocqueville, this working-class revolt against the provisional government's apparent betrayal of the February revolution unleashed class and gender disorder, evident in the ugliness and uncontrolled passions of the women he encountered in the streets during the revolt. When the June revolution failed, de Tocqueville became a member of the new government which, as one of its first acts, clamped down on the clubs and the press that had flourished in the months before, and made women's political participation in the public sphere illegal. Over 11,000 prisoners were taken, including nearly 300 women. In the new post-June 1848 'bourgeois' French republic, some of the political demands of 1848 were met: all men were given the right to vote, but no women. In some ways the 1848 revolutions in France repeated the sequence of the 1790s, 1830s, and of events elsewhere in Europe after 1848: the new governments which represented those demanding revolutionary change established their political legitimacy by enfranchising men but banning women from participation in the public sphere.

In each of the German-speaking states of the Confederation created in 1814, revolt had different political motivations and meanings. But revolution also led to the creation of the Frankfurt Parliament in which they were all represented. The Frankfurt Parliament was an institution convened by middle-class liberals from these different states who identified with a German nation, and who were eager to unify and liberalise Germany by drawing up a federal constitution. A limited number of women were given special passes to observe the debates of the Frankfurt Parliament, but there seems to have been no expectation among the parliamentary delegates that women might directly participate in this political process, despite the public role of women who participated in the revolts at the side of their menfolk or by publishing revolutionary newspapers. Some of the more radical delegates linked their minority ambitions for a German republic with changes in the laws governing the private sphere: equality within the family, and a more equal domestic relationship between men and women. Although the con-stitution decided upon in 1849 was called 'The Rights of the German People', the feminist Louise Dittmar complained that it only addressed the rights of men (Herzog 1990).

Women's rights were not on the Frankfurt Parliament's agenda, but the proper role of women in the revolution *was* the subject of discussion. In these discussions, the moderate liberals who dominated the Frankfurt Parliament and who assumed control of revolution in the various German states, attacked 'public' women. Like de Tocqueville, they relied on images of disorderly women and chaos in the family to express their fear of the threat the working-classes and socialist ideas posed to middle-class political and economic interests. They accepted that women had a patriotic role, but were concerned that this might lead to the neglect of families. The liberal care-takers of the revolts in Germany disliked the idea of women engaging in political debate. Instead, they preferred women to participate in revolu-tionary ceremonies dressed in white in order to symbolically consecrate national flags and banners. Sperber argued that this ritual linked private and public life and identified 'political goals with an idealised family life' (Sperber 1994: 251). Women were also important as an audience for democratic and liberal men's display of their masculinity.

A small number of radical democratic women like Amelia Struve, some of whom were the wives of radical liberals, participated in the revolutions by building barricades and fighting the opposition's military forces. Known as the 'Amazons', they formed their own female gymnastic clubs to work on achieving physical equality with men. Gymnastic organisations had pro-liferated in the early decades of the nineteenth century under the constraints of censorship, as places where men who shared progressive ideals and concerned to develop their physical strength could meet. Members of the 1848 Frankfurt women's gymnastic club believed they were encouraging 'true sisterhood', 'freedom, strength and simplicity' (Zucker 1991: 81). But this club seems to have been atypical. Even those women engaged in the battlefield or in civic organisations accepted conventional ideas of sexual difference and emphasised the domestic virtues of womanhood. Their distinctively feminine participation was encouraged throughout the German-speaking regions by a multiplication of newspapers edited by women, and by the organisation of democratic women's clubs, including Kathinka Zitz-Halein's Humania Association for Patriotic Interests, which aided refugees and impoverished revolutionaries (Sperber 1994: 153). Nine per cent of the women of the town of Mainz belonged to this organisation. The presence of women in the revolutionary public sphere was also evident in the newspapers that they published, for example Louise Otto's *Frauen Zeitung* (*Women's News*) in Leipzig, and Mathilda Franziska Anneke's *Neue Kolnische Zeitung* (*New Cologne Times*) in Cologne.

On the Italian peninsula, the expansion of the public sphere and of political participation was a feature of the revolutionary period, and of rebellion against Habsburg authorities and despotic monarchs. Female clubs and newspapers variously demanded women's education, the right of married women to control property, the right to divorce, the right to work and suffrage (none of which automatically included working-class women). A number of politically inspired women played key roles in the revolts. In the 1840s Princess Cristina Belgiojoso, an aristocrat who was living in exile in Paris and had embraced the socialism of Saint-Simon and Fourier as well as Mazzini's national republicanism, published her own newspapers promoting the creation of an Italian republic. In 1848 she acted as Mazzini's emissary securing arms and ships from France, directing hospital services, and leading a battalion of volunteers from Naples to Milan. However, when Mazzini established the short-lived Roman Republic in early 1849 women's legal or political rights were not considered.

The fervour and varied hopes for sexual revolution in 1848, such as they were among the women involved in the revolutions of 1848, were short-lived. By 1849 there was a return to more conventional gendered modes of political agency across Europe. The hostility towards women's political participation was so pronounced that women activists felt compelled to apologise for or to explain their actions. The German writer Anneke, for example, tried to downplay the extent of her political engagement. Although Anneke admitted belonging to a radical liberal group, she rejected the

Amazon image, denying that she had 'donned a massive cavalry sabre, a hunting pike, a musket and men's clothing'. She claimed instead to have been 'at my husband's side, unarmed, and in my usual woman's clothing, with only the addition of linen trousers for riding'. She defended the legitimacy of her reason for leaving 'the sphere originally assigned to me to become involved in the war', as 'a burning hate generated against tyrants and oppressors of sacred human rights'. Jeanne Deroin (unsuccessfully) nominated herself as a candidate for the Legislative Assembly of the French Second Republic, which only allowed universal manhood suffrage, by announcing that she represented 'the civil and political equality of the sexes'. But she also explained her commitment to politics and participation in the public sphere by drawing on the image of women helping men 'establish order in this badly-administered large household called the State'; women would do for 'the large social family' what they did in her own home, they would expand the egoistic circle of domestic affections and elevate the standing of humanitarian questions (Zevaes 1931: 128). In the 1850s the liberal feminist Louise Otto, like other European female ex-revolutionaries, joined in the condemnation of the emancipated woman 'whose demands for absolute equality between the sexes exceeded the taste and propriety of the journal and its editor and readers', and presented herself as 'the concerned, well-informed, practical, and aware housewife and mother who was above all interested in the proper upbringing and education of her offspring' (Boetcher-Joeres 1979: 4).

Otto's conservative representation of women's proper role was announced against the background of an 1850 Prussian decree which prohibited the participation of students, apprentices and women in the public sphere. In 1854 the same decree was made part of the protocols of the loose German federation structure retained after the revolution's failure. Two years earlier, the new French monarch, Napoleon III, also formally excluded women from the right to publish newspapers or to discuss political subjects. Under the new French anti-association law directed against women and socialists, Deroin ended up in prison. French and German anti-association laws restricted the possible public roles women could take and made clear that women's participation in the public sphere was only legitimate if it could be represented as a social contribution, rather than as an intrinsic right. Women anxious to continue their political and public activities turned their attention to the churches, both Protestant and Catholic, or radical socialist and communist organisations (Herzog 1990). Patriotism continued to provided a legitimate rationale for women to form associations: the Humania Association was allowed to continue its work in the German states after 1850 because its female members were associating for 'patriotic' reasons. In this sense, patriotism had now become synonymous with political conservatism.

Elsewhere in Europe, the post-revolutionary backlash had similar features. In the post-1848 period, statutes were introduced throughout the Habsburg empire that outlawed women's organised political participation. In 1849 wealthy women in 'Lower Austria' gained the right to vote for the Provincial Assembly 'by proxy' (a man had to be sent to do the actual voting), but in 1888 even this right was taken away from them in the interests of national uniformity (Anderson 1992: 39). While liberals and more radical social democrats within the Habsburg empire successfully extended voting rights for men (universal male suffrage was enacted in 1907), the scarce opportunities for propertied women to vote in local or provincial elections were removed.

The historian Dagmar Herzog has pointed out that in the German states '[F]ar from being marginal, debates over gender relations went to the heart of the liberal dilemma, for gender was the primary category around which bourgeois society organised itself ' (Herzog 1996: 57). In Europe generally, the revolutionary atmosphere of 1848 had offered a space for the articulation by some groups of radical democratic ideals – the rights of women or of property-less men to political representation and political participation. The failures of the revolution not only had different consequences for the growing industrial working class and the bourgeoisie, but for women and men. This was particularly so in the French case after 1848, where on the one hand the vote was granted to men as a whole, and on the other, women were formally excluded from the public sphere and political engagement. Sperber argues that:

> the space that had been opened closed again all too soon. The small organised women's movement that emerged in the 1860s was dedicated to women's right to work and to the personal autonomy and political equality with men that would accompany that right to work ... [By 1871] the women's movement had once again turned to arguments about women's superior sensibility and morality in an (amazingly successful) effort to appear less threatening to male liberals – their potential political allies – and to broaden their social base.
>
> (Sperber 1994: 84)

By confirming the symbolic centrality of women and sexual politics to the constitution of conservative and liberal conceptions of social and political order, and to the nation, the 1848 revolutions had also reinforced women's claims to 'superior sensibility and morality'. Thus despite the defeat of liberals, radical democrats and socialists in the 1848 revolutions, and the diminution in women's political and legal rights that had been effected in many European states in the name of liberalism, liberal feminists continued to make demands for women's legal equality with men, even if on the basis of women's difference from men.

The obvious paradoxes and contradictions within this European-wide belief in separate spheres and in the need for women to be immersed within family life and located in the home provided the framework for the many women's organisations which began to emerge in the mid nineteenth century seeking to improve the lot of their sex. The contrast between the belief that marriage was the sacred and social duty of women, and the complete legal, economic and social subordination, even enslavement, of married women, and the obvious fact that while women were assumed to be protected and supported by their husbands or fathers, many women from all social classes, married and single, needed to earn their own living, provided the twin pillars on which most women's organisations were built. Although feminist critiques of women's oppression and of the sexual double standard had been made by a number of people since the 1790s, it was only in the mid nineteenth century that organisations seeking to campaign for reform of the situation of women were created. In Austria, the first organisation to initiate what is referred to as the 'era of the organised woman' was the Viennese Women's Employment Association founded in November 1866. Its immediate impetus was the widespread economic distress that followed the defeat of Austria by Prussia earlier that year, that had made many women, both married and single, destitute and in need of employment. This organisation was followed by a series of other associations dedicated to the improvement of women's education and to the support of lower-middle-class girls by assisting them in obtaining appropriate training. Though essentially philanthropic organisations, these groups nonetheless recognised the need for financial independence for women.

At the very time that in many places on the Continent women were outlawed from political association, in Britain the debate around the 1867 Reform Act was accompanied by the start of a campaign for women's suffrage. As many historians have pointed out, the earlier anti-slavery and anti-Corn Law campaigns had provided the basis for the movement for women's suffrage which was established in Britain in the 1860s and 1870s. Suffrage committees were formed first in London and Manchester and then in a number of other centres. By the 1870s, a national movement with a journal, the *Women's Suffrage Journal*, and a co-ordinating committee, concentrated its lobbying efforts in London. The idea of women's suffrage was supported by some prominent male liberals in England, most notably John Stuart Mill whose book, *The Subjection of Women* (1869) was taken by many English feminists as their basic text and was translated and widely read throughout Europe. Mill insisted that liberal principles should be extended to women, and believed that as societies evolved men and women would become less dissimilar.

In the nineteenth century, feminism was both sustained and constrained by liberal ideals, by the promise of experiences such as the 1848 revolution, and by the shared interest of men and women in the prevention of further social instability. Even in states where there was no specific legislation against the political activism and association of women, the progressive liberal frameworks they increasingly adopted made the question of women's rights more difficult because of the ways in which economic and legal developments limited and reduced women's public role. In the 1870s liberalism inspired women in the new Kingdom of Italy (see Chapter 4) to organise around demands for education, access to professions, the right to claim paternity suits, and suffrage. Anna Maria Mozzoni (a prominent liberal spokesperson for women's rights in Italy and the Italian translator of Mill's *Subjection of Women*) argued that while the French Revolution of 1789 promised the emancipation of women, 'laws, habits, opinion, belief and scientific postulates had undermined that promise' (Mozzoni 1871). As we will see in the following chapters, the small gains made by European feminists in their political and legal campaigns in the late nineteenth century occurred within ongoing debates among liberals, socialists, nationalists and others about the relationship between the individual and the state, and most specifically, about the rights and duties of the national citizen.

References and further reading

Primary sources

Engels, Frederich (1880) *Socialism: Utopian and Scientific*, London.
Fichte, Johann Gottlieb (1968 [1807]) *Addresses to the German Nation*, New York.
Fourier, Charles (1996 [1808]) *The Theory of the Four Movements* (ed. G. Stedman Jones and I. Patterson), Cambridge.
Martineau, Harriet (1983 [1875]) *Autobiography*, London.

Mazzini, Joseph (1966 [1844–58]) *The Duties of Man and Other Essays*, London.
Michelet, Jules (1973 [1845]) *The People*, trans. J. P. McKay, Urbana.
Mill, John Stuart (1869) *On the Subjection of Women*, London.
Mozzoni, Anna Maria (1871) 'La questione dell'emancipazione della donna in Italia', in *La Roma del popolo*, 21 Marzo.
de Tocqueville, Alexis (1893) *Souvenirs de Alexis De Tocqueville*, Paris.
White Mario, J. (1909) *The Birth of Modern Italy* (ed. Duke Litta-Visconti-Arese), London.

Liberalism

Davidoff, L. and Hall, C. (1987) *Family Fortunes, Men and Women of the English Middle Class 1780–1850*, London.
Goodman, K. (1982) 'Poesis and praxis in Rachel Varnhagen's letters', *New German Critique* 27.
Gray, M. (1990) 'From the household economy to rational agriculture: the establishment of Liberal ideals in German agricultural thought', in K. Jarausch and L. Jones (eds) *In Search of a Liberal German: Studies in the History of German Liberalism from 1789 to the Present*, New York.
Hall, C. (1992) *White Male and Middle-Class: Explorations in Feminism and History*, Cambridge.
Hull, I. (1996) *Sexuality, State, and Civil Society in Germany, 1700–1815*, Ithaca, New York.
Nye, R. (1993) *Masculinity and Male Codes of Honor in Modern France*, Oxford.
Pateman, C. (1989) *The Disorder of Women*, Oxford.
Pilbeam, P. (1990) *The Middle Classes in Europe 1789–1914: France, Germany, Italy and Russia*, London.
Polasky, J. L. (1986) 'Women in revolutionary Belgium: from stone throwers to hearth tenders', *History Workshop* 21 (Spring): 87–104.
Poovey, M. (1989) *Uneven Developments: The Ideological Work of Gender in mid-Victorian England*, London.

Socialism and the social

Cook, B. W. (1986) 'Feminism, socialism, and sexual freedom: women in culture and politics', in J. Friedlander *et al.* (eds) *Women in Culture and Politics: A Century of Change*, Bloomington.
Grogan, S. (1992) *French Socialism and Sexual Difference: Women and the New Society, 1803–1844*, London.
Moon, J. S. (1978) 'Feminism and socialism: the Utopian synthesis of Flora Tristan', in M. Boxer and J. Quaetert (eds) *Socialist Women*, New York.
Moses, C. (1982) 'Saint-Simonian men/Saint-Simonian women: the transformation of feminist thought in 1830s France', *Journal of Modern History* 54, 2: 240–67.

Moses, C. (1984) *French Feminism in the Nineteenth Century*, Albany, New York.

Moses, C. and L. Rabine (1993) *Feminism, Socialism and French Romanticism*, Bloomington.

Taylor, B. (1983) *Eve and the New Jerusalem: Socialism and Feminism in the Nineteenth Century*, London.

The state as nation

Hanley, S. (1989) 'Engendering the state: family formation and state building in early modern France', *French Historical Studies* **16**, 1: 4–27.

Lorence-Kot, B. (1987) 'Klementyna Tanska Hoffmanowa cultural nationalism and a new formula for Polish womanhood', *History of European Ideas* **8**, 4/5: 435–50.

Mosse, G. (1980) *Masses and Men: Nationalist and Fascist Perceptions of Reality*, New York.

Mosse, G. (1985) *Nationalism and Sexuality: Respectability and Abnormal Sexuality in Modern Europe*, New York.

Offen, K. (1987) 'A nineteenth-century French feminist rediscovered: Jenny P. de Hericourt, 1809–1875', *Signs* **13**, 1: 144–58.

Paulsell, P. (1976) 'The relationship of "Young Germany" to questions of women's rights', Ph.D. thesis, University of Michigan.

Riley, D. (1988) *Am I That Name? Feminism and the Category 'Women' in History*, Minnesota.

Starr Guilloton, D. (1987) 'Toward a new freedom: Rahel Varnhagen and the German women writers before 1848', in A. Goldberger (ed.) *Woman as Mediatrix*, New York.

Tosh, J. (1991) 'Domesticity and manliness in the Victorian middle class: the family of Edward White Benson', in M. Roper and J. Tosh (eds) *Manful Assertions: Masculinities in Britain since 1800*, London.

Zucker, S. (1991) *Kathinka Zitz-Halein and Female Civic Activism in Mid-Nineteenth-Century Germany*, Carbondale and Edwardsville.

1848

Anderson, H. (1992) *Women's Movement in Fin-de-Siècle Vienna*, New Haven and London.

Boetcher-Joeres, R. (1979) 'Louise Otto and her journals: a chapter in nineteenth-century German feminism', *Internationales Archiv für Sozialgeschichte der deutschen Literatur* **4**: 100–29.

Herzog, D. (1990) 'Liberalism, religious dissent and women's rights: Louise Dittmar's writings from the 1840s', in K. Jarausch and L. Jones (eds) *In Search of a Liberal Germany: Studies in the History of German Liberalism from 1789 to the Present*, New York.

Herzog, D. (1996) *Intimacy and Exclusion: Religious Policies in Pre-Revolutionary Baden*, Princeton.

McPhee, P. (1997) 'Towards a sesquicentennial: the gendered body politic and the French revolution of 1848', unpublished ms Melbourne University.

Secci, L. (1984) 'German women writers and the revolution of 1848', in J. C. Fout (ed.) *German Women in the Nineteenth Century: A Social History*, New York.

Sperber, J. (1994) *The European Revolutions, 1848–1851*, Cambridge.

Strumingher, L. (1987) 'The Vesuviennes: images of women warriors in 1848 and their significance for French history', *History of European Ideas* 8, 4/5: 451–88.

Strumingher, L. (1989) 'The struggle for unity among Parisian women: the voix des femmes, March–June 1848', *History of European Ideas* 11: 273–85.

Zevaes, A. (1931) 'Une candidature feministe en 1849', *La revolution de 1848 et les revolutions du XIXe siècle, 1830, 1848, 1870*, Paris.

FOUR

Sex and Race, Nations and Empires

In the second half of the nineteenth century the ideal of the nation as a democratic and progressive political and social form was transformed by racial and evolutionary theories of national differences and the pressures of 'new imperialism'. Military power was the measure of national strength, and the rivalry between states the measure of national weakness. The new conception of the nation as a collective, and often organic and racial entity, made the question of national belonging and exclusion a critical determinant of the political, legal and social status of those members of a national population who were classed either as 'the people' or as 'different'.

The emergence of race as a major concern in nineteenth-century Europe was signalled by the influence of the French diplomat Arthur de Gobineau, and his infamous *Essay on the Inequality of the Human Races*, published in the 1850s. Gobineau believed that the rise of civilisations depended on racial characteristics, and that their decline resulted from intermarriage with other races. 'The racial question overshadows all other problems of history' he argued, and it holds the key to them all, as 'the inequality of the races from whose fusion a people is formed is enough to explain the whole course of its destiny' (Gobineau 1967: 41). Gobineau created a tripartite division of races in which the 'white' races were absolutely superior to the others, while the 'yellow' races were more advanced and capable than the 'black'. Within these broad racial groups, he also established other divisions. Northern European nations were strong, disciplined, energetic and innovative, southern ones were indolent, sensual and weak. In his discussion of nations, as of races, Gobineau drew on prevailing gender stereotypes. The masculine strength of northern European nations was contrasted with the effeminacy of the south. In Gobineau's view, the mixing of masculine with feminine societies inevitably caused the decline of civilisations.

Gobineau's ideas influenced Charles Darwin, whose theory of evolution dominated late nineteenth-century ideas about racial hierarchy and provided a new framework for thinking about nationalism and national struggle. Darwin's *Origin of Species* (1859) provided a new scientific basis for insisting that some races were superior to others and more likely to succeed in the struggle for survival, which Darwin saw as evident everywhere in nature. By the 1860s the theory of evolution developed by Darwin in *Origin of Species* was being popularised and used to provide a framework for looking at social evolution and at sexual difference. Social Darwinists argued that societies evolved in ways similar to living organisms, from simpler to more complex forms. Sociologists, including the English Herbert Spencer and the French Emile Durkheim, regarded the gendered division of labour and the emergence of public and private spheres as evidence of a more highly evolved culture. The highest forms of society, like the most developed peoples, were those modern European societies which naturally held power over and dominated the simpler and more primitive societies of Africa, Asia and Australasia. The language of Social Darwinism thus provided a powerful intellectual foundation for imperial projects and European domination.

Evolution also provided a new 'scientific' framework for thinking about sexual difference. Women, in the views of Social Darwinist sociologists like Spencer, were less highly evolved and more childlike than men. Spencer often drew parallels between women and children and the 'childlike' and immature races or peoples over whom European men ruled. His ideas were popularised in French and Italian translations and by the last decades of the nineteenth century, liberals, republicans and even socialists inflected their political ideals with Darwinian and Spencerian views of nature and biology. Clemence Royer, the first translator of Darwin into French, utilised Darwin's theory of evolution to argue against women being given the vote until they had evolved through education to the stage where they could responsibly exercise political rights (Fraisse 1986). Those who supported the emancipation of women, including the English liberal John Stuart Mill and the German socialist Auguste Bebel, had to find ways to argue against the now widely held view that women were less evolved and had less brain capacity than men. In what was perhaps the most widely read feminist and socialist text in Europe, *Die Frau und der Sozialismus* (Woman and Socialism, 1879), Bebel went on the offensive, pointing to the physiological differences in the vascular systems, jaws and brain weights of men and women in order to suggest that men might be more closely connected to apes than women. Bebel, like Mill, rejected the argument that men were more intelligent than women because they had larger skulls. He insisted that skull size did not determine brain size, and that the important point was not absolute brain size, but the relative size of brain to body size and weight (Mill 1869; Bebel 1879).

Evolutionary theories which were applied to societies as well as to species gave a central place to the nation, describing the nation as a political form which emerged only in the most developed societies. Hence the emergence of nation-states came to be seen as following natural law and as further evidence of the superiority of Europe over the rest of the world. In 1860 Italy was unified, in 1871 the German nation-state was created, and at the same time, the French nation began a new phase of political life as the Third Republic. These developments, along with the changing nature of political representation in Britain, were accompanied by debates about how the nation was defined and who belonged to or should be represented politically in the nation. These debates in turn provoked intense concern about citizenship rights and about the implications of political exclusion. In France, Germany, England, Italy and elsewhere in Europe, the physiological and biological arguments which dominated debates regarding women's legal position were evident also in discussions about the conditions of their employment. All these debates made clear the increasing acceptance of the authority of 'science' in place of religion as the foundation of nations. As we will see, the legal, medical and political acceptance of the 'incommensurability of the sexes' in the European states meant that men and women were constituted differently as national citizens.

The late nineteenth century was a period of fervid European imperialism and colonialism as well as nation-building. The aims and achievements of imperialism were understood in relation to theories of evolution, which elaborated the 'scientific' bases of racial and sexual differences, and established the hierarchical status of different races and nations through the mutual imagining of race and sexuality. One of the major concerns of anthropologists and sociologists in the second half of the nineteenth century was the classification of national differences on the basis of language, custom, psychology and physiognomy. At the same time, medical interest in gendered bodies provided an important context for understanding popular sovereignty and the constitution of 'the people'. The differences between races and nations, like men and women, were elaborated as characteristics of their respective stages of biological and psychological advance and competitiveness. Depictions of women as psychologically inferior, as being unable to control their passions, reinforced their physiological difference, and made femininity an important metaphor for describing racially marginalised groups like Jews and blacks (Gilman 1993). In Otto Weininger's popular theory of 'sex and character', woman's lack of personality and of a complex psychological self also likened her to the Jew. The success of imperialism was measured in terms of physical health and sexual vitality. Imperial expansion was seen as an affirmation of national virility and health, of racial superiority, and of the higher stage of evolution of the colonising nation. Alternatively, imperial failure was blamed on the growing prominence of 'new women', often themselves eager to join in the imperial adventure in an attempt to secure recognition for their contribution to the nation.

Our focus in this chapter is on the different ways in which concepts of race and gender were involved in the processes of Italian, German, British and French nation-building in the late nineteenth century, and their role in the legitimation of the sovereignty of nation-states and the drive by European nations to expand their empires. We will also explore the connections between race, sexuality, gender identities, family and nation, and the respective political roles they afforded men and women.

Nationalism and citizenship

The failures of the 1848 revolutions did not bring to an end the ideal of national governments legitimated by popular sovereignty. In the early summer of 1857, a young English woman named Jessie White who was closely involved with the Italian nationalist programme of Mazzini, insisted that Mazzini was the man who had been chosen by God to bring 'the new word': 'I believe', she told her interrogators, 'that the epoch of tyranny is finished and that the epoch of the People is about to begin' (White Mario 1857). White believed that the unification of Italian states promised the establishment of a new political entity which would combine social harmony and political inclusiveness. The future Italian state would represent 'the people', rather than the interests of an élite few.

When Italy was unified in 1861, however, it was not in fulfilment of Mazzini's or Jessie White's vision of the nation as a natural unit in which the state coincided with the cultural traditions and identity of its 'people'. On the contrary, the political unification of Italy was engineered by Count Camillo Cavour, premier of the Kingdom of Piedmont. Piedmont became the dominant force in Italy and Piedmont's monarch, Victor Emmanuel, became King of the new Italy, while Cavour himself became first Prime Minister. Moreover, after the successful campaign for Italian unification – known as the

Italian Risorgimento, or the 'renewal of the Italian nation' – 'Italy' existed but, as many people recognised, 'Italians' still had to be made. In Germany too, the illusion that national unification expressed the wishes of a populace who identified naturally with the nation was quickly dispelled. The German nation-state was created as a federation a decade after Italy, in 1871, as a result of the victory of the forces of the German states which had united in a war against the expansionism of the French monarch, Napoleon III. The Prime Minister of the Prussian state, Otto von Bismarck, manoeuvered the other German states into a new political and legal unit dominated by Prussia. The new Emperor was the former Prussian king who maintained control of the army and held executive power.

The new national German and Italian citizenry were drawn together from people with a range of disparate political experiences, social customs, languages, and class and gender expectations. Among the earliest activities of the new national governments was the introduction of legislation and administrative arrangements necessary to make the states governable and which aimed to make uniform the institutions, customs and basic language of the new nation. Those institutional arrangements reflected and reinforced the limited definition of popular sovereignty which accompanied national unification in the second half of the nineteenth century. Only some groups of men were legally and politically recognised as active citizens in these new nations. Women, and those men who lacked adequate property or who belonged to minority religions and ethnic groups, were excluded. In some cases the process of unification even removed the legal and political rights that some women had previously been able to exercise.

The unified Italy of 1860 was a constitutional monarchy, but one in which popular sovereignty was only dimly recognised. Until the end of the First World War less than 7 per cent of the Italian population – literate men with the requisite property – had the right to vote. Before the creation of unified Italy, propertied women living under Austrian law in the Italian-speaking regions of Lombardy, Tuscany and Venice (which were incorporated into Italy) had some form of political representation, most usually in municipal elections. For them, the creation of the Italian state constituted a step backwards. Similarly, in the old Piedmontese state, there had been no explicit exclusion of women from 'the free exercise of civil rights' accorded to all men. With unification, the old 1848 Piedmontese constitution was adapted to become the Italian charter, but women were purposely excluded from the rights they had once legally shared. Like the 1804 French Napoleonic Code, the 1865 Italian Civil Code stipulated that married women had the status of minors, and they, like their property, were subject to their husbands' guardianship. Parental authority belonged to both parents, but the father had precedence. In the absence of the father, women were to be supervised by an (all-male) council of the family. There was no provision for divorce and paternity suits were forbidden. Maternity suits, enforcing maternal responsibility, were, however, acceptable, and adultery was a crime for which wives rather than husbands were punished. Only widowed women enjoyed legal, economic or social autonomy. This sense of sexual hierarchy also extended to the regulation of work. The Italian national government established wage differentials so that women, by law, earned less than male workers and the government strictly supervised the areas in which women could seek employment.

Unlike unified Italy, in the new federal Germany all male citizens were granted suffrage; even male German Jews were granted political rights. The German parliament, however, held no real power, as the Emperor could override its decision-making processes. Similarly, despite universal male suffrage, the middle classes had limited political and economic power in this new state in comparison with the landed classes (the Junkers) and the aristocracy. Women had a distinctive place in this new nation-state. German nationality from 1871 until 1918 was the prerogative of the father of the family. In contrast to France and England where citizenship relied upon the place of birth, in the new Germany the child of married parents took on its father's nationality. The legal and civil codes of the new nation restricted women to the private sphere. The anti-association laws which had been introduced after 1848 in some German states to prohibit the involvement of women and socialists in political life were now extended across the federation. The new German civil code that came into force nationally in 1900 addressed the specifics of gender relations and rights in relation to the role of women in the family, and by extension, in the nation as a larger family. The family was, in theory, the 'natural' foundation for the nation-state. Nevertheless it was the government, not the family, which encoded acceptable forms of behaviour even in the most intimate of circumstances. Women had become legal persons in principle and 'parents' rather than the father were given authority over children. The provision that a wife's earnings from any work remained hers, and that she no longer required her husband's consent before taking a job, reflected a new economic reality – the industrialising German nation needed female workers. The gains that women made in terms of financial independence were constrained, however, by the old Prussian family law, which continued to define women's rights in respect to the patriarchal family. Husbands retained all legal power over decisions affecting children and the marriage, and gained control over their wives' property upon marriage. Further, the new civil code extinguished the right to divorce by consent which had existed in the old Prussian code.

The extent to which domesticity and women's sexual conduct were seen as important to national well-being, as evident in the regulation of prostitution, was a marked feature of late nineteenth-century nation-building. The question of prostitution and the need to regulate it was a major social issue throughout the nineteenth century. Beginning in France under Napoleon at the beginning of the century, and then extending in the second half of the century to Britain, Italy, Russia, Switzerland and Germany, prostitution was regulated in a number of countries. Ostensibly undertaken in the interests of health and morality, regulation generally involved the registration and the regular medical examination of prostitutes who could be confined to locked hospital wards if found to be diseased. While the spread of sexually transmitted disease was undoubtedly a major health concern, the lack of any surveillance of male clients made clear that the regulation of prostitution enshrined a sexual double standard: women were liable to incarceration for activities which men could engage in with impunity. It was women, not men, who were seen as spreading disease right up until the end of the nineteenth century. Judith Walkowitz has argued that by the latter half of the nineteenth century in England the prostitute had become 'the Great Social Evil', both 'an affront to morality and a vital aspect of the social economy' (Walkowitz 1980: 32). Historians have argued that it is no coincidence that the first law introduced by the new Italian Prime Minister (enacted as a ministerial decree) and undertaken while the wars of unification were still underway, dealt with prostitution (Gibson 1986: 13). Cavour's objective in introducing the law was to provide a reliable and medically maintained prostitution service for the Italian army in official brothels – thereby emulating the precedents set by Napoleon during the French wars of 'liberation', and by the British in 1864. Since unregulated prostitution was believed to pose a moral and physical threat to the health of the soldiers engaged in patriotic duty, and men needed to fulfil their heterosexual needs outside of marriage and the family, the prostitute was made the focus of efforts to police 'national' health and respectability. In order to ensure a supply of healthy prostitutes, women suspected of being prostitutes were reduced to the status of state property, organised into a regulated state-sponsored brothel system, and used as a source of government income. Mary Gibson has suggested that the prostitute was a potent symbol of deviance in Italy and '[i]n the context of the economic and social transformations of the period . . . a target for state efforts to assert hegemony and restore order' (Gibson 1986: 23). State control of prostitution clearly complemented laws regarding women and the family, and is evidence of the ways that the authority and legitimacy of the nation were bound up with the tenets of bourgeois respectability, at the same time that the 'double standard' of respectability was being applied in the interests of the nation. The representatives of the nation-state assumed the right to regulate, control and sell the bodies of prostitutes. A similar situation prevailed in Germany, where, even though the organisation of state brothels was illegal, police established local brothels populated with female detainees. In some European states, vice squads maintained surveillance over prostitutes who had to undergo regular examination, carry identity cards, and conform to standards of conduct, dress and behaviour so that they could be clearly distinguished from respectable middle-class women. Registration and police surveillance made it very difficult for women who had once engaged in casual prostitution to give it up, since it publicly marked a woman's social status.

In late nineteenth-century Europe, governments passed decrees and legislation on questions of public order, morality and health because these issues were regarded as vital to national health. Abortion was everywhere illegal, and, as we have already seen, the state took most seriously its task of organising prostitution and of policing women suspected of being prostitutes for evidence of sexually transmitted diseases. In Italy, 'woman was the measure of the conflict between progress and tradition, liberty and order in the liberal state' (Howard 1978: ii). The image of woman that these laws and practices deployed was influenced by the mid nineteenth-century ideas of the French socialist Pierre-Joseph Proudhon, the positivist August Comte and the historian Jules Michelet (Mozzoni 1865: 4), and cloaked in the 'scientific' physiological and psychological theories of a new generation of social scientists like Spencer and the Italian criminologist Cesare Lombroso. Proudhon believed in the idea of the 'spermatic economy'. Men had the power of generation through semen, and women were passive receptacles. But men were also vulnerable to castration and excessive use of sperm. For this reason it was important to maintain the virile energy of men, through soldiering and work, and the passivity of women, who could only catch up with men if 'strength and intelligence' were rendered useless, if the progress of science, industry, work were called to a halt, and humanity were prevented from developing its virile power 'all for the greater glory of this poor little woman's soul, which can neither rival her companion nor follow him'

(Proudhon 1858). By the 1850s Jules Michelet's considerations of class and sexual antagonisms in the French nation had grown increasingly reliant on (highly questionable) developments in the medical sciences. Michelet attacked the idea of female suffrage arguing, in a series of public lectures on the family at the College de France in Paris where he was Professor of History and Morals (or customs), that it would empower the Church and undermine his vision for a secular French Republic (Michelet 1858). In Auguste Comte's second major synthetic study *The System of Positive Polity*, published in 1854, he included not only a dedication to a woman, but a special chapter on 'the feminine influence of positivism' (Comte 1875). Women featured as one of three major groups constituting the positivist community, alongside new philosophers and the working class. In this community, instead of a public sphere of clashing public opinion, the hierarchical order of domesticity would reign. The concern for social order and harmony required the abandonment by women of the political and with it the masculine. Men and women would have their place in a society ruled by chivalry. Women would teach self-sacrifice. Harriet Martineau, Comte's English translator and editor (she condensed six volumes into two and in the process made Comte accessible to a much wider audience), celebrated Comte's emphasis on the social role attributed to women by positivism, because it promised to reunify society. Martineau was ardent in her faith that if Comte's work was made accessible to young men of the middle and 'operative' classes they would give up their antagonistic search for alternative social theories (Comte 1875). Comte's premise, like that of his English contemporary Herbert Spencer, was that by discovering the laws of biology, society could use those laws as a guide to its own natural course. In the 1880s and 1890s Comte's ideas and concerns became an important foundation for the creation of French national social policies and for the national identification of radical republicans. Italian debates regarding legal and political reform that took place in the latter half of the nineteenth century borrowed from conceptions of 'woman's' difference propagated by these intellectuals and scientists, socialists, liberals and conservatives and made them the basis for women's exclusion from politics and citizenship. Alice Kelikian has maintained that the European-wide trend of physiological determinism was taken to an extreme in Italy (Kelikian 1996: 379). In 1889, the description of the prostitute as 'the natural form' of female degeneration popularised by Lombroso was incorporated into the Italian penal code.

In both Italy and Germany, unification also provided a new national political framework for agitation for women's rights and for gender equality

(Howard 1980: 237). For the liberal feminist Anna Maria Mozzoni, national progress meant the attainment of a certain social equality for women (Mozzoni 1865: 4). In unified Italy, men sympathetic to the cause of female emancipation, the rights of women to education and to economic and political autonomy, made attempts to reform family law on a national basis. Although they failed to gain equal parental authority for women, or provisions for divorce and paternity suits, between 1877 and 1893 Italian women were uniformly given the right to bear legal witness, to have their own bank accounts (unless their husband or guardian objected), to sit on boards of directors of charity institutions, and to take part in factory arbitration boards and prisons – positions which were identified with philanthropy and with women's moral or healing influence in a nation riven by economic inequities, regional disparities (particularly a north/south divide) and class discontent.

The restrictions on women's political agency which came with new and more highly centralised government, and the feminist agitation inspired by new ideals of national or political progress, did not occur only in new nations. The gendered features of nation-building were also evident in England, a constitutional monarchy where the first major extension of manhood suffrage in 1832 had specifically excluded female suffrage and where, despite the continual increase in manhood suffrage, all women continued to be excluded from the suffrage until 1918. Even then, while all adult men were given the vote, women's enfranchisement was confined to propertied women over the age of 30. In England, organised feminism, and particularly the women's suffrage movement, was a direct response by women to this continual extension of the franchise to new groups of men, and the continual denial to women of the vote, and of nationality. As new (and old) states on the continent emphasised their national identities, in 1870 British legislation specifically denied women the right to nationality, and insisted that women took the nationality of their husbands. British women who married foreigners were thus no longer entitled to be counted as British. Around this time, the French feminist Jenny d'Hericourt complained about women's place in national 'progress'; d'Hericourt argued that 'among us [women] there can be no foreigners, since *we* are not *citizens*' (Offen 1987: 157). Her view was further reinforced when in 1889 in France, some Algerian and Jewish male residents were allowed to become French citizens, but women still had no intrinsic right to citizenship.

The family and nation

The family with the father at its head was a key element in the nineteenth-century idea of the liberal state and of the organic nation. As Lynn Hunt's psychoanalytic analysis of the French Revolution as an 'unconscious' Freudian 'family romance' has shown, images of the family and of family breakdown played a key role in political representation (Hunt 1992: xiii). For writers as diverse as Auguste Comte, Jules Michelet and the novelist Victor Hugo, the family provided the basis for the resolution of social conflict between the classes and the sexes (Stone 1995: 58). In England, Spencer presented the patriarchal Victorian family as the highest stage in social evolution. In the new nation-states of Germany and Italy, the family was regulated by the state and seen as the site of the reproduction of both national citizens and national values. Emphasis on the family reinforced sexual hierarchy and the maternal role of women. After unification, Italian laws imposed the model of the patriarchal family on a national scale in order to provide the new Italian constitutional monarchy with the authority of 'tradition' and of morality. Like the Catholic Church, the new Italian state belaboured its message that women were mothers, not workers. The definition of woman as mother reinforced the privileged position of men: male social standing (*la bella figura*) it was argued, could be offended by any challenge to *patria potestas*, the authority of the father within the family, over his wife as well as his children (Galoppin 1980).

Adulation of the family was often accompanied by a sense that social and even political and military problems resulted from inadequate family life. In France, physicians argued that women's maternal indifference was the cause of the nation's defeat at the hands of the German states in 1870 (Offen 1984). The crisis brought about by that defeat was imagined by French intellectuals and scientists as a sexual crisis; military defeat was described as the consequence of a lack of masculine virility; falling demographic rates were linked to that defeat and blamed on feminists and effeminate men; Jews, homosexuals and women were all employed as scapegoats for the imagined dissipation of national masculinity; and women's maternal responsibility became the focus of efforts to restore national 'fertility'.

The history of the Paris Commune, the common name for a two-month-long period of revolutionary turmoil in Paris which erupted after the defeat of France and Napoleon III's downfall, illustrates well the predominance of gender themes at the founding moment of the new French Third Republic. The Commune and its communist ideals were defended by armed local working-class women and men, known as *Communards*. For liberals and conservatives, the Paris Commune was a symbol of the menace faced by a society that failed to exert moral standards and maintain national solidarity. Communards seemed to flaunt the institutions of bourgeois respectability: they acknowledged *union libres*, free sexual unions between men and women, and they recognised the children of unmarried women, usually working-class women, as legitimate. Communard society reinforced the shared parental responsibilities of fathers and mothers towards children and raised the idea of secular education for girls as well as boys. In the wake of the post-1848 restrictions on women's involvement in the public sphere, the Commune was important for reinvigorating female activism. At the same time, in the eyes of liberals and conservatives, it stamped that activism with the taint of violence, destruction and revolution. When open conflict broke out between Communards and the official French government in Versailles, it led to widespread fires in the city and the killing of 20,000 Parisians by government troops. French officials blamed the fires on the Communard women. The 'unruly women' of the Paris Commune were branded *petroleuses* and portrayed as ugly, masculine, and bad mothers (Gullickson 1992). Their critics claimed that they had spread danger, disease and destruction of property and order, instead of fulfilling their familial duties and motherhood. The founding fathers of the new French Third Republic that emerged from the defeat of 1870 represented the *petroleuses* as like prostitutes in symbolising both sexual and political disorder.

After 1870, the social significance of the family was most strongly promoted in France by Frederic Le Play who developed the notion of 'familism'. Le Play's 1871 publication *Organisation of the Family* demanded legal recognition of the importance of the family to the social order. He supported the idea that families rather than individual men should have special citizen rights, and modelled his idea of family on the large families of the *ancien régime*, rather than the 'modern' bourgeois nuclear family, the exclusiveness of which he believed was a cause of social unrest. Le Play also wanted fathers to be given a special status as a 'fourth estate', and as citizens requiring specific representation. The legal validation of the strength of paternal authority, he argued, would restore women to their primary reproductive role (Quine 1996: 55–7). Le Play's emphasis on 'familism' and fatherhood suggests that by the late nineteenth century, even the very extensive powers given to fathers in the French Civil Code seemed inadequate. The principles of 'familism' were reflected more broadly in French society, in republican debates regarding a 'family wage' and the role of the male '*chefs de famille*' as the family's spokesperson in all social and political matters. The idea of a 'family vote' (rather than individual votes) was debated in the French parliament alongside measures for the promotion of large families.

In France, Britain, Italy and Germany, support for the family as the foundation of the national community was evident among Catholics, anti-clericals, liberals, republicans and even many socialists. For socialists, many of whom criticised the family as a source of women's oppression while at the same time believing it to be necessary for social order, and (building on the Saint-Simonian legacy) regarded women's right to labour as the solution to the problem of women's emancipation, the predominance of familial ideology placed them in a difficult situation. In 1884 Marx's colleague and co-author Frederich Engels published *The Origin of the Family* in which he stated that property and the desire for men to pass their property to their sons was the basis of family life and of the oppression of women. While arguing that women needed access to paid employment, Engels also saw industrial labour as desexing women and undermining men. Following him, most late nineteenth-century socialists thought the state should provide care for wives and children, for the sick and unemployed, but in the image of a parental rather than paternal state. Secular liberals' support for the family was more straightforwardly self-interested. As Jacques Donzelot argues, the family protected private property, bolstered 'the bourgeois ethic of accumulation, and acted as a barrier against encroachments of the state'; 'the family became ... the point where criticism of the established order stopped and the point of support for demands for more social equality' (Donzelot 1980: 53). For Catholics the family buttressed a religious, moral and social conservatism. In 1880 Pope Leo XIII issued an encyclical reaffirming the procreative purpose of marriage. In 1891 in another encyclical, *De Rerum Novarum*, the Pope supported the 'family wage' for workers as a means of ending class discontent and of keeping women out of the workplace. The family was also fundamental to the social policies of anti-republicans. They, too, idealised the patriarchal (and noble) family as the basis of social order, and criticised republicans for what they saw as support for an egalitarian bourgeois family. At the turn of the century, republicans in France portrayed the family in terms of the key concept of 'solidarism'. Republican Solidarists stressed the importance of the role of the mother within the family, at the same time as they supported the political and legal pre-eminence of the father and the maintenance of patriarchal power. They regarded both these maternal and paternal roles as essential to the ideal of national harmony. In the solidarist view, the state represented a single national community whose class or sex differences were inconsequential in comparison with the health and harmony of the national organism itself.

In 1905, the popular English author Miss Betham-Edwards summed up the bipartisan view of the family in her praise for the French Civil Code which, she stated, 'binds family life into a compact, indissoluble whole, renders unassailable, impregnable, that sacred ark, that palladium of national strength, healthfulness, and vitality, the ancestral, the patriarchal home' (Betham-Edwards 1905: 315). This sense of the primacy of the family, and the widespread belief that the family was necessarily patriarchal, created barriers for those seeking to reform the laws which limited the rights of women and of children. When deputies in the new Italian parliament argued for civil rights for women, and the right of married women to control their own property, they were blocked by the Italian Senate's affirmation of the principle of family unity as the basis of public order. Even the proposed law guaranteeing both sons and daughters equal inheritance, was regarded by the more conservative members of the Italian parliament as a threat to the family. Women as well as men supported family prerogatives. Princess Cristina Belgiojoso, who had assisted both Mazzini and Garibaldi in their campaigns for Italian unification, for example, expressed her concern about the impact of women's liberation on the family. 'What would happen to the family as it is presently constituted', she asked, 'if women were initiated into masculine pursuits, and shared with men public, social and literary activities?' (Brombert 1977: 229).

The German idea of the 'great social household' mirrored French familism and solidarism. In Germany the conception of the state as a family was also used to legitimate welfare measures sought by increasingly strong socialist and trade union movements. These movements argued that the state had an obligation to its citizens, the way a father did to his children. The importance of the family and the prevailing sexual division of labour provided the basis for the introduction of welfare policies in Germany in the late 1880s, such as health and accident insurance for factory workers, and old-age pension schemes. A clear family agenda was inherent in such allowances. For example, in 1891 German legislation gave the married working woman an hour-and-a-half meal break to allow her time to return home and cook a main meal for her family. Similarly, a reduction in hours of paid work was also offered as a means of providing working-class women with more time to fulfil their unpaid domestic duties, such as cleaning and washing. The German strategy of implementing welfare reforms to avoid class conflict and support traditional gender relationships inspired similar legislation in

France, Italy and England in the decade before the First World War.

The social reforms of the Third Republic were also directed at the increase in the number of working women. These women were employed in the expanding industrial base and on the fringes of government institutions. After the 1848 revolutions, census reports had consistently indicated the significant numbers of women working in France, more than in any other Western nation. From 1856 to 1906, the number of women employed in non-agricultural areas doubled, most of them either young and single or older and widowed (Stone 1995). However, by the turn of the century nearly 40 per cent of working women were married with children. The phenomenon of working married women was associated with a significant dependence on wet-nurses, and high rates of child abandonment and infant mortality. Concerned observers demanded the payment of a family wage to men so that women would not have to work and could resume their domestic responsibilities. They were heavily influenced in these views by the growing support of doctors, who had become, along with lawyers, a powerful professional lobby group in deciding the state's interests, and nowhere more so than in France, where they made up a higher proportion of the parliament than in Britain, Germany or the United States (Fuchs 1995: 181). The medical profession – regarded as the representative of objective and apolitical science – confirmed fears that paid labour was destructive to women and disruptive of family life. The direct links between the institutional organisation of science and medicine and the state, and the development of welfare policies under pressure from organised socialist movements, had given the medical profession a new political status. In Italy in the 1890s, socialists like Anna Kuliscioff and Filippo Turati, co-founders of the Italian Socialist Party, campaigned for the introduction of laws regulating the work of woman and children in factories. Kuliscioff, a doctor, believed that overwork by women could pose a biological threat to the human species (La Vigna 1987: 158). This view corresponded with the strategies of successive governments which legislated women's industrial work as the earliest of their measures for reform – usually in the interest of the nation and in accord with the kind of biological argument put forward by Kuliscioff. Yet, all-female unions, which demanded the same right to work as men, rejected the paternalist legislation enacted by governments as too interventionist. Even the liberal feminist Anna Maria Mozzoni rejected special protection because she thought it would perpetuate gender inequality.

Women were a key focus of new welfare policies, but in ways that constituted them as national citizens and workers quite differently from men.

Rachel Fuchs argues that 'the social reforms leading to the development of the welfare state embodied a blurring of the lines between the public and private spheres'. The governments of welfare states could as easily 'conceive of state fathers for single-mother families and more generally working-class families', as conceive of 'state mothers producing healthy children for the nation' (Fuchs 1995: 159, 160). The familial and gendered precepts of late nineteenth-century welfare policies reinvented the state as both paternal and maternal. In the last decades in the nineteenth century, at the same time as married women of many European countries were given more legal rights – to act as witnesses in law courts, or to control their own wages – special laws were introduced in European countries that made the state responsible for the regulation of pregnancy, birth and child care, as well as for the protection of working women and children. Switzerland enacted unpaid maternity leave as early as 1877, and Germany in 1878, allowing women time away from employment in order to have their children. Other European countries would follow suit much later. In 1913 the French government instituted payment for the duration of maternity leave. The French government was also unique in offering social assistance to unmarried and married mothers, possibly a reflection of the widespread anxiety about demography.

The development of gendered welfare and work policies was related to pronatalism, and to the image of the nation as an extended family, and as an organism. Statistical fertility rates were used as indicators of national virility and success. It is in this context, as Anna Davin argues, that in the latter half of the nineteenth century there was an important shift in the definition of women as mothers rather than wives (Davin 1997). The emphasis on the responsibility of women for the success or failure of national health and the future of the race, rather than social or political policies, was an important basis of imperialist ambitions. The expanding importance of the medical profession, combined with the concerns about national or racial efficiency which accompanied imperial expansion – concern about falling population, and the declining quality of the race, Britain's defeat in the Boer War (1899–1902) – meant that by the last two decades of the nineteenth century in Britain, mothers were being advised on the best ways to bear and rear large numbers of healthy children, as well as being supervised in their activities and provided with training. The working class became the key focus of provisions for child and maternal welfare. Middle-class women were recruited by governments to train working-class mothers in bringing up healthy children. A spate of voluntary welfare societies sprang up to teach, supervise and enforce public health and hygiene, including the National League of Health, Maternity and Child Welfare, and the Women's League for the Service of Motherhood. Child-rearing was reinvented as a national duty and a direct form of female patriotism. Women were bestowed with the nomenclature 'mothers of the race'. The British National Insurance Act 1911 included support towards the expenses of childbirth. In the Netherlands, uplifting the working-class and emphasising child-rearing and education were targeted as strategies for the promotion of Dutch national identity and imperial ambitions (Stoler 1997: 203). European governments elsewhere increasingly took responsibility for supervising and directing reproduction and mothering under the influence of new important actors in the public sphere: the 'scientific expert', and organisations such as the *Alliance nationale pour l'accroisement de la population française* (National Alliance for French Population Increase), and the German *Bund Mutterschutz* (League for the Protection of Mothers). The creation of the *Bund Mutterschutz* by Helene Stocker, is only one example of a trend pursued in many European states in the early twentieth century. Influenced by the ideas of the Swedish feminist Ellen Key, Stocker's organisation not only aimed to protect motherhood for unmarried as well as married women, but petitioned the German *Reichstag* (parliament) to recognise maternity as a form of national service. In France, debates about maternity drew very directly on the fears of depopulation and of French decline as a European power which had followed on the Franco-Prussian war of 1870. The equation of the maternal with the national was promoted not merely by the state, but advocated by certain feminist groups, including the *Ligue des Meres de Famille* (League of the Mothers of Families) created in 1901. Some feminists construed government actions on behalf of women as attention to national well-being. The identification of women with motherhood also provided women with a basis for influencing national policies and politics. It was through their claims as mothers that women established positions for themselves in welfare organisations and in education.

Although governments and doctors increasingly represented women's maternal capacity as requiring guidance and surveillance from the medical profession and the state, they also viewed the devotion of women to their children as being distinctive to middle-class European women. Just as the freeing of women from arduous labour was equated with social progress and development, for Europeans, maternalism served to underline the sexual differences between European women and men, and to demonstrate the differences between European middle-class women and those belonging to other classes and races. It was generally assumed that middle-class European women showed a highly developed consciousness of their proper duty and were dedicated to the care of their young. Other women – working-class, or black women, so-called 'savage' Indian and African women – were thought to be lacking in this maternal care and devotion. With the development of ideas about social evolution in the second half of the nineteenth century, the European ideal of separate spheres, of patriarchal fathers and husbands and of women devoting themselves to family life, were regarded as the pinnacle of social development. Those ethnic or racial groups which still expected women to work were seen as less civilised because they treated their womenfolk as 'beasts of burden', rather than protecting them in the ways that they 'naturally' required. English discussions of motherhood showed the virtues of 'civilised' English mothers over the 'savage' women of other countries, and even of the English poor (Fee 1974). In a similar way, discussions of motherhood in France constantly emphasised the importance of middle-class women caring for their own children, and protecting them from contamination from poorer women. In both countries, the stress on breast-feeding was accompanied by an attack on the widespread practice of wet-nursing and of leaving children in the care of paid servants, practices which were seen to carry the risk of exposing children to the moral and physical dangers posed by women of lesser social status and moral virtue (Donzelot 1980).

Late nineteenth-century French feminists exploited the new nationalist and imperialist emphases on maternalism as a basis for insisting on legal and political recognition for mothers. 'If you want children, learn to honour their mothers', insisted Maria Martin, editor of the *Journal des dames* (*Ladies Journal*) in 1896 (Cova 1991: 120). For socialist feminists in the organisation *La Solidarité des femmes*, the central issue was financial support for mothers, provided by the state. The suffragist Hubertine Auclert, who was also the first woman to use the label 'feminist', demanded a new form of 'mother state', which would provide maternity endowment and children's allowances, financed by a paternal tax on men. Arguing that motherhood was a state service of the same importance as military activity, Auclert insisted that it be supported by the state. Few other French feminists were prepared to demand as much as this, seeking rather welfare services and motherhood centres that would provide education and training and advice for mothers (Cova 1991: 120–3). Governments in turn were able to utilise this support for a 'maternal state' to instigate the demographic policies that were meant to solve what were seen as national crises. As states developed new bureaucracies to deal with their health and social concerns, and directed attention to the family, women and children, middle-class women gained national significance and legitimate work employed on the nation's fringes in education, social work and health.

The voluntary and government agencies which spread new health practices also disseminated ideas of 'race hygiene' and eugenics (see Chapter 5). Throughout Europe the new science of eugenics affirmed fears of racial and national degeneration, and offered regulation of the working-class population as the solution. It was no coincidence that the architect of Solidarism, the republican Leon Bourgeois, was also the first honorary president of the French Eugenics Society in 1912. Patriotism was the calling card of middle-class women's promotion of the duty of motherhood and of racial hygiene, through organisations like the *Ligue des Femmes Françaises* (League of French Women), and the *Ligue Patriotique des Françaises* (Patriotic League of French Women) (Offen 1984: 179). In Germany, support for eugenics was fostered by the fear of racial degeneration and by widespread intellectual interest in the ideas of Gobineau and Darwin. Italy did not experience the same intensity of pronatalist debate since there was little evidence of population decline. Instead, the improvement of the quality of the 'race' and of social conditions focused on the problem of southern Italy. While the population rate in the north of Italy declined under the influence of the nuclear family, in the south high mortality was matched with high fertility. This situation only helped to emphasise for northerners that the 'peasant' south threatened the superiority of a bourgeois northern Italian national identity.

The late nineteenth-century emphasis on national sovereignty and the identification of the nation-state with the family translated reproduction into an issue of national or political control. States developed policies to protect the national body through the control of women's bodies, supervising maternity practices and the acceptable conditions for women's work as it affected their reproductive capacities and family responsibilities (Stone 1995: 175). Seth Koven has argued that maternalism had a 'protean character'; it could be employed 'in the service of women' or to serve 'the needs of paternalists' (Koven and Michel 1993: 5). Feminists often dressed their demands in the language of motherhood as persistently as their opponents did. Liberals and conservatives, republicans and monarchists competed for a political voice, but they shared a common emphasis, across national boundaries and political causes, of the importance of policing sexual differences and controlling sexuality.

Imperialism

By the end of the nineteenth century, population concerns dominated political foreign policy in the form of imperialism and colonialism, just as pronatalism ruled domestic agendas in most European states. Since the seventeenth century, French, Spanish, Portuguese, Dutch and British governments had been engaged in the search for extra-European territories in order to provide new markets. In the late eighteenth and first half of the nineteenth centuries Britain and France had both built up substantial colonies in India, the Caribbean and northern Africa. The 1870s, however, marked a new stage in aggressive imperial expansion as most of Africa and significant parts of Asia and the pacific were subject to colonial conquest. This period, sometimes referred to as 'the age of empire', saw the development of a 'new imperialism' that some historians argue culminated in the First World War. By 1914 more than three-quarters of the earth was under the control, either directly or indirectly, of the colonial powers: Britain, France, Germany, Spain, Portugal, Belgium, Italy, the United States and Japan. The 'new imperialism' had an impact on gender identities, gender relations and ideas about appropriate spheres and conduct for men and women in the colonies as well as in Europe. Women as well as men participated in imperial ventures, and the cause of imperialism shaped *fin-de-siècle* feminism.

In the early nineteenth century British imperialism influenced definitions of English national identity and of bourgeois masculinity. The notion of 'muscular Christianity' distinctive of nineteenth-century English middle-class manhood, derived as much from the Christian missionary endeavours associated with early imperialism as from the changing values of family and home in Britain itself. In the 1860s the development of institutions such as public schools, team sports, and colonial bureaucracies encouraged the development of more aggressive masculine virtues which were closely associated with the adulation of homosocial or all-male spheres and with the changing nature of the empire and nation (Tosh 1991). Throughout Europe, in the late nineteenth and the early twentieth centuries team games, fencing and gymnastics gained in popularity as bases of national identification for men. In England, the Boy Scout movements aimed to make the experiences which upper-class boys gained at school available to lower-middle- and working-class boys and to prepare young men for the imperial frontier. Scouts were familiarised with military drill and military hierarchy. Many historians have argued that the appeal of the new imperialism among Englishmen can be explained through its close connection with public school homosociality and the celebration of sport, and the encouragement in both of the instinct to compete and win. Public schools, like the Boy Scouts, advocated the values of empire and the bonds of fraternity and encouraged young men to believe that the best life was not to be found in the domestic sphere and family, but in the adventure of empire.

According to John Mangan, by the end of Queen Victoria's reign the British empire was run by English public school men who saw themselves as 'its ruler and guardian, and not infrequently its teacher and its missionary' (Mangan 1986: 44). Middle-class men flocked into the colonial service in search of adventure and escape. Most imperial senior administrators were drawn from the ranks of Oxford and Cambridge. Their qualifications were 'character', an honours degree, and athletic distinction. Colonial service replicated the British class order: the assumption of British superiority to the 'darker race' paralleled middle-class assumptions of superiority to the working class within Britain.

Throughout Europe, imperial expansion was seen to prove 'national virility'. In 1906, following a destructive colonial war in southwest Africa, the German parliament dissolved over disagreement regarding the type of colonialism which Germany should be practising. Failure to colonise was interpreted by some contemporaries as a weakness of national character. In France, some commentators argued that the French were not as enthusiastic about imperialism as the British or Germans and regarded this as another sign of the unhealthy state of French society, even though between 1880 and 1895 the French colonial empire had significantly expanded from one million to nine and a half million square kilometres of territory – in Tunisia, Indochina, Madagascar and sub-Saharan Africa.

Britain was widely recognised as the ideal colonising and imperial force. In Britain itself, however, there was some anxiety about the success of British imperialism and about its possible impact on national traditions. The Boer War (1899–1902) aroused considerable consternation about the state of the British nation/empire. In 1899 Cecil Rhodes, the Prime Minister of the British Cape Colony, intervened in a dispute in the neighbouring former Dutch colony, the Boer Republic of Transvaal, over the conditions of gold production, and the desire by mining companies to reduce the cost of black labour. Rhodes saw himself as the defender of British mining interests and engaged in provocations which ultimately led to the outbreak of war between British and Boer troops. Some critics were dismayed by what they saw as the aggressive and 'unEnglish' means employed by British imperial forces in support of commercial interests. Other criticism focused on the great difficulty experienced by the British government in finding healthy recruits for the war, raising questions about the overall well-being of the British people. Moreover, despite the fact that British forces outnumbered the Boers by about five to one, they found it extremely difficult to subdue the Boers and the conflict only ended in May 1902, when a treaty was finally signed establishing civil government under British rule. The historian Joanna Burke has argued that the Boer War led to a crisis of 'masculinity' in Britain 'as men's weakening virility was thought to be threatening British imperial prowess and national efficiency' (Bourke 1996: 13).

By the early twentieth century ambivalence towards imperialism was discussed largely in terms of its effect on national 'virility'. The aggressive imperial expansion of the late nineteenth century made extensive use of the language and rhetoric of gender and sexual difference, equating virility with masculinity. Contemporaries debated whether or not imperialism sapped the resources of national strength or expanded them. In the 1890s, the French parliament had rejected imperial expansion because it was believed to dissipate national virility. By contrast, in 1912 Charles Regismauset, a supporter of imperialism, blamed what he saw as the lethargic indifference to the competitive aspect of imperialism predominant in France on neurasthenia, or nervous debility. In Italy, the failure to conquer Ethiopia in 1896 confirmed fears of degeneration among the ruling class who made the conquest of empire a top priority. By contrast, the Italian invasion of Libya in 1911 was represented as the beginning of a new Italian 'Roman' Empire and the regeneration of Italian virility.

The emphasis on masculinity and on the virility of imperial activity was accompanied by hostility towards women's claims for political participation, and a persistent emphasis on the sexual nature of imperial engagement. Imperial rule was naturalised by the stereotyping of indigenous men as weaker and more 'effeminate' than their British counterparts and hence as being like women in their natural subordination to European men. 'Sometimes,' as John Tosh has argued, 'the feminine was ascribed to whole regions as in the allure of the Dark Continent awaiting penetration and mastery' (Tosh 1994: 197). This sense of the empire as feminine is best exemplified by the novel *She* (1887). In the story of *She*, its author Rider Haggard revealed a dark feminine Other at the heart of imperial conquest. The journey by a civilised Englishman to the heart of Africa leads to an encounter with a place where 'woman' reigned, kept men in thrall, and had to be destroyed.

This sense of the sexual nature of imperial conquest had as its counterpart an extreme anxiety about interracial sexual unions and miscegenation. Evolutionary theories and biological racism made contemporaries view miscegenation as a threat to the health and virility of the European colonisers themselves, whether British, French, German, Dutch or Italian. Fears about the consequences of interracial sexual encounters encouraged discussion of the colonising role of white European women who could establish a moral framework and reproduce the race beyond national borders. Miscegenation was to be warded off by the incorporation of more white women into the colonising processes of imperialism.

Although imperialism forged a new breed of men who strongly opposed feminist claims to legal and political rights in the public sphere, and even in empire, towards the end of the nineteenth century women were increasingly encouraged to undertake imperial activities or to settle in far flung parts of the empire for racial reasons. Feminists pursuing their own political and social interests were quite easily co-opted by the English government into the tasks of empire. English feminists gained self-confidence and a sense of their own historical mission by seeing themselves as forging a path for all the women of the empire. In the process, they reinforced the sense of British superiority by contrasting the status of women in Britain with the situation of indigenous women in its colonies. English women involved themselves particularly with the emancipation of Indian women as part of their imperial civilising mission. In India, they set up schools, attempted to provide women doctors and fought against what they saw as dangerous native customs, such as child marriage. Feminists often claimed rights for women on the basis of their devotion to imperial duty. Their own demands for university education for women, municipal suffrage, marriage-reform law and the abolition of the Contagious Diseases Acts in England were all achieved against this imperial background (Burton 1994: 1).

French feminists took up the cause of Algerian women. Algeria had been made a French colony in 1830. Between 1888 and 1892 the French feminist Hubertine Auclert plied French newspapers with articles on the condition of Arab women in Algeria. Her aim was to equate the French civilising mission with republican secularism. Auclert argued that the presence of white women on the councils of French administration in Algeria would elevate a *potentially* 'gifted and beautiful race' (Scott 1996: 115). Auclert connected the cause of female enfranchisement to women's national role in the colonial sphere. She idealised the extension of universal suffrage to colonials, but objected to the enfranchisement of 'natives' before suffrage was extended to French women like herself (Scott 1996: 117).

Despite the extraordinary range of women's organisations at the turn of the century, in most European states, continental and British feminists all shared a readiness to annex the cause of female emancipation to imperial service. Thus in 1901 the prominent English feminist Millicent Garret Fawcett headed the Ladies' Committee appointed by the British Secretary of State for War to inquire into the conditions in the civilian concentration camps which had been set up throughout the South African colonies in the course of the Boer War. These camps were used to accommodate Boer women and children, including those who had been left destitute by the systematic burning of Boer villages and homes by British troops. Fawcett's committee had not been sent to question the existence of the camps but to find out why tens of thousands, mainly children, had reputedly died in them, and to decide on the best use to which charitable funds from England could be put in improving conditions. Her report (Fawcett 1902) was sanguine in its conclusions and recommendations. Although critical, Fawcett saw the ignorance of Boer women, their bad maternal practices, as a major cause of the child mortality. For Emily Hobhouse, a stern critic of Fawcett's report, Englishness was no guarantee of justice (Hobhouse 1902). Hobhouse's concern that English women could fail to sympathise with these Boer women, posited a feminism that transgressed patriotism and national differences (at least among Europeans). It also ignored the plight of the 'native races', a third position taken up by another feminist, Josephine Butler. Butler maintained in regard to the Boer War, 'Great Britain will in future be judged, condemned or justified according to her treatment of those innumerable coloured races, over whom her rule extends' (Butler 1928: 216). But Butler's own admonition was complemented by support for the British in the Boer War and for the Christian missionary cause, and criticism of the Boers on patriotic grounds.

In the first decade of the twentieth century the participation of French women in empire was the concern of the French government as well as civilian enthusiasts. In the aftermath of the plans by the English government to organise women for settlement in South Africa as a means of replenishing the British presence after the Boer War, the French press – colonial newspapers and 'women's' magazines – compared English imperial success with the apathy of French colonialism. Ironically, French women were now seen to be at fault and the relative failure of France to compete in the imperial struggle was attributed to the excessive dependency of French women. The assumption was that all could be rectified with a shift in social attitudes, and in the greater independence of French women. Although the question of women's role in the colonial endeavour cannot be said to have dominated discussion of imperialism, in France at least the intermittent reappearance of the topic of '*le rôle colonial de la femme*' led to the coining of the concept '*feminisme coloniale*'. The French Colonial Ministry voiced its interest in populating its colonies with the children of French women. Patriotic middle-class women took up the task of organisation, setting up societies for the emigration of women and disseminating propaganda. In the years leading up to the First World War, the pacifying role of middle-class women, both in the nation and in the colonies, was emphasised in French papers like *Colonia*. Feminists argued that there were obvious rewards for the French woman who ventured abroad. She was likely to share in a greater income. Magazines like *Le Conseil des Femmes* (*Advice for Women*) claimed that by exploiting indigenous customs educated middle-class women could establish themselves independently in the colonies as doctors and dentists in ways prohibited to them in Europe. When French male doctors were prohibited from attending to the native élite (particularly women), French female doctors could easily take over. Ironically, it was the perceived 'backwardness' of colonial spaces that would allow women to escape the limitations placed on their activity by civilised Western society. The 'modern', even scientific, French woman was supposed to realise her ambitions by exploiting the traditional gender role of the native colonial woman. French women, feminists argued, could displace the indigenous midwife in the same way that European men had usurped the traditional medical role of European women.

By 1907 German imperialism was showing belated signs of similar trends: the German Colonial Women's League was founded, and within five years had 12,000 members. The Women's League was composed of a mixed membership – patriots, eugenicists, feminists, conservatives and colonists, categories which were not always mutually exclusive. Their aim was to preserve 'the purity of the white race in the colonies through the export of white women from the mother country' and to expand German settlement as an ambition for working-class women as well as the middle-class women whose domestic skills would civilise and pacify the colonies (Evans 1979: 147). Although the German Colonial Society had attempted to encourage the settlement of women in southwest African areas of German colonisation, it was not until the German Colonial Women's League was organised by women that the project was in any way successful. The German middle-class woman who went to the colonies to reproduce German children and values was expected to rely on the 'white female servant'. That servant was to protect the German settler household from possible contamination by the seductive presence of native girls – the source of racial threat in the colonies that the white woman was meant to displace. As in the Dutch, Italian, British and French examples, the success of racially defined German imperialism and colonialism relied upon the transplantation of women's bodies as the source of whiteness and national or racial identity.

Empire offered women of all classes and colonising nations a legitimate space beyond national borders as 'colonisers', both at the side of their husbands, and on their own. Programmes of colonisation that accompanied imperialism provided single unemployed (lower-middle-class and working-class) women with a justification for independent (and often necessary) travel in search of work. It meant that women could exercise independence beyond the confines of local communities. In this context, women's independence, whether working-class or middle-class, was inevitably linked to the propagation of the premised racial inequalities on which imperialism was based. The implications of this relationship are not straightforward. As we will see in the next chapter, the involvement of women in empire coincided with the rise of anti-suffrage and anti-feminist movements. The existence of these movements brought new debates about the extent to which women should take on patriotic roles in an imperial, national or political context, and about the nature of citizenship in the age of empire.

References and further reading

Primary sources

Bebel, August (1892 [1879]) *Die Frau und der Sozialismus. Die Frau in der Vergangenheit, Gegenwart und Zukunft*, Stuttgart.

Betham-Edwards, M. (1905) *Home Life in France*, 2nd edn, London.

Butler, Josephine (1928 [1909]) *An Autobiographical Memoir* (ed. George W. and Lucy A. Johnson, intro. James Stuart), 3rd edn, Bristol.

Comte, Auguste (1875) *The Positive Philosophy of Auguste Comte, vol. 2*, trans. H. Martineau, London.

Darwin, Charles (1872 [1859]) *Origin of Species*, 6th edn, London.

Engels, Frederick (1954 [1884]) *The Origin of the Family*, Moscow.

Fawcett, Millicent Garrett (1902) 'Report on the concentration camps in South Africa by the Committee of Ladies Appointed by the Secretary of State for War', London.

Gobineau, Arthur Comte de (1967 [1853–5]) *Inequality of Human Races*, trans. Adrian Collins, New York.

Haggard, Rider (1886) *She*, London.

Hobhouse, E. (1902) *Brunt of the War*, London.

Michelet, Jules (1854) *Les Femmes de la Revolution*, in *Oeuvres Complètes* (ed. P. Viallaneix) (Paris, 1985), vol. 16: 353–570.

Michelet, Jules (1858) *L'Amour*, in *Ouvres Complètes* (ed. P. Viallaneix), vol. 18, Paris.

Mill, J. S. (1869) *On the Subjection of Women*, London.

Mozzoni, Anna Maria (1865) *La Donna in Faccia al progetto del nuovo codice civile italiano*, Milano.

Proudhon, Pierre-Joseph (1858) *De la Justice dans la revolution et dans l'Eglise*, Paris.

Spencer, Herbert (1876) *Principles of Sociology*, London.

Weininger, Otto (1903) *Sex and Character: An Authorised Translation*, London.

White Mario, Jessie (1857) Busta 407/1(1), *Archivio Jessie White Mario*, Museo Centrale de Risorgimento, Rome.

White Mario, Jessie (1909) *The Birth of Modern Italy: Posthumous Papers of Jessie White Mario* (ed. Duke Litta-Visconti-Arese), London.

Nationalism and citizenship

Bochachevsky-Chomiak, M. (1980) 'Socialism, feminism and nationalism: the first stages of women's organisations in the Eastern part of the Austrian Empire', in T. Yedlin (ed.) *Women in Eastern Europe and the Soviet Union*, New York.

Evans, R. (1976) 'Prostitution, state and society in Imperial Germany', *Past and Present* 70: 106–29.

Evans, R. (1979) *The Feminists: Women's Emancipation Movements in Europe, America and Australasia, 1840–1920*, London.

Fraise, G. (1986) 'Natural law and the origins of nineteenth century feminist thought in France', in J. Friedlander *et al.* (eds) *Women in Culture and Politics*, Bloomington.

Gibson, M. (1986) *Prostitution and the State in Italy 1860–1915*, New Brunswick, New Jersey.

Gilman, S. (1993) *Freud, Race, and Gender*, Princeton.

Hackett, A. (1972) 'The German women's movement and suffrage, 1890–1914: a study of national feminism', in R. J. Bezucha (ed.) *Modern European Social History*, Lexington, Mass.; Toronto; London.

Howard, J. (1978) 'The woman question in Italy 1861–1880', Ph.D. thesis, Ann Arbor.

Howard, J. (1980) 'Patriot mothers in the post-Risorgimento: women after the Italian revolution', in C. R. Berkin and C. M. Lovett (eds) *Women War and Revolution*, New York.

Kelikian, A. (1996) 'Science, gender and moral ascendancy in liberal Italy', *Journal of Modern Italian Studies* **1**, 3: 377–89.

Lorence-Kot, B. (1987) 'Klementya Tanska Hofmanowa, cultural nationalism and a new formula for Polish womanhood', *History of European Ideas* **8**, 4/5: 435–50.

Offen, K. (1987) 'A nineteenth-century French feminist rediscovered: Jenny P. de Hericourt, 1809–1875', *Signs* **13**, 1: 144–58.

Walkowitz, J. R. (1980) *Prostitution and Victorian Society*, Cambridge.

The family and the nation

Accampo, E. A., Fuchs, R. G. and Stewart, M. L. (eds) (1995) *Gender and the Politics of Social Reform in France, 1870–1914*, Baltimore.

Bock, G. and Thane, P. (1991) *Maternity and Gender Policies: Women and the Rise of the European Welfare States 1880s–1950s*, London and New York.

Brombert, B. A. (1977) *Christina: Portraits of a Princess*, New York.

Cole, J. A. (1996) 'There are only good mothers: the ideological work of women's fertility in France before World War 1', *French Historical Studies* **19**, 3: 639–72.

Copley, A. (1989) *Sexual Moralities in France, 1780–1980: New Ideas on the Family, Divorce and Homosexuality*, London.

Cova, A. (1991) 'French feminism and maternity: theories and policies 1890–1918', in G. Bock and P. Thane (eds) *Maternity and Gender Policies*, London and New York.

Donzelot, J. (1980) *The Policing of Families*, trans. R. Hurley, London.

Fee, E. (1974) 'The sexual politics of Victorian social anthropology', in M. Hartman and L. Banner (eds) *Clio's Consciousness Raised*, New York.

Fuchs, R. G. (1995) 'France in a comparative perspective', in E. A. Accampo, R. G. Fuchs and M. L. Stewart (eds) *Gender and the Politics of Social Reform in France, 1870–1914*, Baltimore.

Fuchs, R. G. (1996) 'Population and the state in the Third Republic', *French Historical Studies* **19**, 3: 633–8.

Gallopin, A. (1980) *Il Lungo viaggio verso la Patría*, Rome.

Gullickson, G. (1992) 'The unruly woman of the Paris Commune', in D. O. Helly and S. M. Reverby (eds) *Gendered Domains: Rethinking Public and Private in Women's History*, New York.

Hunt, L. (1992) *The Family Romance of the French Revolution*, Berkeley.

Klaus, A. (1993) 'Depopulation and race suicide: materialism and pronatalist ideologies in France and the United States', in S. Koven and S. Michel (eds) *Mothers of a New World*, New York.

Koos, C. A. (1996) 'Gender, anti-individualism, and nationalism: the Alliance Nationale and the pronatalist backlash against the femme moderne', *French Historical Studies* **19**, 3: 699–723.

Koven, S. and Michel, S. (eds) (1993) *Mothers of a New World: Maternalist Politics and the Origins of Welfare States*, New York.

La Vigna, C. (1987) 'The Marxist ambivalence toward women: between socialism and feminism in the Italian Socialist Party', in M. Boxer and J. H. Quataert (eds) *Socialist Women*, New York.

Nelson, C. and Sumner Holmes, A. (eds) (1997) *Maternal Instincts: Visions of Motherhood and Sexuality in Britain, 1875–1925*, London.

Offen, K. (1984) 'Depopulation, nationalism, and feminism in fin-de-siècle France', *American Historical Review* 89: 648–76.

Pedersen, J. E. (1996) 'Regulating abortion and birth control: gender, medicine, and republican politics in France, 1870–1920', *French Historical Studies* 19, 3: 673–98.

Quine, M. S. (1996) *Population Politics in Twentieth Century Europe*, London and New York.

Stone, J. (1995) 'The Republican brotherhood: gender and ideology', in E. A. Accampo, R. G. Fuchs and M. L. Stewart (eds) *Gender and the Politics of Social Reform in France, 1870–1914*, Baltimore.

Imperialism

Blakely, B. (1981) 'Women and imperialism: the Colonial Office and female emigration to South Africa, 1901–1910', *Albion* 13, 2: 131–49.

Bourke, J. (1996) *Dismembering the Male*, London.

Brantlinger, P. (1988) *Rule of Darkness: British Literature and Imperialism, 1830–1914*, Cornell.

Burton, A. (1992) 'The white woman's burden: British feminists and "The Indian Woman", 1865–1915', in N. Chaudhuri and M. Strobel (eds), *Western Women and Imperialism: Complicity and Resistance*, Bloomington.

Burton, A. (1994) *Burdens of History*, Chapel Hill, North Carolina.

Chickering, R. (1988) ' "Casting their gaze more broadly": women's patriotic activism in Imperial Germany', *Past and Present* 118: 156–85.

Davin, A. (1997) 'Imperialism and motherhood', in F. Cooper and A. L. Stoler (eds) *Tensions of Empire: Colonial Cultures in a Bourgeois World*, Berkeley.

Mangan, J. A. (1986) *The Games Ethic and Imperialism: Aspects of the Diffusion of an Ideal*, Harmondsworth, Middlesex.

Mosse, G. L. (1996) *The Image of Man: The Creation of Modern Masculinity*, New York.

Scott, J. W. (1996) *Only Paradoxes to Offer: French Feminists and the Rights of Man*, Cambridge, Mass.

Stoler, A. L. (1997) 'Sexual affronts and racial frontiers: European identities and the cultural politics of exclusion in Colonial Southeast Asia', in A. L. Stoler and F. Cooper (eds) *Tensions of Empire: Colonial Cultures in a Bourgeois World*, Berkeley.

Tosh, J. (1991) 'Domesticity and manliness in the Victorian middle class: the family of Edward White Benson', in M. Roper and J. Tosh (eds) *Manful Assertions*, London.

Tosh, J. (1994) 'What should historians do with masculinity? Reflections on 19th century Britain', *History Workshop* 38: 179–202.

Wildenthal, L. (1997) 'Race, gender, and citizenship in the German Colonial Empire', in A. L. Stoler and F. Cooper (eds) *Tensions of Empire: Colonial Cultures in a Bourgeois World*, Berkeley.

Zantop, S. (1997) *Colonial Fantasies: Conquest, Family, and Nation in Precolonial Germany, 1770–1870*, Durham.

FIVE

The *Fin-de-siècle*

The period from 1880 to the outbreak of the First World War was a watershed for ideas about gender. The very term '*fin de siècle*', as the Hungarian writer Max Nordau argued, implied decadence and changing views of sexuality, morality and personal life (Nordau 1895). Questions about sexual difference and sexuality achieved a hitherto unknown prominence evident in the changing legal regulation of homosexuality and a number of widely discussed sexual scandals. The new scientific discourses of sexology and psychoanalysis showed the importance of sexuality and sexual development from the earliest stage of infancy and made sexuality into a special domain which warranted extensive investigation. Proponents of these new sciences proposed that sexuality established the framework of individual identity and underlay emotional and mental disorders. Emphasis on sexuality was closely associated with the considerable anxiety aroused by the declining birth-rates in European states. The focus on demography brought particular urgency to discussions about marriage, family life and sexuality. These varied developments made some contemporaries regard the *fin-de-siècle* as a period of 'sexual anarchy'.

In order to understand the intensity of concern aroused by the new scientific and popular views of sexuality and gender, it is necessary to place them in the wider context of the paradoxical and often contradictory social and political developments of the period spanning the late nineteenth century up to the outbreak of the First World War. In this period, socialism and organised labour movements attracted broad-based interest and adherents, at the same time as many states experienced unparalleled imperial expansion, relative political stability and economic growth. This growth was accompanied by a pervasive concern about decadence and decline. As Eugene Weber has argued in regard to France, no other period exhibits so marked a 'discrepancy between material progress and spiritual dejection' (Weber 1986: 2). How, asks Eric Hobsbawm, can one account for the fact that what appears now to economic analysts to have been a period of spectacular economic growth, was seen by contemporaries as one of deep economic depression? For Hobsbawm, what needs to be understood are the fundamental structural changes which occurred as economies changed gear, and industry took over the predominant place once held by agriculture in Europe (Hobsbawm 1987: 2–25). The establishment of a global economy dominated by industrialised European nations, which harnessed the raw materials from their imperial possessions to their manufacturing developments and used their empires as markets to sustain economic growth, was accompanied by a decline in agricultural prices and profits.

The growth and expansion of European economies did not lead to benefits for all, nor was there a constant pattern of either financial difficulty or ease. The marked depression in agricultural prices and profits of the 1870s and 1880s began to shift in the 1890s, when agricultural prices increased so that landowners and wealthy groups experienced a new sense of ease and luxury. From the view of urban workers, the agricultural depression of the period 1873–96 may have been accompanied by wage rises, but they experienced declining wages and harsher conditions in the two decades before the First World War, and missed out entirely on the economic benefits of agricultural recovery. The phenomenal industrial growth was often achieved at the expense of farmers, workers and the urban poor within Europe as well as in the colonies.

The term 'modern' is often used to differentiate European history from the *ancien régime* to the time of the French Revolution. As this discussion of economic change makes clear, the late nineteenth century saw a new stage in the shaping of modernity. The most marked feature of this new modernity, and greatest cause of middle-class concern, was the rise of 'mass society'. Hitherto unimaginable crowds of people now worked in factories, lived in close proximity in cities, demanded political rights and access to resources and engaged in new patterns of consumption, communication and daily life. The language of Marxism, the bloody Paris Commune of 1870, the strikes and industrial unrest evident in Britain and France in the 1880s, all provoked a sense of unease among the European middle classes. Law and order and the prevailing social and political hierarchy seemed to be threatened by the uncontrollable and irrational 'masses'. The most influential analysis of the 'masses' was that provided by the French social psychologist, Gustave Le Bon in his book *The Crowd* (1895). Urban life for Le Bon was characterised by crowds, which exhibited high levels of credulity, irrationality and emotional instability, characteristics Le Bon regarded as specifically feminine. Even the educated and rational individual was liable to behave in an irrational manner once subject to the mental contagion which came from absorption into the crowd. Fear of the masses fed into the ✳ particular demographic concern of the late nineteenth century. This was a period of marked decline in the birth-rate across Europe. Decline was not uniform, however, as the middle class seemed to be reducing its birth-rate much more rapidly than did the working class and the urban poor. Widespread belief that hereditary diseases among the poor were increasing, that some sections of the population were 'degenerating', increased concerns that European civilisation would be engulfed by an ineducable and unruly mass.

Anxiety about mass society, social decline and population provided the framework for extensive scientific and popular discussion of changes in family life, in sexual norms and practices and in the situation of women. Feminism and the demands for sexual freedom, and freedom to live without family ties, seemed to undermine completely the established family order. But it was not only women's desires that were at issue. Military scandals in Germany, and the widespread coverage of the trials of Oscar Wilde in England, brought homosexuality, already of great concern to legislators and to the medical and psychological professions, into everyday discussion.

In this chapter we will examine the new ideas about gender and family life evident in the late nineteenth century. We will look at the debates about sexuality and sexual difference which emerged through sexology and psychoanalysis in the 1880s and 1890s and at the changing legislative framework concerning homosexuality. We will discuss changing ideas about femininity, the emergence of the 'new woman' in literature, and the new issues raised by feminists. Finally we will explore the city and the new patterns of gender evident within the urban world.

Eugenics, degeneration and the decadent modern world

Imperial expansion after 1870 brought a renewed sense of European superiority in intellect and physical strength as well as a belief in the high level of European social development. Nonetheless, many European social theorists and writers, doctors and psychologists were preoccupied with a fear of mental and physical degeneration, which they saw as evident in many parts of Europe. Although few could deny the extent of economic and social change and the material progress which had been evident since the late eighteenth century, for many writers and social theorists throughout the nineteenth century, there was a nagging doubt whether this progress was accompanied by moral and intellectual advances, or had rather brought spiritual and moral decline. Expansion in the fields of medicine and especially psychology and psychiatry in the late nineteenth century encouraged the classification and labelling of a new range of mental disorders and sexual pathologies, all of which seemed to provide evidence of a deterioration in the mental, moral and physical health and stability of national populations throughout Europe.

The idea of degeneration – of the hereditary transmission of physical and mental disorders, which could ultimately end in cretinism, idiocy, or forms of compulsive criminal behaviours – was first articulated in France by the psychiatrist Benedict Augustin Morel in the 1850s. Morel's main concern was with the phenomenon he labelled 'cretinism', a congenital and incurable condition in which 'all that constitutes human nature from the point of view of perception, feeling, love, will, speech, action and caring for one's own life is destroyed' (Pick 1989: 46–8). Morel and his followers used 'cretinism' as a label for people with a vast range of different physical abnormalities and patterns of behaviour, which he saw as the external signs of internal illness or mental and moral deformity, including stunted growth, pointed ears, rickets, cranial abnormalities, scrofula, deafness and alcoholism. Morel, like the novelist Emile Zola, believed that degeneration was the result of unhealthy individuals reproducing and spreading their hereditary illnesses or disabilities.

By the late nineteenth century, there was a growing sense that cities and urban life contributed to the development of diseases and instability which fostered degeneracy. Scientists and doctors diagnosed and named a whole series of disorders including agoraphobia (fear of crowds), claustrophobia (fear of confined spaces), and kleptomania (a compulsion to theft) as *urban* phenomena, and as illustrative of how crowded city life undermined the mental balance of its inhabitants. Gustave Le Bon argued that degeneration was a result of nineteenth-century urban developments. He believed that the herding of people together in cities brought into being an irrational and hysterical mass, and increased the mental instability and deterioration of the entire urban population. Social theorists, like Le Bon, or popular novelists, like Zola, regarded poor living conditions, the accessibility of drink, and the hysteria associated with crowds as contributing to what they saw as the prevalence of degeneration. Others saw degeneracy in the increasing numbers of criminals, sexual perverts and prostitutes who were thought to roam city streets.

Degeneration was regarded as a specifically nineteenth-century phenomenon. Max Nordau, the writer who developed the most comprehensive analysis of this phenomenon, traced it in every aspect of nineteenth-century life and culture. It had historic roots, Nordau argued, and had developed in France as a result of the cataclysmic events of the past century. The loss of life in the French Revolution, the Napoleonic Wars and the upheavals of the nineteenth century culminating in the devastating defeat in the Franco-Prussian War of 1870, led to 'nervous strain and morbid derangement' (Pick 1989: 95). The concept of degeneration also derived much of its strength from the idea that human life was connected by evolution with animal life. Lombroso believed that some people lacked the intellectual and moral qualities of normal humans, and had the propensity to cruelty which characterised animals lower down the evolutionary ladder. If criminal behaviour, like cretinism, was the result of heredity, then, by implication, education was unavailing and reform impossible. What was needed was the isolation of the criminal and the degenerate from the rest of society.

Gender provides a crucial framework for understanding the various discourses of degeneration. Many of the characteristics identified by Le Bon and Nordau as signs of degeneration – nervousness, neurasthenia, excessive emotion and hysteria – were regarded as feminine. The increasing influence and prominence of women in the public sphere, on the one hand, and the apparent increase in the incidence of feminine characteristics in men, on the other, were often used as evidence of degeneration. For Le Bon, the masculine capacity for rational analysis and action was completely lost in crowds who engaged in hysterical behaviour. Crowd behaviour was also characterised for him by its credulity, its tendency to inaccuracy and false perception, and its violence. Women's potential for violence was illustrated by the novelist Emile Zola in *Germinal* (1885). In this novel, Zola depicted a strike in a mining village in which the men concentrated on destroying the mines, while the women turned on an individual shopkeeper who had harassed and raped some of them. The women castrated and murdered the shopkeeper, and then marched through the streets with his penis on a pole. For Zola, as for Le Bon, the most frightening aspect of crowd behaviour was that crowds behaved like women in their hysteria, irrationality and extremism. Le Bon, Zola and Nordau regarded the phenomenon of crowds as illustrations of the deleterious consequences of women's political participation. The participation of women in the French Revolution, the revolutions of 1848, or the Commune of 1870, in their view, served to make these events particularly violent and destructive. This fear of women's political behaviour was echoed by Lombroso. Once involved in revolution, Lombroso insisted, 'women become terribly infuriated'. They were the most ferocious revolutionaries, descending to acts of murder and cannibalism (Pick 1989: 93).

Concern about physical and mental degeneration had as its cultural corollary the perception of Europe's moral decline. The term 'decadence' was applied by philosophers, sociologists, theorists and political figures to describe broad social developments. The German philosopher Nietzsche, the pioneering French social scientist Emile Durkheim and the French syndicalist Georges Sorel all used the term 'decadence' to describe what they saw as the corruption of bourgeois society. In various ways, they pointed to the declining sense of community, the loss of spiritual values, the expansion of state power and the development of mass culture as evidence. In the late eighteenth century, many philosophers and middle-class radicals had regarded the aristocracy as decadent and degenerate. By the late nineteenth century, this charge was levelled against the bourgeoisie itself by writers like Nietzsche, who argued that contemporary Western bourgeois society was decadent because of its lack of vitality. In his view, European society lacked strength, vigour and self-assurance. Its moral values were based on what he regarded as the 'old ladies' morality' of Christianity, with its praise of meekness and humility, and its rejection of virility, strength and courage. The nineteenth century lacked the energy and strength to develop a great culture like that of the Renaissance. Taking up a very different tack, Durkheim sought to explain the connection between the increasing incidence of suicide and the nature of urban life. Although Durkheim believed that many modern social developments were progressive and desirable, he also argued that modern urban society destroyed the common bonds and beliefs which in traditional societies were embedded in family life, religion, local and vocational loyalties. In place of community values, in Europe, and especially in European cities, there was the development of what he called *anomie*; that is a general collapse of collective conscience or sense of shared cultural and spiritual values, which brought isolation of individuals and a lack of any sense of connection. It was this sense of *anomie* which provoked suicide (Durkheim 1951: 70).

European intellectuals and scientists who embraced opposing political views concluded that social decline was produced and illustrated by changes in the traditional sexual hierarchy and the growing participation of women in the public world – despite the laws which in many parts of Europe prohibited women from political association. As Arno Mayer argues, their ideas provided a comprehensive attack on liberal, modern society, and expressed extreme fear of the direction of democracy; a hatred of common man and of 'mass society' (Mayer 1981: 230–6). At the very root of this attack lay a fundamental opposition to any move towards the emancipation of women and any questioning of the hierarchical and authoritarian family.

Concern about degeneration was central to discussions about the size, health and nature of the population in the later nineteenth century. If degeneracy was an hereditary problem, it became imperative in the eyes of some to try to find ways to discourage the degenerate from reproducing and to encourage those healthy people who could contribute to the overall health of the racial stock. This argument was the basis for the development of eugenics, yet another new field which claimed scientific status in the late nineteenth century.

The term 'eugenics' was coined in 1883 by the man who first attempted to develop it as a science, Sir Francis Galton. A nephew of Charles Darwin, Galton built very closely on his own understanding of Darwin's theory of evolution. Darwin argued that evolution occurred through random selection of those traits or characteristics most fitted to survive, but Galton and his fellow eugenicists wanted to remove the randomness, to intervene in natural processes, to establish precisely what traits should be perpetuated and how this was to be done. Accepting the view that all human characteristics were inherited from parents, Galton argued that through proper selection or control of human reproduction, one could ensure an improvement in the human race. Galton lacked any understanding of genetics, or of the ways in which genes combine to determine hereditary characteristics. He tried to prove his theory by undertaking interviews with the descendants of talented and influential men, and then by drawing up tables of the statistical like- lihood that particular characteristics would be inherited. Though Galton accepted that characteristics from parents passed to children of both sexes, his major interest was to establish the inheritance pattern for the sons of famous fathers.

Eugenic concerns increased markedly in Britain in the 1880s and 1890s, when it became clear not only that the birth-rate was declining, but that it was declining most rapidly and most markedly among the urban middle and upper middle classes, while increasing among the working class and the poor and among immigrants. Fears were expressed that the Anglo-Saxon race would be outbred by Celts and East European Jews. The quality of the 'British' population seemed to be visibly declining in the late 1890s when almost 60 per cent of the young men who volunteered for service in the Boer War had to be rejected as unfit. This concern about the health and well-being of populations became a European-wide matter in 1905 in the Russo–Japanese War when Russia became the first European nation to be defeated by an Asian army. Eugenics seemed to offer a possible way out of the fear of degeneration and decline, and was taken up very widely by upper-middle-class professional men and educated women. There was considerable interest in eugenic ideas in Germany, where a eugenics journal and a racial Hygiene Society were established in 1905. By 1910, there was an international eugenics society, which encouraged the setting up of national societies in France and Italy as well. The extreme forms of racist eugenic practice carried out by the Nazis in the 1930s and 1940s was not contemplated at the turn of the century. Nonetheless, Eugenics certainly carried with it designs for social engineering, which could include the idea that those deemed 'unfit' be sterilised in order to ensure that they did not reproduce. Some of these schemes were carried out in the United States at this time, but not in Europe until the inter-war period.

The implications of eugenics for women are complex. As several historians have shown, the eugenic preoccupation with the birth-rate led to an insistence that maternity was women's primary duty to the nation and the race. Galton, and a number of his followers, opposed feminist campaigns for higher education and political rights for women, arguing that women's primary social duty lay in motherhood. Galton's British successor, Karl Pearson, insisted that if women's subjection as mothers was necessary for the general good, then they had better remain in subjection. Pearson, like Galton, believed that higher education during adolescence might impair a woman's reproductive capacity. What would happen, he asked, if in seeking emancipation, women reduce their maternal capacities and 'injure the race?' (Solloway 1990: 110–15). Leading male eugenicists opposed women's emancipation, but, as Richard Soloway and Lucy Bland have shown, many women, particularly in Britain, were attracted to eugenics and became very active in eugenic societies (Bland 1995: 29). Eugenic activities gave some women a cause connected with a new and progressive science, and many of them were very willing to be engaged to explain the importance of 'responsible motherhood' to other women. As we have already seen, feminists were not immune to the imperialist and racist ideas of the time. In Germany, the popular *Bund for Mutterschutz* led by Helene Stocker, drew on eugenic ideas. In a similar way, British feminists saw the health of the British race as a major concern. Eugenics also offered feminists a way to combat the prevailing sexual double standard. Feminists had long criticised the prevailing moral and social system, which allowed men to engage in promiscuous sexual activity, while women were required to remain chaste. They sought not to give women new freedom, but to control men. Women involved with eugenics had begun to discuss the threat that male promiscuity posed to virtuous wives and unborn children. The novels of Sarah Grand and Emma Brooke, like Henrik Ibsen's play *Ghosts*, showed in graphic detail the ways in which promiscuous men could infect their wives and children, thus destroying the very families and homes they were supposed to protect (Grand 1992: Ibsen 1977).

Sexuality, sexology and psychoanalysis

Towards the end of the nineteenth century, as Jeffrey Weeks has argued, sexuality began to be seen as deserving of serious study. Sexual desire and behaviour were important not just as an aspect of moral laxity or disease, but because of their 'significance for the whole existence of the individual and society' (Weeks 1977: 3). The new discussions about sexuality reflected anxiety about family life, and served also to undermine many deeply held beliefs about the family. Demographic concern about national population sizes and birth-rates provided one framework for contemporary interest in questions about the basis of the sexual instinct.

In the early nineteenth century, debate about sexual behaviour had been dominated by clergy, by moralists and by the ideas of philosophers and social theorists like Rousseau. In the late nineteenth century, by contrast, these debates were dominated by medical and legal specialists: by doctors, psychologists, sexologists and psychoanalysts, on the one hand, and by lawyers and those concerned with criminal justice and law reform on the other. The new fields of knowledge developed by these specialists, such as sexology, endocrinology and psychoanalysis, all had sexual difference or sexual desire as their primary investigative focus. Professional and popular literature on sexology and psychoanalysis in particular encouraged intensive discussion of women's sexuality and the nature and origins of homosexuality. They brought new theories of the sexual basis of intellectual and emotional disturbance or illness and of infantile sexuality which called into question many prevailing ideas about the nature of family life.

The intensity of concern about sexuality at this time is also evident in the proliferation of a new descriptive vocabulary of sexuality. In the eighteenth century, new words had been invented to describe female genitalia; in the late nineteenth century, a series of terms were devised to describe those who desired sexual relations with members of their own sex. The term 'homosexuality' was coined in 1869 by a German-Hungarian writer and translator, Karoly Maria Benkert, but was little used until the turn of the century. The English social and sexual reformer, Edward Carpenter, preferred the term 'intermediate sex' to apply to both men and women who desired sexual relations with members of their own sex. The most common label was 'sexual invert'. The German sex reformer, Karl Ulrichs, devised a whole taxonomy to characterise different forms of 'sexual inversion'. He differentiated between a normal heterosexual man, a *Dioning*, and an invert, or *Urning*. Ulrichs gave the term *Mannling* to those inverts who preferred effeminate male partners, *Zwishen-Urning* to those who sought adolescent partners and *Weiblings* to those who were attracted to powerful adult males. Those who were attracted to either sex he called *Uranodioninge* (Weeks 1989: 164–5).

Discussions about homosexuality were inseparable from the changing legal framework of European states in the late nineteenth century. A great deal of debate in the German-speaking states in the 1860s was occasioned by the Prussian penal code, which outlawed male homosexual activities. When Germany became unified in 1870, this penal code was extended throughout the empire. Sex reformers like Ulrichs worked to amend the German law. In Britain, all male homosexual activities were outlawed by the Criminal Law Amendment Act of 1885, which declared that 'Any male person who, in public or private, commits, or is a party to the commission of, or procures or attempts to procure the commission by any male person of any act of gross indecency with another male person, shall be guilty of a misdemeanour' (Weeks 1989: 221). Such a misdemeanour was punishable by two years' imprisonment, with or without hard labour.

The regulation and prohibition of indecent acts between men in the late nineteenth century stands in striking contrast to the legislative concerns of the earlier part of the century, which sought to ensure that there was no sexual indecency in public. Despite their extensive regulation of family life and women's activity, the early nineteenth-century Napoleonic Codes mentioned neither sodomy nor any form of homosexuality, hence in France, these acts were not illegal (Copley 1989: 24–5). Article 330 of the Napoleonic Criminal Code set out a new offence against public decency, which was punishable by imprisonment or a substantial fine. Homosexual acts became punishable only if they involved minors or occurred in a place that could be construed as public. But from the 1870s onwards, in France, too, discussion about the causes of homosexual behaviour and about the people likely to engage in it became widespread.

One major preoccupation in scientific and legal circles centred on the question of what profession was best equipped to understand and regulate homosexuality, and this in turn involved discussion of how homosexuality was 'caused' or came about. Many legislators and police saw homosexuality as a crime, appropriately dealt with by the criminal justice system. Doctors, psychiatrists, sexologists and psychoanalysts all argued against this view, insisting that whether homosexuality was congenital or acquired, it was properly the province of the sciences and the forms of medical speciality which dealt with nervous and sexual disorders.

One of the new disciplines which became prominent in this debate about homosexuality was sexology. Although only named in 1907, this new science which sought to study the sexual life of the individual, was established in the late nineteenth century largely by the Austrian Richard von Krafft-Ebing and the English Havelock Ellis. Working largely through case studies, sexologists accumulated examples of every kind of sexual desire and behaviour. Krafft-Ebing believed that 'sexuality is the most powerful factor in individual and social existence' and his monumental *Psychopathia Sexualis*, published in Austria in 1886, was an encyclopedic survey of sexual tastes, desires and perversions. He itemised 'pathological manifestations' (such as 'sexual neuroses' or 'nymphomania'), and sought to establish whether particular kinds of social behaviour or tastes in dress accompanied abnormal forms of sexual desire. Krafft-Ebing viewed sexual perversion as dangerous to society, and devoted much of his work to showing how in the highest civilisations of northern Europe sexual energies had been mastered and controlled. In his early work, he argued that homosexuality was a sign of degeneration and needed control. By the 1890s, however, Krafft-Ebing was persuaded of the need for reform of the laws which made homosexuality criminal. Other sexologists were active participants in the struggle for homosexual law reform. Havelock Ellis, for example, was closely associated with a group of left-wing radicals in England actively seeking new approaches to sexuality and family life, and sympathised with the need for reform. Indeed, Ellis felt that homosexual men were often superior in artistic and intellectual gifts to heterosexual ones and that homosexuality 'made civilisation possible' (Ellis 1903).

Both sex research and legal debate served to produce new homosexual identities. Michel Foucault and Jeffrey Weeks have both explored the social and cultural impact of the legislation outlawing homosexuality and the

extensive discussion of it by sexologists. Weeks argues that, far from reducing the incidence of homosexuality, the naming and constant speaking about
homosexuality, the detailing of its many forms by sexologists, the establishment of a regulatory legal apparatus for its control, all served to make it more
widely known. Those whose lives were discussed in this way became increasingly aware of themselves as particular kinds of people. Hence this attempt at
regulation was one factor in the development of distinctive homosexual
identities and of the quite visible homosexual subcultures evident in major
European cities by 1900.

The place of women within the discussion of sexuality, and the impact of
these late nineteenth-century developments on women remain a matter of
debate. Krafft-Ebing and Ellis, like Freud, devoted a great deal of time to
exploring the nature and extent of the differences between men and women
in terms of their sexual desires. Their investigations brought profound
changes in ideas about women's sexuality. Both Ellis and Freud insisted that
nineteenth-century conceptions of women as lacking sexual instincts and
desire were false. Freud insisted that the silence about sexual matters which
was customary in middle-class homes assumed an innocence and an ignorance of sexual matters among girls that was both false and damaging; young
girls had powerful sexual feelings and many gained extensive sexual knowledge from maids, from their own activities and from observing others (Freud
1907: 179–81). Ellis argued that Victorian morality, with its belief that
women were 'sexually anaesthetic' and had no sexual feelings, had been a
major factor in women's oppression (Ellis 1903: 155–79). But their ideas on
the nature of women's sexuality are still controversial. In Ellis's view,
women's sexuality was essentially responsive: it was diffuse and not directed
at any single object and usually developed in response to male attentions.
Men automatically took the active and aggressive role in sexual courtship
and encounters, while women adopted the passive role. Women's passivity,
Ellis argued, must not be taken as absence of sexual desire; rather, it served
to increase male aggression and sexual activity. Moreover aggression, power
and the capacity to inflict pain, were for Ellis integral to the sexual impulse in
man, while women's sexual pleasure was itself very like pain. For Freud too,
women's sexuality was generally passive, and the pathway women had to
travel from the active infantile sexuality of girls through to the vaginal and
passive sexuality of adult women was tortuous and difficult.

One of the most important new ideas, and the one which comprehensively
undermined nineteenth-century family values, was the insistence on infantile

sexuality. The growing preoccupation with 'adolescence' as a special stage in life, which emerged in the 1870s and 1880s, heightened the attention paid to adolescent sexuality. The traumas and crises faced by adolescents unable to deal with their own sexual desires in a culture which offered them no guidance or assistance was a major theme in German literature of the 1890s (Neubauer 1991). Psychoanalysis pushed the borders back even further, stressing the importance of sexual feelings from earliest infancy. 'The new born baby', Freud insisted, 'brings sexuality with it into the world.' Sexual sensations accompany the baby's development as a suckling and throughout early childhood (Freud 1907: 174). Freud's discussion of the development of erotogenic zones and of infantile sexual aims, his description of the phases of development of sexual organisation through childhood, radically undermined earlier notions of childhood sexual innocence. At the same time, Freud's discussion of the child's sexual feelings about its parents, his belief that 'falling in love with the mother and jealousy of the father [was] ... a universal event of early childhood', and his elaboration of the need to resolve the conflict set up by this desire for a parent, involved a new analysis of the family in which sexual feelings were not confined to the central married couple, but underlay all relations between children and parents.

Sexologists and psychoanalysts engaged in sexual discussion with considerable freedom and frankness, arguing both that it was scientifically imperative for them to do so, and that greater openness would benefit society as a whole. In England, the outrage aroused by the trials of Oscar Wilde in 1895 meant there was immense hostility to any publication even mentioning homosexuality. In the aftermath of the trials, which resulted in Wilde being sentenced to two years' hard labour, the work of sexologists was frowned upon. Havelock Ellis's and John Addington Symonds's *Sexual Inversion*, in which they explored and attempted to defend homosexuality, was seized immediately after its publication in 1897. The authors were not put on trial, but the bookseller who had sold it to an undercover policeman was. Even Krafft-Ebing's work, which used Latin to describe sexual acts, was described as 'medical pornography' (Porter and Hall 1995: 163). At the same time, new ideas about sexuality and a demand for greater sexual freedom influenced many progressive groups, including socialists in England, Germany and Russia, and young educated professionals who saw greater openness and preparedness to discuss sexual questions as definitive of their own modernity.

Feminism and the 'new woman'

In the 1890s and the early twentieth century women's rights finally became a matter of major public and political debate throughout Europe. After decades of discussion of the 'woman question' among feminist activists, socialists, writers, artists, scientists, moralists and educators, the nature and the situation and the demands of women began to feature in the popular imagination. In England, *Punch* cartoons of the late 1880s and 1890s featured powerful and athletic women cycling or playing cricket, and bullying effeminate men at cocktail parties. With the advent of militancy and the massive suffrage demonstrations after 1907, public discussion and press coverage of the 'woman question' was even more extensive.

The nature of the 'woman question' also changed in the *fin-de-siècle*. In late nineteenth-century literature discussions of the 'new woman' coincided with new public debates about marriage and sexuality. First coined in Britain in 1894 by the novelist Sarah Grand, the term 'new woman' was used to describe fictional characters and to refer to actual women who sought to lead lives very different from those of their mothers by engaging in activities which proclaimed their independence, their sense of personal worth, and their entitlement to a public role. Grand insisted on the rejection of the middle-class feminine ideals by defining the 'new woman' as a woman who refused to be treated either as a breeding machine or a prostitute, who rejected the idea that 'Home-is-the-Woman's-Sphere' and who sought a wider world of thought and activity (Grand 1898: 5–10).

Though most vociferous in Britain, by the turn of the century debates about the 'new woman', marriage and sexuality occurred throughout Europe. The extent of this debate and its similarity across Europe are best illustrated in the widespread controversy which surrounded *The Doll's House*, the play by the Norwegian dramatist Henrik Ibsen, which was staged in theatres in London and Paris, in Berlin and Vienna throughout the 1880s and 1890s. Nora, the heroine of Ibsen's play, comes to realise that her marriage and her role as mother are built on fantasy and illusion. As a woman, Nora is kept ignorant of the laws which govern commercial dealings, and is not deemed sufficiently adult to make moral decisions or indeed to take a serious role in the moral education of her children. She is supposed rather to ensure that their home continues happy and loving, and to embody an idealised maternal figure. When Nora comes finally to see that she has been living in a 'doll's house', in which she is the doll-wife of her husband, as previously she had been the doll-child of her father, she rebels and walks out, leaving home, husband and children behind. Many established critics saw Nora as epitomising the selfishness, self-indulgence and even irrationality of the 'new woman'. But others, including Janet Achurch, who acted Nora on the London stage in 1891, regarded her as the clearest possible example of the problems women faced and the need for a new approach to marriage and family life and to women's education (Achurch 1889: 124). For many women and feminist sympathisers, *The Doll's House* illustrated the demeaning nature of women's place, even within loving marriages and families. For others, the resounding slamming of the door as Nora left was evidence of the extent to which marriage and family life were being threatened and undermined by the selfishness of contemporary women and by all those seeking change or reform in the sexual order.

The connection between the demands of women, on the one hand, and the critique of marriage, on the other, helps explain the intensity and even virulence of the debate about the 'woman question' at the turn of the century. Few feminists absolutely rejected marriage or women's maternal duty. But any discussion of women's autonomy, any hint of a demand for education, political rights, employment was seen by the opponents of feminism as a rejection of women's traditional sphere and duties, and as a demand that women become like men. Even the mildest discussions of women's rights brought visions of domestic and familial chaos and of women as desexed and threatening. The aims and the campaigns of feminists had met fierce opposition throughout the nineteenth century. At the turn of the century, however, this opposition became more organised and vocal. This was evident in Britain in the formation of an anti-suffrage society, which conducted public meetings, lobbied members of parliament and moved around the country mobilising opposition to women's claim for enfranchisement. But in the eyes of some historians, hostility to women's demands was mobilised not only at a political level. Bram Djikstra has argued recently that the theme of a 'sex war' pervaded the visual and literary representations of women at this period. Writers and painters, supported by psychologists and social theorists, dedicated themselves to depicting women as simultaneously helpless, wicked and destructive (Djikstra 1986: vii).

The intensity of opposition to women's emancipation coincided with what some historians describe as 'the flowering of feminism' across Europe in the 1890s (Offen 1987: 356). In this decade the terms 'feminism' and 'feminist' first came to be used in both France and England. The new language of feminism accompanied a proliferation of national feminist organisations across Europe, and the establishment of international bodies to co-ordinate various campaigns for women's rights. At the same time, many feminists became increasingly radical in their demands, seeking an end to the sexual double standard, reform of prostitution, rights for both single and married mothers as well as political and legal rights.

The capacity of European women to participate in these debates and campaigns varied. In Germany, women were forbidden to engage in any form of political association until 1907. In Britain, by contrast, an extensive feminist movement emerged during this period. The British women's suffrage movement had begun in the 1860s, and, by the 1890s, some women felt that they had campaigned for 30 years with little obvious effect. During the 1890s, however, British women's participation in local government extended, as did their involvement in education and in some forms of professional employment. Moreover, women were becoming more and more visible and influential in national political concerns. In the course of the 1880s, all major British political parties established women's groups and used women in electoral campaigns. In the 1890s, some women played a prominent role in the debates about Irish Home Rule and the Boer War. Suffrage activity became better organised in 1897, when the major provincial and local suffrage societies united to form the National Union of Women's Suffrage Societies under the leadership of Millicent Garrett Fawcett.

The nineteenth-century British approach to the suffrage campaign, with its drawing-room meetings and genteel lectures, was dramatically transformed in the early twentieth century with the formation in 1903 of the Women's Social and Political Union (WSPU). Scorning the peaceful, moderate and genteel approach of the NUWSS, the WSPU took the question of women's suffrage into the public arena by interrupting political meetings, organising mass demonstrations and marches and arranging open-air meetings. The WSPU courted arrest and imprisonment and used the dock as a venue to deliver their message. They had a genius for publicity and for drama, introducing colourful and choreographed mass marches and making suffrage demonstrations into visual spectacles attracting crowds of onlookers and gaining extensive press coverage. Taken up by other suffrage organisations, this new approach gave great vitality to the suffrage campaign and helped to bring it thousands of new members and substantial amounts of money. As the British government remained opposed to women's suffrage, the campaign of the militants escalated, and they moved from peaceful marches and demonstrations to campaigns of window breaking and arson. At the same time, imprisoned suffragettes embarked on hunger strikes, which brought increased publicity, especially when hunger strikers were forcibly fed.

The activities of the WSPU were subject to considerable critical comment in Britain, but were watched with great fascination by feminists in France, Russia, Finland, Italy and Germany. Britain, as Linda Edmondson has argued, 'exercised a special fascination for feminists abroad during the last decade before the First World War, because it was the only country in the world where the suffrage campaign seemed to be assuming the proportions of a revolutionary upheaval' (Edmondson 1984: 120). The French feminist Madeleine Pelletier was so impressed by the giant suffrage demonstration in which she participated at Hyde Park in London in 1909 that she set about organising public demonstrations among her own countrywomen.

No other European country developed a militant suffrage movement on the British model, but just as other political movements, like the socialists, developed mass bases in this period, feminist organisations in most countries increased markedly in size and became more outspoken in their demands. As we have seen, increasing numbers of women became involved in eugenic societies concerned to promote motherhood. Women also joined peace movements. But what was most remarkable was the growing number of women insisting on legal and political rights.

In France, earlier feminist organisations had concerned themselves primarily with education and philanthropy. In the 1890s new groups emerged, demanding political rights for women and adding their voices to that of Hubertine Auclert in *Suffrage des femmes*. Suffrage groups remained very small in size, but were accompanied by the growth of moderate groups and of national bodies, like the *Conseil National des Femmes Françaises* (National Council of French Women), which brought together many different women's groups, from trade unions to philanthropic societies. They aimed to expand campaigns for educational reform and for moral reform, including an end to legalised prostitution. Though the majority of Catholic women continued to hold aloof from feminist organisations during the first decade of the twentieth century, it is still estimated that some 100,000 French women were active in feminist groups prior to the First World War.

Most other European countries also saw the formation of national women's groups fighting for particular rights, but all aiming to expand the claims of women as citizens. In the Netherlands, a National Association for Women's Suffrage was formed in 1894, which boasted 62 branches by 1909. In Germany too, a number of the middle-class groups which had existed since the 1860s now combined to form national bodies. All the women's philanthropic organisations founded in the 1880s and early 1890s combined to form the Federation of German Women's Associations in 1894, and, as in

France, this unified group extended its programme. Initially a very small moderate group, within a few years of its formation, its members had begun concerted campaigns to reform the Civil Law Code of 1896 in order to increase the rights of women within marriage and family life. In Habsburg, Austria, the 1890s was a critical period for women's organisations and for feminism. A range of new specialist organisations were established alongside the General Austrian Women's Association, which aimed to go 'to the roots' of the 'woman problem' by addressing the economic, political and ideological basis of women's oppression. It campaigned particularly on questions about the sexual double standard and sexually transmitted diseases (Anderson 1992: 60–89). In Italy, industrialisation in the north brought a stirring of feminism. A Society for Women's Work and an Association for Women, seeking to secularise girls' education, were both established in the early 1890s, and women were active in new Italian-based international organisations which combined pacifist demands with a consciousness of the 'woman question'.

In the late nineteenth century a range of working-class and socialist women's organisations took up these women's rights issues and linked them to their participation within socialist politics. The women's organisation associated with the German Social Democratic Party (SPD), led by Ottilie Baader and Klara Zetkin, was established in 1896 and soon became the largest women's organisation in Europe. Originally designed at least in part to circumvent the legislation which prevented women from joining the SPD itself, the establishment of a separate women's group which gave them the freedom to speak and act away from men, was clearly very attractive to women. By 1908, when women were permitted by law to join the party, thousands did so and women made up nearly 10 per cent of total party membership. The success of the German model suggested that, if women were to be involved in socialist politics, they needed a separate organisation which would allow them the capacity to speak and to deal with questions about women's work and women's rights alongside their general socialist concerns. In the socialist movements of other countries that followed this model, such as Finland and Austria, separate socialist women's organisations also attracted significant numbers of women. In France and Italy, by contrast, there was no separate women's group, and hence only a very small number of women were involved in socialist political activities. Britain had a different pattern again. Though no separate women's organisation was connected to the Labour party or to most socialist groups, the women's suffrage movement did include Labour supporters. But the importance of separate organisations for women was also very clearly demonstrated through the Women's Co-operative Guild, the largest organisation for working-class women. Intended initially as a way of bringing women into the co-operative movement, the Women's Co-operative Guild had its own organisers and local branches and its own national conferences and campaigns. It became a forum in which married working-class women could campaign for reform of the divorce laws, for improved maternity services and for equal pay (Gaffin and Thoms 1983).

Demands for legal and political rights for women were accompanied by demands for the rights of mothers, whether married or single, and demands for women's control of their own bodies through contraception and abortion. In England, where feminists had long sought for women to have the freedom not to marry, and for a wider range of opportunities for single women, an increasingly radical critique of marriage emerged. Some feminists, including the militant suffragettes, depicted marriage as a prison for women and set up an alternative ideal of female celibacy. A small number of 'advanced women' insisted also on the entitlement of women to engage in sexual relations without marriage. These outspoken criticisms of marriage and conventional femininity coincided with more dramatic and confrontational feminist campaigns. The French socialist Madeleine Pelletier, one of the few feminists who also had a professional practice as a doctor, was in some ways the most radical of all. As an independent woman, Pelletier felt particularly strongly about the need to connect the demand for women's economic independence with the demand for the vote. She also demanded access for women to contraception and abortion, which would give them control over their own bodies and free them from the burden of continual child-bearing (Scott 1996: 144–5).

Although few women were as radical as Pelletier, feminists became more outspoken and far more critical of conventional morality at the turn of the century than at any time earlier in the nineteenth century. Feminist activists in the mid-nineteenth century had attempted to emphasise their moderation, their endorsement of family values and their philanthropic concerns with unfortunate women. By contrast, feminists at the turn of the century demanded legal and political rights for women, and social and sexual freedoms which had hardly been addressed at all since the 1790s. In France, Germany and Austria, as in the Scandinavian countries, it was not so much marriage, as the right of a woman to her children, whether she was married or not, which inspired debate. French feminists fought for the equality of rights and responsibilities of both parents to their children. Many targeted the Napoleonic Code, demanding the repeal of article 340, which had prevented a woman who bore children out of wedlock from attempting to find or to demand support from the father of their child. The idea of voluntary motherhood, involving both the idea that married women should be free to limit and control their fertility, and that single women should be able to have children without facing legal and social barriers, was strongly advocated in these years. It was put forward in Sweden and Norway by Ellen Key and Katti Anker Moller, and in Germany by Ruth Bre. The German *Bund Mutterschutz* (Society for the Protection of Motherhood) defended the idea of voluntary motherhood through the provision of contraception and abortion, as well as demanding support for single mothers and an end to legal discrimination against them.

The issue of motherhood was always a complicated one for feminists. In demanding a higher status for mothers and greater recognition of the social contribution of motherhood, feminists often sounded very much like the eugenicists who demanded that women eschew the struggle for rights and devote themselves entirely to their maternal duties. Most of those advocating voluntary motherhood supported some eugenic ideas: all of them wanted the fittest women to reproduce and saw in voluntary motherhood a measure that would allow this. But in some cases, the needs of single women got lost. Their concerns were directly related to the broader social and political concerns of each society, in particular anxieties about decadence, degeneration and decline, and the rise of nation-building institutions that concentrated on managing reproduction as well as production. Feminists were as influenced by these concerns as the broader population, but they also contributed to them through their challenges to the political and legal *status quo*.

Gender and the city

The city occupied a central place both in the social development of late nineteenth-century Europe and in contemporary debates about the nature of modernity. The unparalleled growth in the size of cities is one of the distinctive features of the *fin-de-siècle*. At the same time that falling birth-rates and massive migration contributed to the slowing of the overall rate of European population growth by the end of the nineteenth century, urban populations increased dramatically. By 1890, there were 1,709 cities with a population greater than 10,000, accommodating almost 30 per cent of the total population. In the two decades between 1880 and 1913, the number of cities with populations over 100,000 increased from 14 to 48. England was the most urbanised country, with 60 per cent of its population living in cities by the turn of the century; in Germany, France and Belgium more than 25 per cent of the population lived in cities (Hobsbawm 1987: 343). The cities which dominated popular imagination were becoming vast in size. London and Paris, the two largest European cities, had populations of 7 million and 4 million respectively by the turn of the century, and Vienna had a population of 2 million.

Concern about mass society was most clearly focused on cities in which vast numbers of people, unknown to each other and often not clearly demarcated in terms of class or occupation, mingled in city streets. In late nineteenth-century Paris, for the first time, workers as well as the wealthy could patronise a wide range of leisure institutions including music halls, circuses, cafés, dance halls and street fairs. For the middle classes, the more concentrated presence of the working and poor sections of the population only added to their anxieties. The numbers of people engaged in crime, prostitution and begging seemed to grow, and encouraged the view that cities provided a magnet for the criminal and the deviant, gathering together the darker side of life. City life was often portrayed as brutal and vicious, promoting criminal activity among the poor, and restlessness and instability among the wealthy.

The phenomenon of the city produced new forms of housing, transport, work and entertainment and captured the imagination of writers, artists and social theorists. Although cities offered a multitude of new pleasures for people of all classes, as the primary location of the workplaces and the political and social activities that made up the public sphere, the city was also clearly gendered. The expanding range of activities, facilities and pleasures associated with the city were largely a masculine affair. From the late eighteenth century onwards, the development of business, economic and political facilities, banks and offices, chambers of commerce, learned societies, political groups and social and dining clubs had meant that middle-class men both worked and undertook some of their social life in cities, while their wives and daughters remained at their suburban homes. In the mid and late nineteenth century, the proliferation of shops, clubs, restaurants, hotels and theatres catering primarily to men extended the range of activities which cities offered. But middle-class women whose primary location was the home, had limited access to this city life.

Historians usually discuss the distinctive nature of masculine life in the city in terms of the new figure which began to feature in literature, art and social criticism: the '*flâneur*'. First described by the French poet Baudelaire in the mid nineteenth century, the *flâneur* was an urban stroller, an unattached single man freely exploring city streets, observing shops and shoppers, partaking of whatever entertainments were offered, gazing at women and sometimes purchasing sex, but anonymous and in absolute control of his own life. Although discussed mainly in relation to Paris, the figure of the *flâneur* served for writers, painters and cultural critics to illustrate the complex and ephemeral nature of city life across Europe, with its combination of spectacle and pleasures, on the one hand, and its lack of connection to society, on the other. Recently feminist historians have emphasised the extent to which the figure of the *flâneur* is explicitly masculine. For the *flâneur* some of the city sights and pleasures are the women whom he can watch or use as he chooses.

The location of women within this new urban world has been a matter of much recent historical discussion. Moving to a city offered many women an opportunity to leave the family home and to engage in an independent life, which might include philanthropic or feminist activity for women with their own income, or paid work for others. The fact that city pleasures for men had always included sexual access to women through dance halls, bars, brothels and street prostitution meant, however, that women seen alone in city streets had to mark their respectability very carefully. Otherwise they ran the risk of being regarded as prostitutes or at least as being sexually available. Working-class women were subject to continual harassment as they went about their daily lives. As Anne Shapiro (1996) has shown, the visibility of women and of women's work within French cities led to concern about the extent both of prostitution and of female criminality. City life was seen as corrupting to working-class women, offering them a life of vice which appeared easier and more lucrative than honest toil.

Writers like Rachel Bowlby (1985), Janet Wolff (1989), Elizabeth Wilson (1991), Judith Walkowitz (1992) and Mica Nava (1996) have argued that while the city was often seen as hostile and threatening to women, the emergence of department stores and the activity of 'shopping' alongside the expansion of philanthropic activities and social work offered a range of activities and facilities for women. Many middle-class women utilised libraries, visited art galleries or went to the theatre in cities. Although throughout the nineteenth century, middle-class women seeking access to city streets and shops had to indicate their respectability by the presence of chaperones, or maids, cities also offered them specifically feminine domains. The department store, as the French novelist Emile Zola showed in his book *The Ladies Paradise* (1883), gave middle-class women a whole new way of life. The expanding range of consumer products made 'shopping' or 'window shopping' into an activity. Department stores enabled women to become aware of new products and new fashions, which in turn brought not only new patterns of consumption, but also new ways of getting to know about the social and commercial world. Many department stores also offered reading rooms, talks and lectures, dining rooms and cloak rooms, providing sufficient activity to fill the whole day of a middle-class woman. It also is clear that in the later part of the nineteenth century, increasing numbers of women worked in shops and offices or provided cleaning and other services for city businesses.

In the 1880s, as Judith Walkowitz has argued, 'marginalised groups comprising working men and women of all classes, repeatedly spilled over and out of their ascribed, bounded roles, costumes, and locales into the public streets and the wrong parts of town, engaged on missions of their own' (Walkowitz 1992: 41). While women may have lacked the freedom of men in city streets, they had their own pastimes and focal points. The autobiographies of late nineteenth-century women emphasise what city life offered them. The move from the country or from small towns into cities immediately brought a range of new social, economic and political activities and the freedom of a life away from close surveillance by parents and community. Many of these women relished precisely the freedom of movement and the anonymity seen as characteristic of the *flâneur*. They may not have indulged in all the same pleasures as the masculine *flâneur*, but in many cases, women commented on their enjoyment of solitude, combined with the opportunity to organise a social life of their choice and in some cases the freedom to transgress bourgeois sexual norms.

Cities played an important part in feminist campaigns, as indeed in all political campaigns of the early twentieth century. Like socialists, trade unionists and political radicals, feminists needed the transport and communications cities offered in order to stage their mass demonstrations. In city spaces they could appeal to the largest audiences and be most visible. Capital cities also offered closer access to governments and important officials. In England, the militant WSPU, which began in Manchester, realised early on that it would have to move its headquarters to London in order to be effective. In a similar way, French feminist organisations became more vocal and radical in Paris in the 1890s and the early twentieth century than anywhere else in France. Militant suffragettes also utilised the backdrop of the city to emphasise the vulnerability of women and the brutality of men by insisting that women demonstrate in delicate white gowns – the kind of apparel normally worn within a genteel home – while engaged in street demonstrations. This strategy simultaneously underlined and contested the masculine monopoly of public space. By showing these delicate women in white alongside burly policemen dressed in heavy dark clothes, they emphasised the sexual basis of women's oppression and the menace of male violence and brutality.

References and further reading

Primary sources

Achurch, Janet (1889) 'On the difficulty of being Nora', in M. Egan (ed.) (1972) *Ibsen: The Critical Heritage*, London.

Durkheim, Emile (1951 [1897]) *Suicide*, New York.

Nordau, Max (1993 [1895]) *Degeneration*, trans. George L. Mosse, Lincoln.

Le Bon, Gustav (1952 [1895]) *The Crowd*, New York.

Freud, Sigmund (1907) 'The sexual enlightenment of children', in S. Freud (1977) *On Sexuality*, Pelican Freud Library, vol. 7, New York.

Ellis, Havelock and Symonds, John Addington (1897) *Sexual Inversion*, London.

Ellis, Havelock (1903) *The Analysis of the Sexual Impulse: Studies in the Psychology of Sex, Vol. III*, Philadelphia.

Grand, Sarah (1898) *The Modern Man and Maid*, London.

Ibsen, Henrik (1935 [1889]) *The Doll's House*, London.

Ibsen, Henrik (1973 [1889]) *Ghosts*, trans. M. Meyer, London.

Zola, Emile (1956 [1887]) *Germinal*, London.

Zola, Emile (1995 [1883]) *The Ladies Paradise*, trans. Brian Nelson, Oxford.

Eugenics, degeneration and the decadent modern world

Bland, L. (1995) *Banishing the Beast: English Feminism and Sexual Morality, 1885–1914*, Harmondsworth.

Foldy, M. S. (1997) *The Trials of Oscar Wilde: Deviance, Morality and Late Victorian Society*, New Haven.

Grand, S. (1992) *The Heavenly Twins*, Ann Arbor.

Hobsbawm, E. J. (1987) *The Age of Empire 1870–1914*, London.

Mayer, A. J. (1981) *The Persistence of the Old Regime: Europe to the Great War*, New York.

Mosse, G. L. (1996) *The Image of Man: The Creation of Modern Masculinity*, New York.

Nye, R. A. (1984) *Crime Madness and Modern Politics in France: The Medical Concept of a National Decline*, Princeton.

Pick, D. (1989) *Faces of Degeneration: A European Disorder c1848–c1918*, New York.

Searle, G. R. (1976) *Eugenics and Politics in Britian, 1900–1914*, Leyden.
Shapiro, A. L. (1996) *Breaking the Codes: Female Criminality in fin-de-siècle Paris*, Stanford.
Soloway, R. (1990) *Demography and Degeneration: Eugenics and the Declining Birthrate in Twentieth Century Britain*, Chapel Hill.
Vidler, A. (1994) 'Psychopathologies of modern space: metropolitan fear from agoraphobia to estrangement', in M. S. Roth (ed.) *Recovering History: Culture, Politics and the Psyche*, Stanford.
Weber, E. (1986) *France: Fin de Siecle*, Cambridge, Mass.

Sexuality, sexology and psychoanalysis

Copley, A. (1989) *Sexual Moralities in France, 1780–1980: New Ideas on the Family, Divorce and Homosexuality*, London.
Jackson, M. (1994) *The Real Facts of Life: Feminism and the Politics of Sexuality, c. 1850–1940*, London.
Neubauer, J. (1991) *The Fin-de-Siècle Culture of Adolescence*, New Haven.
Porter, R. and Hall, L. (1995) *The Facts of Life: The Creation of Sexual Knowledge in Britian, 1650–1950*, New Haven and London.
Walkowitz, J. (1992) *City of Dreadful Delight: Narrative of Sexual Danger in Late Victorian England*, London.
Weeks, J. (1977) *Coming Out: Homosexual Politics in Britian from the Nineteenth Century to the Present*, London.
Weeks, J. (1989) *Sex, Politics and Society: The Regulation of Sexuality since 1800*, London.

Feminism and the 'new woman'

Anderson, H. (1992) *Women's Movement in fin-de-siècle Vienna*, New Haven and London.
Bock, G. and Thane, P. (eds) (1991) *Maternity and Gender Policies: Women and the Rise of the European Welfare States 1880s–1950s*, London and New York.
Caine, B. (1997) *English Feminism, 1780–1980*, Melbourne.
Cova, A. (1991) 'French feminism and maternity: theories and politics, 1890–1918', in G. Bock and P. Thane (eds), *Maternity and Gender Policies: Women and the Rise of the European Welfare States 1880s–1950s*, London and New York.
Djikstra, B. (1986) *Idols of Perversity: Fantasies of Feminine Evil at the fin de siècle*, Oxford.
Edmondson, L. (1984) *Feminism in Russia 1900–1917*, London.
Gaffin, J. and Thoms, D. (1983) *Caring & Sharing: The Centenary History of the Co-operative Women's Guild*, Manchester.
Gordon, F. (1990) *The Integral Feminist: Madeleine Pelletier, 1874–1939, Feminism, Socialism and Medicine*, Cambridge.

Offen, K. (1987) 'The theory and practice of feminism in nineteenth-century Europe', in R. Bridenthal, C. Koonz and S. Stuard (eds) *Becoming Visible: Women in European History*, 2nd edn Boston.

Reagin, N. R. A. (1995) *German Women's Movement. Class and Gender in Hanover 1880–1933*, Chapel Hill.

Scott, J. W. (1996) *Only Paradoxes to Offer: French Feminists and the Rights of Man*, Cambridge, Mass.

Sowerwine, C. (1987) 'The socialist women's movement from 1850 to 1940', in R. Bridenthal, C. Koonz and S. Stuard (eds) *Becoming Visible: Women in European History*, 2nd edn Boston.

Stoehr, I. (1991) 'Housework and motherhood: debates and policies in the women's movement in Imperial and Weimar Germany', in G. Bock and P. Thane (eds) *Maternity and Gender Policies: Women and the Rise of the European Welfare States 1880–1950s*, London and New York.

City life

Bowlby, R. (1985) *Just Looking: Consumer Culture in Dreiser, Gissing and Zola*, New York.

Kern, S. (1983) *The Culture of Time and Space 1880–1918*, Harvard, Mass.

Miller, M. B (1981) *The Bon Marché: Bourgeois Culture and the Department Store, 1869–1920*, Princeton.

Nava, M. (1996) 'Women, the city and the department store', in A. O'Shea (ed.) *Modern Times: A Century of English Modernity*, London.

Williams, R. H. (1982) *Dream Worlds: Mass Consumption in Late Nineteenth Century France*, Berkeley.

Wilson, E. (1991) *The Sphinx in the City: Urban Life, the Control of Disorder, and Women*, Berkeley.

Wolff, J. (1989) 'The invisible *flâneuse*: woman and the literature of modernity', in A. Benjamin (ed.) *The Problems of Modernity*, London.

SIX

War and the New World Order

In this chapter we will explore the ways in which gender was at issue in different political and social contexts before, during and immediately after the First World War. The social and political circumstances in which the First World War broke out in 1914 are as much debated by historians as the different significance for men and women of the war, and of the post-war 'new world order'.

The close connection between imperialism and virility, and the emphasis on masculinity in the discourses of nationalism and work, were apparent throughout Europe in the late nineteenth and early twentieth centuries. The historian Robert Nye has argued that in France, 'the shock of military defeat, the fear of depopulation, and the corrosive effects of the gender revolution focused medical and scientific attention as never before on the bodies and masculine qualities of men' (Nye 1993: 97). The state of the nation was commonly assessed in terms of the masculinity of its male population. The popularisation of racial and evolutionary theories, and apprehension about national degeneration, also focused the attention of governments and of voluntary organisations on the biological and social roles of women – women as the reproducers of population, and of the cultural values on which political and national legitimacy rested. Fears of decline and degeneration were exacerbated by the growing awareness of homosexuality and by the demands of feminists and 'new women' for independence from family ties. Feminist agitation, particularly in the form of suffragette activism, was portrayed as threatening national strength and even racial survival. In *La Question de la Population* (1913) the French sociologist Paul Le Roy Beaulieu argued that as French women became more numerous in public posts, administration, medicine and law, they were becoming increasingly similar to men. Unlike the liberal John Stuart Mill who had argued half a century earlier that the increasing dissimilarity between men and women was the mark of an evolved society, Beaulieu maintained that the masculinisation of women was the greatest threat to modern civilisation. He assumed that women who became involved in paid employment rejected their reproductive role. Moreover, the more masculine women became, the less masculine and virile men could be.

These political, social and cultural anxieties were compounded by the international effects of the scramble for colonies, in particular the militarisation of Europe, and confrontations in Europe and the colonies, which involved the death of large numbers of soldiers and in some cases civilians. The major European powers, France, Germany, Britain, the Habsburg empire and Russia variously took part in these conflicts, including the Boer War (1899–1902), the Russo–Japanese war (1904–5) in which Japan trounced Russia, the Moroccan Crises (1906 and 1911), the colonial war between Italy and Libya (1911), and the battles provoked by the so-called 'Eastern Question' in the Balkans and Mediterranean. The many imperial conflicts, increased military spending by almost all European governments and improvements in the technology of killing, and the frequent insistence on the 'struggle for survival' as a law of political and social life in the years before the war, point to a growing belief in the inevitability and the benefits of war. In some intellectual and scientific circles, military conflict was presented as the source of social renewal and of the regeneration of the masculine virility of the nation or state. In this context, historians have argued that anxieties about masculinity, and the popularity of a militaristic form of masculinity, may have contributed to the prospect of war. Some of the new aesthetic movements which emerged over this period celebrated aggression and violence as masculine virtues. The Futurist manifesto, composed and launched in Paris by the Italian Marinetti in 1909, enjoined men to seek out violence and death in the battlefield and to show contempt for women, in order to prove their own masculinity and the virility of the nation (Marinetti 1909). Intellectuals cited Nietzsche and Darwin in order to argue for the qualities of conquest and the 'will to power' through war. Will was regarded as a masculine characteristic. The concept of a nation's will to power, like national virility, linked masculinity and men explicitly to the status of the nation.

These examples suggest that at the turn of the century the question of sexual difference and normative gender relations had a significant place in international and national concerns throughout Europe. Socialists, for example, were viewed as a menace to the stability and respectability of nations because of their perceived revolutionary threat to liberal and middle-class social and family values. Socialists were also most strongly identified with anti-militarism and internationalism in the pre-war period. Between 1908 and 1914 the mass-based German socialist party conducted an explicitly pacifist campaign. At the same time that many socialists identified with an iconography that idealised the figure of the masculine worker who radiated 'manly strength' (Mosse 1996: 123), the humane socialist presented himself as the antithesis of the militaristic warrior type. The pacifism and internationalism of socialists were commonly characterised as extensions of feminine or maternal virtues. Feminists were divided on these issues. By the end of the nineteenth century some feminists in Britain and on the continent sought the vote in order to expand the sway of pacifism and to make their opposition to war feature more prominently on the political stage. However, these groups were often in a minority, as many feminists endorsed national ambitions and supported war as a means of displaying their patriotism and, in some cases, of claiming citizenship.

The importance of gender, and indeed of a 'gender crisis', during the First World War is now widely accepted. Historians have long had an interest in the nature of women's experience of war, and especially in the range of new opportunities for work it offered. There is now a much stronger sense that gender conflict was intrinsic to the war experience and that there was a 'sex war' on the home front which paralleled the battle front. The extent of the 'sex war' continues to be disputed, but there is overwhelming evidence that conventional forms of femininity and masculinity were placed under threat during the war. The stagnation and emasculating effect of trench warfare called into question the idealisation of the heroic soldier figure and the aggressive forms of masculinity unleashed by the war. On the home front, male status in civilian contexts was being challenged. As women were called upon to take up civil and military duties for the war effort, questions were raised about acceptable forms of work for women, and of public participation in war and in civilian society. At the end of the war, the restoration of a post-war order required the renegotiation of the place of men and women in public and work contexts, a renewed emphasis on gendered separate spheres as the social norm, on women's maternal patriotism, and on the overlapping threat of gender and class revolution.

Militarism and masculinity, patriotism and citizenship

Historians such as Arno Mayer have highlighted the enthusiasm for war generated by European intellectual, scientific and middle-class élites in the years before the First World War. Perceptions about the naturalness of aggressive or physical masculinity were shared across political, class and national boundaries, and encouraged by predominant theories of biological and social evolution (see Chapters 4 and 5). John Hobson's famous study of *Imperialism* (1902) provides evidence of the influence of militarism at this time. Modern society and English imperialism were, in Hobson's view, responsible for a new militaristic type of male, which he believed threatened prospects for a peaceful society. The 'new way of life' began in the 'nursery', which had become a 'miniature scouting ground'. It was reinforced at school where boys participated in military exercises, were taught that history was the story of blood and iron, and read the poems and stories of Rudyard Kipling. In this way, Britain was being transformed from a nation of 'sportsmen' into one of hunters (Hobson 1902: 280). Conversely, Hobson argued that imperialism was also equated with sport because 'in its stronger or 'more adventurous' forms [it] involves a direct appeal to the lust of slaughter and the crude struggle for life involved in pursuit' (Hobson 1902: 225). In Hobson's view, militarism and jingoism had pervaded the lower classes of English society, and had negatively influenced English masculinity. The best of English manhood, which in his view was the skilled worker rather than the upper-class gentleman or officer, was being conscripted into colonial forces and transformed into a servile soldier. As a result, Hobson believed that English men were losing their individualism, the source of English strength and of the nation's entrepreneurial and democratic characteristics.

Looking at France in this period, Robert Nye argues that there, too, team games were considered a crucial training ground for civilian manliness and physical courage. English sporting models were imported into France by various organisations in the late nineteenth century (Nye 1993). The Catholic Women's organisation *Action Sociale des Femmes* (Catholic Social Action) approved of the creation of a Boy Scout movement, which would introduce young boys to the military values of loyalty, endurance and devotion, and offer them physical and intellectual training. The League of National Education was introduced into France in 1912 and modelled explicitly on the British Boy Scout movement. In the decades before the First World War in France, the ideals of heroism, of 'physical courage' and its equation with an essential masculinity, were also spread in religious teaching, school textbooks and public statuary. The predominance of the militaristic model in Europe was made obvious in a study published in 1913 of male students between the ages of 18 and 25 in France. The authors of *Les jeunes gens d'aujourd hui* (The young people of today), Henri Massis and

Alfred de Tarde, showed that the students preferred action to abstract thought. For them war was a source of national regeneration, a declaration of the spiritual over the material and over rationalism.

The popularity of duelling in most European nations at the turn of the twentieth century (excluding England, where duels had been legally abolished in 1844) assisted in the promotion of militarism as a fundamental expression of the masculine self, and as an important aspect of men's capacity and duty as citizens. In the Habsburg empire and Germany particularly, duelling was associated with the military code of the officer class or élite. As both states extended entry to the officer class from the upper-class to the middle-class male population, so these codes increased in importance. At the same time, military education that integrated ordinary soldiers into a national army disseminated not only reading and writing skills and personal hygiene, but the values and interests of the state and of military ideals of masculinity. In Germany there was other evidence of widespread support for military values. On the eve of the First World War, German Soldier associations had three million members, drawn mainly from the lower-middle-classes and working-classes (Stargardt 1994). However, the emergence of the *Bund* movement suggests the existence of a quite opposite trend. Some young men banded together in a new youth movement as a form of rebellion against the militarism and industrialism of their elders, and to revitalise German national identity. Youth *Bund* idealised the classical image of the male body and male company, in erotic as well as social ways (there were some female *bund* but these were a minority). They celebrated ancient origins and nature through the organisation of hiking groups such as the German Wandervogel, and had a crucial role to play in idealising the naturalness and racial origins of the German nation (Mosse 1996). Despite their initial anti-militarism, the *Bund*'s emphasis on a *Volkisch* or folk nationalism complemented the nationalist message of the more militaristic organisations.

To some extent the acceptance and even adulation of war was moderated by the growing (if marginal) support in some social and political circles for pacifism and internationalism. In the early twentieth century, pacifism was a popular basis for female participation in the public sphere. It was also associated with so-called feminine qualities, the desire to nurture and protect life. The most famous pacifist in this period was indeed a woman, a Prague-born Austrian named Baroness Bertha Von Suttner. In her most famous novel *Lay Down Your Arms*, Von Suttner dealt with the problem of the widespread female admiration for soldiers and military heroes. She argued that girls learned 'all the military and glorifying odes' and envisaged for themselves the role of 'the Spartan mothers of old, the women who present battle-flags and regimental colours, and are the admired and happy belles during the ball season, when they receive the attentions of the brass-buttoned officers' corps' (Suttner 1894: 7). By 1905 *Lay Down Your Arms* had been translated into more than a dozen languages and published in 37 editions. Its impact was far-reaching. It also contributed to the popular association of the cause of pacifism with women. As a result, pacifism was commonly charac-terised as excessively idealistic and impossible in the face of the 'hard' (masculine) facts of international politics. This was despite the fact that some pacifist and internationalist organisations were run by men. For example, the editor of the Milan-based Italian review *La Vita Internazionale*, which was sympathetic to socialism and to 'patriotic pacifism', was Teodor Moneta. Moneta was a good example of the limits of early twentieth-century notions of pacifism when they came into conflict with the cause of national virility. Moneta found no contradiction in espousing on the one hand socialist and internationalist ideals, and the other hand the justice of the Italian colonisa-tion of Libya in 1912 as an affirmation of Italy's national virility and national civilising duty.

Pacifism and internationalism did not preclude what was often termed patriotism. From 1900 to 1914 the espousal of liberal–feminist aims in Europe included a significant enthusiasm for patriotism. Feminists argued that despite 'maternal' pacifist inclinations that arose from the desire to protect their sons from war, women could be patriotic. In the French Third Republic, politicians supported the education of women in state institutions (rather than Catholic convents) in order to have them trained by fellow women to be patriot mothers who would educate their own children in the same republican principles of patriotism. In Britain, Queen Victoria was exemplary of the possibility that women could be patriotic, public and feminine; in Germany it was Queen Luise of Prussia, King Frederick William III's wife who, Roger Chickering says, 'had reportedly managed, without compromising her piety or femininity in any way, to help rally patriotic resistance to the French occupa-tion of her country' (Chickering 1988: 164). In the final two decades of the nineteenth century, the number of German women's patriotic organisations had almost doubled – from 400 in 1877 to nearly 800 in 1891 (Chickering 1988: 162). The key task of these organisations was preparation for war by training nurses, building hospitals, and public relief charity work. By the early twentieth century the majority of women expressed their patriotism in terms of preparation for war. The Catholic Church's canonisation of Joan of Arc in 1909 also reflected the depth of the appeal of a female version of direct militaristic sacrifice. Thus in the years immediately preceding the war, Catholic French women spoke of participation in war as a means of expressing their patriotism, and of defending France from the threat posed to national unity by socialism and class dissent. From 1907 English women could join the First Aid Nursing Yeomanry, which trained nurses to ride horses into the battlefield from their field hospitals. From 1910 women could participate in Voluntary Aid Detachments set up by the Army Medical Services and the British War Office to mobilise women who would be trained to aid the sick and wounded on the home front in case of war. Other voluntary organisations were established by individual women keen to prepare their sex for war.

Though women's military organisations were not widespread in England, for some women, they were intended to show that women could be patriotic, and that patriotism deserved some political recognition in the form of rights or votes (Gould 1987: 116). Female patriotism was used to signal the capacity of women to be active citizens, and to exercise other political and legal rights that accompanied citizenship. This trend in feminist politics has been noticed in other European states. For example, in Italy, the early issues of the Italian monthly review *L'unione femminile* (Feminist Union) first published in 1899, discussed education, work, divorce, prostitution, union organisation and parliamentary debates. Over the next decade, however, the review gave over more and more space to the call for voluntary mobilisation of women, and discussed the idea that women might achieve equality through their military contribution in wartime (Bigaran 1982).

The popularity of the image of the virtuous and patriotic mother, and its significance for feminist as well as anti-feminist politics, increased in direct relation to the tensions between European nations over territory and influence: in particular the 1911 Morocco crisis involving Germany and France, and the two Balkan Wars in 1912–13 involving the Habsburg empire and southeast European states. In 1912 the *Action Sociale des Femmes* was addressed by a visiting speaker from the Red Cross on the topic of 'Women and the War'. What is surprising about this talk is not only the urgency with which the possibility of war was discussed, but the comparisons made by the speaker between the French lack of preparation and the examples set by Japan, Russia and Britain, each of which could draw on the organised support of women in war. At this meeting, and in other European contexts, Florence Nightingale, the English heroine of the mid nineteenth-century

Crimean War, was consistently evoked as an emblem of the woman who embraced her duty on the battlefield by nursing the wounded. The historian Mary Poovey has argued that Nightingale was more concerned with enhancing her personal power than being dutiful, but there is little doubt that at the beginning of the twentieth century the legend of 'the lady with the lamp' permeated many women's organisations across the continent (Poovey 1989: 164). The image of Florence Nightingale, along with the popularity of the soldier-figure of Joan of Arc, illustrate the social significance attached to military participation as a duty of citizenship. They also belie the fact that citizenship was normatively regarded as a masculine prerogative. Women's exclusion from citizenship rights had conventionally been linked to their physical difference from men. Just as men's bodies equipped them to be both defenders of the realm, and invaders of other realms, women were commonly imagined as defenceless territory (Gatens 1996: 79). As we will see in the following section, it is no coincidence that during the First World War the participation of women in war raised concerns about gender norms, and became the conspicuous basis of feminist claims to equality and citizenship.

The sex war?

When war broke out in Europe in August 1914 between the members of two opposing alliances, numerous patriotic organisations rallied to the cause on both sides. Some historians have argued that the diplomatic flurries of the years preceding 1914 prove the extent to which European governments were concerned to avoid war. In this context the prevalent cultural emphasis on militarism, the high esteem awarded to military men, may have been decisive in the descent into war.

George Mosse suggests that 'the quest for masculinity' cut across all the different motivations for going to war (Mosse 1985: 115). This claim had different nuances for the men setting off for battle, the women preparing to 'man' the home front, and the governments of states seeking validation for their involvement in war. Masculinity was not only an attribute to be claimed by men (and women) for reasons of personal stature, but a means of advocating and legitimating decisions at a national level. The French volunteer Ernest Psichari wrote to his mother in August 1914, two days before he died, that war 'was necessary for the honour and greatness of France' (Cross 1988: 226). Debates in Italy during 1914 and 1915 on whether to enter the war (and on which side) drew attention to Italy's effeminate reputation in Europe, and the need for Italians to prove their masculinity. Italy's European image as a culture which was good only for sightseeing and gelati, an effeminate lesser power, rankled the patriotic Italian intelligentsia, spurring among them, according to the historian Richard Bosworth, a broad acceptance of imperialist foreign policy and war (Bosworth 1991: 53).

The quest for affirmation of the nation's masculinity was matched by the desire of individual men for affirmation of their own masculinity. Many writers have also commented on the way the war was welcomed by men of all classes. Believing it would only last a short time, some men imagined war as a heroic escapade, and saw in its challenges a means of personal fulfilment, and of proving their personal virility. Michael Adams offers the examples of middle-class figures like Rupert Brooke and his Cambridge contemporaries. Brooke's view that the outbreak of war would give his life heroic direction was echoed in the pronouncements of his peers that manly chivalry was only to be found in the trenches, and that war offered escape from the 'the quiet humdrum of home life with all its dull humanising but often vulgar influences' (Adams 1990: 79). Similarly, the war was supposed to consummate the bond between men, and between men and their country. Brooke's popular English war poetry, like the German novel *A Wanderer Between Two Worlds* by Walter Flex, published posthumously in 1917, gave homoerotic form to the war experience (Cross 1988: 115). In 1917 two French doctors, Louis Huot and Paul Voivenel, published a study of military courage in wartime in which they concluded that 'one love's one's country as one loves a woman, and fights for it as one would fight for a woman. It is a point of sexuality to love's one country' (Nye 1993: 227).

It was not only men who looked forward to war, as the young English girl Vera Brittain wrote in her diary after 1914. With her fiancé and brother at the front she desperately felt the limitations imposed by her femaleness, complaining that their confinement to the English 'Homefront' had made her feel impotent. She wished that she were a man who could train herself 'to play that "Great game with Death" ':

> But whether it is noble or barbarous I am quite sure that had I been a boy I should have gone off to take part in it long ago; indeed i have wasted many moments regretting that I am a girl. Women get all the dreariness of war and none of its exhilaration.
>
> (cited in Layton 1987: 73)

When war was announced, the majority of socialist and feminist organisations relinquished their commitments to internationalism and pacifism in order to support their particular country. While individual men and women may have made their decision desiring adventure and heroism, most often their choice was validated in the name of national patriotism. In an anti-interventionist feminist journal like *L'unita italiana* (1914–19) the liberation of the Trieste and Trento regions under Habsburg rule, believed by Italian nationalists to 'belong' to Italy, was regarded as a valid basis for women's patriotic support of the war. Similarly, French and British feminists gave up their suffrage campaigns to support national aims and needs. Marguerite Durand, the editor of the liberal feminist journal *La Fronde*, which had ceased publication in 1903, brought out special issues of the journal in August and September 1914 in order to enjoin French women to temporarily abandon their demand for rights and carry out their wartime social duties (Thebaud 1986). Many feminists encouraged women to participate fully in the war effort. The mobilisation of women, wrote Gertrude Bauer, the President of the Federation of German Women, was vital to 'becoming a people' (Frevert 1989: 151). In 1914, the Federation of German Women had 3,300 members in approximately 600 branches. Its executive proposed that a National Women's Service should be mobilised on the basis of compulsory contributions to deal with the wartime welfare needs of society. Privileged women would assist families whose breadwinners were fighting at the front, while the unemployed would take over social welfare functions from the state (Sachsse 1986: 163). In a 1915 address to the Congress of the Union of German Women Teachers, Baumer's good friend Helene Lange expounded on the ways that women could contribute to the war effort:

> The national service of men reaches its ultimate destiny only in times of war, while the national service of women is essentially destined for constant duties throughout times of peace. The efforts of women in war are basically the same as their efforts in peace.
>
> (Lange 1915 in Bell and Offen 1983: 262)

Patriots argued that even women with limited education could participate by undertaking courses in household management and stressed the national economic responsibilities of housewives. In the view of Lange and the Federation of German Women, 'woman's' contribution to the war would be an extension of the 'social' role attributed to women in the nineteenth century.

When the massive casualties began to occur, and advances on all sides stagnated in trench warfare, the experiences of war began to undermine rather than reaffirm the virility of individual soldiers and of participating nations. In 1918, the French writer Henri Barbusse exposed the ugly realities of trench warfare in his novel *Le Feu* (*Under Fire*), and argued that those realities had turned so-called soldier warriors into mere mortal men. The incongruities between the expectations of glory, the reality of static and degrading trench life, and the powerlessness of soldiers, were difficult for many men to sustain. The resort by governments to conscription to maintain recruitment levels similarly undermined the ideal of patriotic male citizenship. Military institutions and medical practitioners stigmatised disillusion with and rejection of the war as a form of national treachery, and as an expression of effeminacy. A new medical term, 'shell-shock', was invented to deal with this reaction. Elaine Showalter argues that for soldiers 'shell-shock' was a psychological condition: 'the body language of masculine complaint, a disguised male protest, not only against the war, but against the concept of manliness itself' (Showalter 1987: 64). By contrast, doctors and military authorities used 'shell-shock' as a way of explaining away soldierly apathy or disillusion with the war. Although little was known about the condition, 'shell-shock' was medically defined as a form of 'male hysteria' – despite the fact that hysteria had until then predominantly been portrayed as a female illness. After the English poet Siegfried Sassoon published a pacifist denunciation of war ('A Soldier's Declaration'), he was diagnosed as having shell-shock, or a war neurosis. Sassoon's doctor, W. H. Rivers (an early exponent of psychoanalysis in Britain) argued that his pacifism was a psychological condition brought on by physical distress (Showalter 1987). The cure was to assist the patient in regaining his active masculine qualities. The treatment for male hysterics was activity and occupation, the opposite of the recommended cure for female hysteria (associated with an excess of masculinity), which was the restoration of normative feminine qualities through extended periods of rest.

While men's initial enthusiasm waned, women continued their energetic support for the war effort with the increasing endorsement of national governments. In reporting on her visit to the 'War Capitals' to the International Congress of Women held at the Hague in 1915, the American peace activist and feminist Alice Hamilton remarked on the uniformity of women's involvement in the war throughout Europe. In Brussels, Berlin, Paris and London, women were active in social welfare tending to the poor and displaced (Addams, Batch and Hamilton 1972), a public role that had long been acceptable for women. By 1916, with the war bogged down in the trenches, and the casualty lists growing at a rapid rate, governments began to adopt more intensive strategies for dealing with a long-term war that included the mobilisation of women. In England women entered occupations previously limited to men, such as engineering and transport, and on the production line in munitions factories. The Ministry for Munitions even found a place for middle-class women as supervisors of women workers in munitions. Supervisors were expected to help avert strikes at the factories, and to organise clubs and hobbies to provide social activities for young girls who would otherwise loiter around soldiers' camps. Single women were recruited into the civilian workforce and were able to take up special positions in the organisations that had been established before the war, such as the Voluntary Aid Detachments, First Aid Nursing Yeomanry, and new units such as the Women's Convoy Corps and the Women's Legion. These organisations were established to assist men on the front line, not to create female fighters (Gould 1987: 118). Women also donned uniforms as the inspectors of common lodging houses, music halls, cinemas, dancing halls and police courts. Khaki became a favoured uniform for women in military-style organisations as well as in civilian contexts (Wollacott 1994: 331).

Women had worked in the armaments industry in Germany since 1915, but it was only in the winter of 1916/17 that the German military attempted a new level of integration of the women's movement into the military administrative apparatus of the Reich. Women were mobilised for 'Service of Help to the Fatherland'. By then organisations such as the Federation of German Women had separately mobilised around 1,000 women to under-take war welfare work. The government's official mobilisation programme aimed to further remove all obstacles to women working in other less conventional areas. The result was the overall relocation of women's work in Germany from textiles and clothing to the steel and chemical industries, and to transport and communications.

In France during the course of the war, 8 million men were mobilised, half of them at the front in combat units. Not only was there a social vacuum for women to fill, but women now comprised the majority of breadwinners. Françoise Thebaud argues that the replacement of men with women was less rapid and less systematic in France than in England and Germany because there was no co-ordinated organisation of women's contributions (Thebaud 1986: 31). The mobilisation of nurses, peasant women and small business women who took over their husbands' tasks was immediate, but it was only later that larger businesses, banks and transport services resorted to women. By 1918 the number of women employed in the state railways rose from 6,000 before the war to 57,000; before the war 124 women worked for the Paris metro, 3,037 at its end. The French Ministry of Posts more than doubled its population of working women (to nearly 40,000), and the

Ministry of Education increased the number of its female employees by nearly 50 per cent. Before the war women were mainly employed in primary education, during the war they were also placed in the secondary education sector. The French munitions industry had 684,000 women working in its factories in 1917, whereas two years prior, only 15,000 women had worked there (Hause 1987: 104). At the same time, the war also meant significant unemployment for women who had worked in the textiles and garment trades.

The new kinds of work for women were not always accompanied with changed attitudes to the worth of women's work. In England particularly, working-class women had long provided labour in factories; what the war had changed for them was the kind of factory in which they worked. The new munitions work was dangerous rather than glamorous, and the excessively long days and poor conditions often resulted in accidents and fatalities. In France, women often worked for 12- to 14-hour days, with two days off a month. The abrogation of legislation limiting the hours and conditions of women's work allowed for immense exploitation. While canteens and nursing rooms were provided in factories, amenities for workers were limited. Private industries also tried to maximise their profits by taking advantage of their control over an unregulated labour reserve, which they could employ in home work as well as in the factories. Although in the early stages of the war women received higher pay than they had before the war, in both England and France this pay was soon eroded by rises in the cost of living. In Germany, a member of the National Liberal party complained of the difficulties experienced by women taking up new professional posts previously occupied by men. These women demurred they were made to feel like intruders and usurpers (Trott cited in Bell and Offen 1983: 278). The fact that women received only half of the wages previously paid to their male counterparts underlined the fact that their 'advance' was temporary and fragile.

The moment women were called upon officially to participate in the war effort, some women began to discuss what this might mean for women's future, and for gender relations. According to Marie Bernays, of the Federation of German Women, the war had made women feel like 'citizens with obligations towards the general public' (Bernays cited in Frevert 1989: 152). In England the feminist Helena Swanwick noted the change of heart with suspicion and irony:

It has been dinned into the ears of women for ages past that 'a woman's place is the home', and that her first duty is a private and individual one. Now suddenly, women are told that they must come out of the home and that their country has first claim upon them, as upon men. Appeal is made even to mothers with husbands at the front to leave their children and go out to work.

(Swanwick 1916: 11)

A view existed that the war would irrevocably affect the gender of some forms of employment. One Italian woman argued that 'distribution of tickets in a tram, the registration of correspondence, money, and goods behind a counter, scribbling in offices, measuring out ribbons, weighing spices in a shop, would no longer seem worthy of masculinity' (Paola n.d.: 287). In May 1916, the French paper *Le Petit Echo de la Monde* (*The Little Echo of the World*) stated that:

The longer the war lasts ... the more this situation develops which forces women to take on men's roles ... What could be less astonishing than to find their bearing and language changed: they adopt a resolute, independent air because they have the responsibility and also the freedom of being in charge.

(Horne 1993: 125)

In a report on 'Women of the War' published in 1917, the former Prime Minister and leader of the British Liberal party, Henry Asquith, described women as having done and doing things 'which, before the war, most of us would have said were both foreign to their nature and beyond their physical capacity' (MacLaren 1917: vi). Asquith also predicted that 'these experiences and achievements will, when the war is over, have a permanent effect upon both the statesman's and the economist's conception of the powers and functions of women in the reconstructed world'.

The post-war status of women in Europe suggests that there was no inevitable link between women's participation in the war effort and acceptable images of femininity, and that the reasons why the war did not 'permanently affect' conceptions of women may lie in the predominant wartime validations for women's participation in the war effort. When Italy joined the war on the side of England and France in 1915, government discussions of the role of women were carefully balanced between an explicit emphasis on women's maternal responsibilities and their patriotic wartime duties. Women, it was stressed, were *temporarily* taking on male tasks to help the men out in their real work at the front. Following the example of other nations, Italian women could nurse with the Red Cross under the jurisdiction of the War Ministry. They could also assume responsibility for convalescing soldiers and the families of soldiers, or looking after the children of mothers forced to work. That work could include mining and farmwork, or involve service industries in the cities. Yet women's organisations as well as government organs made clear that woman's place was in the home, even if that 'home' was now more broadly defined as the nation (Barbera 1916). Italian women answered to 'country' rather than to husband, and shared an equal subservience as well as responsibility to the nation. Those women who could not work could exert their maternal influence at home, and they could sacrifice their sons for the national cause.

In England, the similarities in the employment and the public participation of women in the warring states did not detract from the masculine prerogatives associated with the war. John Horne claims that '[T]he supremacy of the soldier defined the officially-endorsed hierarchy of wartime social morality. Not only some women ... but the entire homefront was morally subordinated to the male authority embodied in the warrior' (Horne 1993: 122–3). The suffering and sacrifice of men in the trenches were often juxtaposed to the comforts of women on the home front. The trenches were the world of masculinity; the home front, although not the exclusive domain of women, was an effeminate world that many believed was increasingly controlled by women. The war had decimated countless male lives in the most inglorious of trench conditions, and had brought about radical changes in the appearance of the home front, most obvious in the public predominance of women. Disillusion with the war spurred anti-war feelings among men, which were sometimes vented against women on the home front. The anti-war poetry of the lesser-known French writer Marc de Larreguy Civrieux depicted the consequences of war, death and revolution, as feminine, its victims as masculine (Cross 1988). Women's wartime contribution only intensified the estrangement between men and women. According to Vera Brittain, the war had placed a 'barrier of indescribable experience ... between men and the women whom they loved' (Brittain cited in Gilbert 1987: 200). Patriotic women urged the participation of women in the public sphere to keep civilian society functioning for their absent husbands, fathers and brothers. But many women revelled in their new duties and experiences, and men felt their public presence as an unambiguous form of betrayal. The Schoolmasters Association in England, for example, rebelled against the increasing influence of women in their profession (Bourke 1996: 193). These schoolmasters saw the war as the moment in which the leadership and supervisory functions usually assumed by males had been expropriated by women. They also believed that the expanded employment of women in the teaching profession would have an exaggerated and damaging feminine influence on the upbringing of Britain's young men.

The wartime empowerment of women was signalled less by the opportunities that individual women had for unleashing their sexual energy, than by the changed gender definitions of certain jobs. The aristocratic writer Vita Sackville-West, for example, not only delighted in dressing in her Women's Land Army outfit, but after eloping to Paris with her female lover Violet Trefusis, assumed the name Julian and the guise of a wounded soldier (Gilbert 1987: 218). Sandra Gilbert has used this example to argue that female eroticism was 'energised by the war' not as the complement of male homoeroticism, but as its usurper (Gilbert 1987: 219). But the image of usurpation may have been more powerful than its reality. At a time when the least sign of women's sexual indulgence was regarded as a form of depravity which threatened national survival, the extent to which most women – particularly those who lacked the financial independence and security of class granted Sackville-West – could flaunt the conventions of sexuality is questionable. Women may have gained new experiences from the circumstances of the war, but as the historian Susan Kent reminds us, during the First World War in England, women were depicted as the terrain of war in representations that decried the rape of Belgium and France; women were the objects of war in propaganda and recruiting posters; women were the victims of war in reports of German atrocities; they were the parasitic beneficiaries of war in *Punch* cartoons or irate letters to newspaper columns; they were the wagers of war in tributes to women's wartime service, particularly that of munitions workers; women were even the cause of the war in some accounts of pre-war suffrage militancy (Kent 1993). The empowerment either of individuals or of gender groups cannot be considered in isolation from the very real legal restraints which delimited the social and political activity of men and women, or the demoralising spectre of death which intruded on their daily lives for four years. The wartime introduction of laws such as the English Defence of the Realm Act, which gave the state absolute powers, affected both men and women critical of the government. Similar laws throughout Europe were used to stifle feminist pacifists, and to hinder their movement. In 1915, for example, when feminist pacifists from across Europe and North America tried to attend the founding meeting of the Women's International League for Peace and Freedom, many of them found their passage to the congress at the Hague blocked or sabotaged. In this context, Claire Tylee has also questioned the extent to which women were practically empowered by the wartime conditions:

. Prevented by votelessness and the government's ruthless use of the Defence of the Realm Act from exercising the one power which really counted, the power to influence the course of the war, were any women tricked by brief bribes into believing themselves suddenly publicly powerful enough to 'man the machine of state'?

(Tylee 1990: 206)

Men and women were victims of a war in which they lost their lives, their livelihoods and their illusions of European civilisation. Men who did not want to participate in the war encountered practical obstacles, such as disenfranchisement and rejection by the labour market, and found themselves attacked for their lack of patriotism and masculinity (Bourke 1996: 77–8). Women who protested against economic hardships, like the men who strayed from the institutional control of the military without returning to the hearth, loomed large on the political landscape as a very real and awesome threat to the existing social order. The question of what they may have gained, as men or as women, is, however, more complicated, because of the ways in which the sense of loss experienced by men during the war and after was often projected onto women (Theweleit 1987), and the extent to which women themselves felt guilty about benefiting from the war at the expense of men. As Joanna Bourke argues, '[a]lthough historians are divided about the extent to which the war led to any change in the status of women, it is clear that most people in the 1920s *believed* that the war had dramatically altered the relationship between the sexes' (Bourke 1996: 193).

The new world order: reconstruction, revolution, counter-revolution?

The war is sometimes regarded as a watershed between the remnants of *ancien* Europe with its aristocratic privilege, and a new modern Europe whose personality was split between its liberal democracies, and its fascist and communist totalitarian regimes. Some historians argue that the war brought about the overturn of traditional values and their replacement with the new amoral mass politics of communist and fascist versions of totalitarianism. Historians have also used a class analysis to argue that the post-war period was marked by the promise of revolution and the processes of counter-revolution. In this view the war brought about the ultimate triumph of the values of the old Europe, the extension of which were the inter-war authoritarian right-wing regimes of Italy, Germany, Spain and central Europe. It is only very recently that historians have begun examining the importance of gender in their more general assessments of the war, and its impact on the post-war period, on whether the post-war period brought

revolution or counter-revolution (Hause 1987: 103). The changes and con-
tinuities in gender representations during the war and after, and the changing
ways in which an individual's life-chances were influenced by his or her
gender, have warranted particular examination. The 'reconstruction of
gender' is now viewed by historians as the 'necessary corollary' of post-war
political and economic restructuring (Kent 1993: 3). Just as gender norms
framed images and discussions of the war, in the post-war period gender
relations and identities were affected by social upheaval and attempts by the
victor governments (Britain and the United States and to a lesser extent
France) to establish a liberal-democratic 'new Europe'. Contemporaries
employed gender conventions to signal the acceptable limits of revolutionary
or radical political change, and gender identities were at issue in the national
and international formulations of post-war reconstruction.

The success of the Bolshevik revolution in Russia in autumn 1917, four
years into the war, had highlighted for European governments the threat
posed to their national and political *status quo* by the discontent in their own
states. The revolution in Russia inspired foment among political and social
radicals throughout Europe and was followed by worker strikes in the
warring states, and troop mutinies in the French, British, Italian, German
and Austrian armies. Many radicals and conservatives believed that the
communist-inspired Bolshevik revolution had made real the possibility that
war might be followed in the rest of Europe by class and even gender
revolution.

As we saw in Chapters 3 and 4, socialist criticism of capitalism and of the
social relations and conventions that supported property ownership, had
long included a criticism of marriage and family as bourgeois institutions.
The communists Marx and Engels, like their political forebears the Utopian
Socialists, had all singled out in their social planning a reassessment of the
gender relations reinforced by existing social norms (regarding the family
and marriage in particular), and the legal forms of submission imposed on
women in accordance with those norms. Following in this tradition, and
under the influence of feminists like Alexandra Kollontai, the Bolshevik
government in Russia had introduced a new code of marriage and decrim-
inalised abortion and homosexuality. Leon Trotsky (who soon after the
revolution found himself in disfavour) went so far as to describe the Bolshevik ideal of new communist man as 'strong, wise, and subtle; his body
would become more harmonious, his movements more rhythmic, his voice
more musical' (Mosse 1996: 127). In Europe, reformist socialists – that is
socialists who were willing to participate in parliamentary systems in order

to bring about change, rather than resort to revolution like communists – discussed alternatives to the dominant modes of masculinity associated with the individualism of bourgeois capitalism and with the aggression of right-wing groups. Their reassessment of masculinity included support for the political redefinition of femininity. In post-war Austria, the ruling socialists accepted the 'new woman' with her short masculine hair; in Italy Filippo Turati, the leader of the Italian socialists and partner of the feminist Anna Kuliscioff, supported female suffrage as an extension of the Enlightenment ideal of self-determination, which he saw as integral to socialism. Nonetheless, for all the support socialists offered the 'emancipated woman', it was unusual to find women in the leadership ranks of the socialist parties after the war. Despite the perceived, and to some extent legalised different status of gender identities and relations in communist, socialist and liberal states, in practice conventional conceptions of sexual difference still operated as the foundation of state authority, and of national identification, even in Bolshevik Russia. Many communists, including the leader of the Bolshevik government, Lenin, distrusted sexual permissiveness and disliked the overly emancipated woman. As George Mosse points out, 'for all the difference in emphasis between the Bolshevik man and bourgeois manliness, masculinity was used by both as the predominant symbol of strength, of work, and of the dynamic that must inform modern society' (Mosse 1996: 130).

Gender and class overlapped in different ways in general perceptions of the prospect of revolution, and of the political and social upheaval that the war had generated. In England, John Hobson argued that the general climate of anarchy in the final exhausted phase of the war was permeated by 'sex consciousness':

> The rapid ferment of thought and feeling on the status of woman and sex problems during recent years has been at once an index and a source of revolutionary energy directed to the very foundations of society. Coincident with the new and startling ebullitions of revolt in the world of labour, this new sex consciousness has transformed the whole nature of social discontent, and helped to turn it into broader channels. The shattering experiences of war will have broken the taboos and sanctities which warded off close scrutiny into the basic institutions of State, Property, and Industry, the Family, Religion and Morals.
>
> (Hobson 1917: 160)

Just as gender was an important ingredient in socialist and communist ideals of reform and revolution, among political moderates and conservatives in the victorious nations, concern about reconstruction, about satisfying the interests of returned soldiers, and about rebuilding national populations for

defence and labour, included a familiar gender and class order. The governments of Britain, France and Italy responded to the success of the Russian
revolution and the epidemic of strikes and mutinies in factories and armies
with the promise of greater democratisation, economic assistance for workers and a more inclusive society. But in the post-war period, the differing
needs of returned soldiers, national political agendas and working women
were difficult to balance. As steps were taken to avert class revolution, the
demands of women were often rejected because they were regarded as
symptomatic of the threat of disorder, and in conflict with meeting the
demands of men, and the needs of the nation.

In post-war England it was official government policy to deter women
from participation in the workplace. At the end of the war the women who
had taken on prominent roles in civilian society during the war, were forced
to retreat. Women were made to feel guilty if they refused to accept their
natural roles as wives and mothers, and women who persisted in taking up a
man's place were made the targets of hatred and intimidation. As Gail
Braybon has shown, the media contributed to the redefinition of the role of
women (Braybon 1981). Thousands of women lost their positions in metal
and chemical industries, in construction and engineering, in the civil service,
and transport, and even in waitressing. Women were still visible in the
workplace, but their participation rates declined and they were found mainly
in lower-level and service sector jobs. In Germany, the government issued
regulations calling for women to be dismissed before men if necessary. In
France too, women were offered bonuses to leave their jobs. Thus, although
during the war French women had worked in munitions factories, or served
as mayors or on councils, by the mid 1920s French women made up a smaller
percentage of the national labour force than they had in 1911 (Hause
1987).

The requirements of reconstruction, and the desire to restore political and
social order, led some European governments to deny women the vote – even
though many women had already been granted some form of suffrage in
former European colonies. In most European countries, support for the vote
for women was commonly justified as a form of reward for women's wartime
work, rather than as an inherent right to direct political representation.
However, even this argument was not very successful. In Britain, as some
historians have commented, the women who had performed patriotically in
the munitions factories were mainly under 30 years of age, and the vote was
extended in the first instance only to women over the age of 30, until 1928
when universal suffrage was finally applied. The 1919 Belgian constitution

extended suffrage only to the widows of soldiers who had died in the war before the first of January 1919 and who had not remarried, the widowed mothers of such soldiers, or women whose patriotism had led to their incarceration by the enemy. These conditions implied that it was only the association of Belgian women with dead soldiers, or their physical suffering, which earned them the right of political participation. In Italy, a range of commentators emphasised that the war had finally brought to life the latent Italian national spirit, and most importantly proven that women too could be reliable and enthusiastic patriots at the service of the nation – but these kinds of observations did not eventuate the vote (much demanded by Italian bourgeois feminists) for Italian women. Neither did the French government give women the vote, despite the expectation on the eve of the war that the majority of male parliamentarians had accepted female suffrage in principle. In France, fears of demographic depletion had been revived by the decimation of male populations and by the demands for women's self-determination. The French republican government reacted not by granting women more rights, but by instituting mothers' day as symbolic of their support for motherhood. This celebration of motherhood testified to the specific maternal contribution of women to the nation; women, the French government claimed, 'contributed the most to maintaining through their descendants, the genius and civilisation, the influence and radiance of France' (Letter from the Minister of Hygiene Jules-Louis Breton, 'The French Decree Establishing Medals for Mothers', Journal Officiel de la republique Francaise, 28 May 1920, cited in Bell and Offen, 1983: 308). The state dispensation of medals for motherhood, later emulated in both Weimar and Nazi Germany and Fascist Italy. Further in 1920, the French government passed a law which made the promotion of abortion or dissemination of advice about abortion (let alone the act) a crime.

The expectations of feminists who had sought equality and recognition as national citizens through wartime work were not entirely disappointed. After the war, European women gained the vote in Holland, Sweden, Russia, Latvia, Lithuania and Estonia, in the defeated and territorially depleted Austria and Germany, and in the new Czechoslovak state. In the new republic of Austria that had been created out of the defeated Habsburg empire and the decimation of vast numbers of the male population, the war had brought the 'fatherless society' in more ways than one. 'Emancipated women' had the support of the socialist-dominated National Assembly, where women could vote and stand for office, in gratitude for their war work. In December 1918, twelve women took up positions on the Vienna City council, and about three months later women occupied ten seats in the Provincial National Assembly (in comparison with 170 men). In 1920, the Social Democrat Adelheid Popp gained national office on behalf of her party. As of that year, Austrian women had the right to full legal equality, to enter professions, and to a secondary education. The new liberal-democratic states of Czechoslovakia and 'Weimar' Germany wrote women's legal and political equality with men into their new constitutions. However, these constitutions explicitly compromised political gender equality by obligating state and local authorities to 'perfect, purify and promote family life', and to protect motherhood.

Despite their varying attitudes to women's suffrage, what post-war European governments shared was a disinclination to recognise women's equal right to work, and a persistent interest in validating the image of women as reproducers of the nation rather than as sex-neutral citizens. The political position of women in the post-war period was further compromised by the new significance attached to nationality (rather than just the vote) as definitive of citizenship. The privilege of nationality was denied to women as an intrinsic right. Most nation-states had laws which forced women who married 'foreigners' to renege their nationality and assume that of their husbands. Only in France, where the government was pressured by demographic fears to allow French women married to foreigners (by necessity) to retain their French nationality – so that their children could also be counted as French – was the privilege of nationality unqualifiedly granted to married women.

In the immediate post-war period gender roles and relations were shaped not only by national governments reconstructing their societies and economies, but by new international bodies, which emerged in response to liberal-democratic calls for the application of 'universal' ideals of democracy. These new bodies included the League of Nations and the International Labour Organisation (ILO). The ILO encouraged discussion among national governments of international standards for the maximum working week, the prevention of unemployment, a living wage, protection against sickness, provisions for old age and injury, and protection of children, young people and women. In 1919, the ILO organised an international conference in Washington which was successful in having European governments accept the general principle of equal pay for equal value work (a notoriously ambiguous equation). Yet, the extent to which the ILO acted as the harbinger of change in the conception of women workers and their rights is contestable, since discussions about women workers were limited primarily to the question of maternity benefits, women's employment before and after childbirth and at night in unhealthy conditions. These concerns echoed those of the congresses on protective legislation convened by the avidly industrialising European nations in the late nineteenth century out of concern for national health and demography.

The League of Nations with its headquarters in Geneva was much more a vehicle for the specific interests of women's organisations in Europe. Having promoted the idea of national self-determination, and the creation of an international form of government, alongside the demand for female suffrage during the war, members of the International Women's League for Peace and Freedom regarded the League as their particular cause. Women's organisations also turned to the League of Nations for representation in the international arena on the basis that since women were commonly denied the intrinsic right to forms of citizenship such as suffrage and nationality, they had no 'fatherland'. Where men had governments to represent them on particular issues, bourgeois women's groups looked to the League to provide them with representation and a forum for discussion of a range of social questions. They also believed that under the guidance of the League of Nations the new world order would invest women throughout Europe with more authority. The League of Nations supported the principle of equal employment, the League itself employed women in its bureaucracy (usually as secretarial staff), and women were the subject of special League conferences. Throughout 1919 and 1920 there was even intense discussion about whether or not a separate organisation for women should be set up within the League, and whether there was any need to appoint a woman within the secretariat (neither of these recommendations were pursued). The League of Nations bureaucracy became the key advocate of many of the rights demanded by middle-class European women's organisations, including the right to nationality. Such was the optimism regarding the space that the League of Nations had created for the participation of women in international affairs, that in 1920 the journalist Constance Drexel wrote that 'there is now no further doubt that women have been given the right of creating a leading part in the new world organisation. What will they do with it?' The partial answer to this question is that feminists exploited the existence of the League of Nations to promote married women's nationality rights (the League's male executive refused to be involved in what it regarded as the more delicate problem of women's suffrage), and to raise international awareness of 'the white slave trade' and the 'problem' of miscegenation in the new colonial mandates that the peace process had shared out among the victorious nations.

As with the erratic introduction of women's suffrage in Europe, the new internationalism seemed to have little effect on the more fundamental forms of gender identification that were possible in the post-war period. Patriotism, like work, women discovered, did not guarantee their legal and political citizenship. When bourgeois women's movements sacrificed their campaigns for rights to the national good they had only bolstered the association of woman with nation through her 'social' (rather than any political or individual) role. In Germany, France, England and Italy, various bourgeois women's movements had reasserted women's identification with social work and with charity organisations as one of the most important bases for their national wartime contribution. Across Europe women's contribution to the national good during the war, and in its aftermath, merely extended the more familiar role of woman as social pacifier, as emblematic of the nationally defined social good itself. Alternatively, for those Europeans who sought explanations of national failure and the post-war social disorder, women, feminised Jews and communists (categories that were not mutually exclusive) provided convenient general scapegoats. Connections between the figure of the emancipated woman and the racial other, in particular the 'Jew', and their combined threat to bourgeois and national respectability and virility continued to be manipulated by governments and political groups for their own purposes. In most of Europe, the 'new woman' was regarded as the explicit antagonist (and emasculator) of the male war hero, and of patriarchal authority. This image of the 'new woman' could conflate both the androgynous and sexually liberated 'flapper', and those women who had dutifully taken responsibility for the home front. Demoralised and worn out, returning soldiers perceived the new public roles of women as a further threat to their civilian and domestic status as men. In Erich Maria Remarque's post-war fictional autobiography, *All Quiet on the Western Front* the German hero is alienated from both the trenches and the society to which he returns. The male bourgeoisie felt threatened by working women in particular, even though the death and severe injury of so many men meant that large numbers of women still had to work in order to survive. Joanna Bourke argues that most older British soldiers and working-class men were eager to return to domestic life, preferring to forget the war, and to resume their previous lives within the hearth of the family (Bourke 1996: 22, 24). Their desire to resume a normal life included a preference for a pre-war gender order. When in 1919 returning soldiers rioted in England, the fear of sexual attacks on women was rife. Newspaper columnists suggested 'that social peace and order would depend upon minimising the provocations of men to anger', that is by restoring women to their 'traditional' social roles and status (Kent 1993: 98–9).

At the same time, the war, it has been argued, set a pattern for new forms of masculine activity which continued into the 1920s and 1930s. In 1915 the American peace activist and feminist Jane Addams insisted that on pre-war visits to England she had noticed that the younger maturing generation of men were being influenced by a new type of masculinity and were, as a result, 'more inclined to be more practically internationalist in their world outlook' (Addams 1972). Historians such as Klaus Theweleit have focused on the way that wartime experiences had brutalised men and encouraged nationalism, and a fundamental misogyny (Theweleit 1987). They have shown how in Germany and Italy, disaffected soldiers refused to exchange their comradely military existence for domestic life and transformed themselves into merce- naries and hit squads – such as the *Freikorps* in Germany and the Fascist *arditi* and *squadristi* in Italy. These paramilitary or militia troops drew their inspirations from their war experiences and offered their services to those political forces that expounded the values of militarism and nation. Accord- ing to Mosse, when the Fascist party took power in Italy within a few years of the war on the back of these hit squads, it elevated masculinity to new heights: 'the hopes placed upon it, the importance of manliness as a national symbol and as a living example played a vital role in all fascist regimes' (Mosse 1996: 155). The nationalist orientation of Italian Fascism also attracted some women to its ranks as activists as early as 1919. Some of these early adherents (older women, teachers, mainly from working- and lower-middle-class back- grounds) still believed that their application to the national cause would earn them political equality with men. The earliest Fascist movement in Milan even included the vote for women without restriction – however, this right was eradicated as Fascism expanded. At the same time, the Fascist cultivation of masculinity meant that even its female supporters accepted that they had a marginal place in the cause. In 1924, Ines Donati, a famous female *squadrista*, wrote on her deathbed, 'I wanted to be too virile and I forgot that I was, ultimately, a damned woman' (Detragiache 1983).

'Reconstruction' in Europe included the renegotiation of the place of men and women in public and work contexts, and a renewed emphasis on gendered separate spheres as the social norm, on women's maternal patriot- ism, and on the overlapping threat of gender and class revolution. The war had brought about change, but that change was worked out according to existing vocabularies and conceptions of gender and gender relations, and often in nostalgia for the pre-war world. Despite the variations in the political situation of women in Europe after the war, and the liberating influence of cultural modernism, the propensity of liberal and totalitarian governments to focus on women and gender relations as symbols of revolution and anarchy, and of reconstruction and order, illustrates that even where women were given the vote, conventional conceptions of femininity or the place of women in national communities could still be effectively manipulated and exploited by governments and political groups for the purposes of shoring up their own authority. In 1929, the year after female suffrage was made universal in England, an English journalist wrote:

> The tide of progress which leaves woman with the vote in her hand and scarcely any clothes upon her back is ebbing, and the sex is returning to the deep, very deep sea of femininity from which her newly-acquired power can be more effectively wielded.
>
> (*Woman's Life* cited in Braybon 1981: 222)

In post-war Europe political access and public opinion had been broadened, but there was no straightforward economic or political progress for women. In states subscribing to the values of the predominant political ideologies, liberalism, communism, or fascism, masculinity remained the axis of political rights, and of predominant conceptions of citizenship. Indeed, the forms of aggressively virile masculinity associated with pre-war militarism assumed social and political priority, even where they had to be physically enforced by new totalitarian regimes. Similarly, representations of sexual difference, and the preference for masculinity, remained a fundamental framework for denial of and demand for citizenship and political agency. When the feminist Madeleine Pelletier protested the introduction of anti-abortion legislation in post-war France, she also insisted that in order to claim 'self-determination' women had to 'virilize' themselves, to become more like men, and to gain sovereignty over the territory of their bodies (Scott 1996: 143). The legitimacy of the nation-state – regardless of the ideological orientation of its political institutions – was still defined around the moral economy of sex, and demographic economy of reproduction, concerns which depleted the individual rights of women in the face of national needs and preferences. Most governments clung to their authority over women and women's bodies in the interests of family and nation. Despite the availability of new conceptions of sexual difference, new images of gender ambiguity and expectations of the inevitability of greater democracy even for women, men continued to make history by exploiting inequities and representations of difference, more often than they addressed the relationship between difference and equality.

References and further reading

Primary sources

Addams, Jane, Balch, Emily G. and Hamilton, Alice (1972 [1915]) *Women at the Hague: The International Congress of Women and its Results*, intro. by Mercedes M. Randall, New York.

Barbera. P. (1916) *Le Donne e la guerra*, Firenze.

Barbusse, Henri (1918) *Le Feu: journal d'une escouade*, Paris.

Brittain, Vera (1978 [1933]) *Testament of Youth: An Autobiographical Study of the Years 1900–1925*, London.

Cross, Timothy (1988) *The Lost Voices of World War I*, Bloomsbury.

Crewe, Marquess of (1918) *Problems of Reconstruction: A Symposium*, London.

Donna, P. (n.d.) *La Funzione della Donna in tempo di Guerra*, Florence.

Graziani, G. (1914) *La Diana della Nuova Italia: Nazionalismo e politica coloniale. L'Italia nel 1911*, Rome.

Hobson, John A. (1902) *Imperialism: A Study*, London.

Hobson, John A. (1917) *Democracy After the War*, London.

Hobson, John A. (1921) *Problems of A New World*, London.

Labriola, Teresa (1919) *I problemi sociali della donna*, Florence.

Le Roy Beaulieu, Paul (1913) *La Question de la Population*, Paris.

Lombroso, Gina. (1921) *L'Anima della Donna. Riflessioni sulla vita*, 2nd edn, Bologna.

Marinetti, F. T. (1909) 'The founding and Manifesto of Futurism', in U. Apollonio (ed.) *Futurist Manifestoes* (1973), New York.

McLaren, Barbara (1917) *Women of the War*, London.

Paola, D. (n.d.) 'La donna della nuova Italia', *Documenti Del Contributo Femminile Alla Guerra*, Milano.

Reich, Emil (1905) *Imperialism: Its Prices, Its Vocation*, London.

Swanwick, Helena (1916) *The War and its Effect upon Women*, London.

Von Suttner, Bertha (1894) *Lay Down Your Arms: The Autobiography of Martha von Tilling*, trans. T. Holmes, London.

Militarism and masculinity, patriotism and citizenship

Adams, M. (1990) *The Great Adventure: Male Desire and the Coming of World War I*, Bloomington.

Bigaran, M. (1982) 'Mutamenti dell'emancipazionismo alla vigilia della grande guerra', *Memoria* **13**, 2: 125–32.

Blom, I. (1993) 'Equality and the threat of war in Scandinavia, 1884–1905, in T. G. Fraser and K. Jeffery (eds) *Men, Women and War*, Dublin.

Chickering, R. (1988) '"Casting their page more broadly": women's patriotic activism in imperial Germany', *Past and Present* **118**: 156–85.

Costin, L. B. (1982) 'Feminism, pacifism, internationalism and the 1915 International Congress of Women', *Women's Studies International Forum* 5, 3/4: 301–15.

Dawson, G. (1994) *Soldier Heroes: British Adventure, Empire and the Imagining of Masculinities*, London.

Evans, R. J. (1980) 'German Social Democracy and women's suffrage 1891–1918', *Journal of Contemporary History* 15, 3: 533–57.

Gatens, M. (1996) *Imaginary Bodies: Ethics, Power and Corporeality*, London.

Gould, J. (1987) 'Women's military services in First World War Britain', in M. Higgonet *et al.* (eds) *Behind the Lines: Gender and the Two World Wars*, New Haven.

Mosse, G. L. (1996) *The Image of Man: The Creation of Modern Masculinity*, New York.

Nye, R. (1993) *Masculinity and Male Codes of Honor in Modern France*, Oxford.

Poovey, M. (1989) *Uneven Developments: The Ideological Work of Gender in mid-Victorian England*, London.

Sherrick, R. (1982) 'Towards universal sisterhood', *Women's Studies International Forum* 5, 6: 655–61.

Stargardt, N. (1994) *The German Idea of Militarism*, Cambridge.

Wiltsher, A. (1985) *Most Dangerous Women Feminist Peace Campaigners of the Great War*, London.

The sex war?

Bell, S. G. and Offen, K. (eds) (1983) *Women, the Family and Freedom*, Stanford.

Bosworth, R. (1991) 'Mito e linguaggio nella politica estera italiana', in R. Bosworth et al. (eds) *Politica Italiana 1860–1988*, Bologna.

Bourke, J. (1996) *Dismembering the Male: Men's Bodies, Britain and the Great War*, London.

Braybon, G. (1981) *Women Workers in the First World War: The British Experience*, London.

Cooper, H. (1989) *Arms and the Woman; War, Gender, and Literary Representations*, Chapel Hill.

Frevert, U. (1989) *Women in German History*, Oxford and New York.

Gilbert, S. (1987) 'Soldier's heart: literary men, literary women and the Great War', in M. Higgonet *et al.* (eds) *Behind the Lines: Gender and the Two World Wars*, New Haven.

Gould, J. (1987) 'Women's military services in First World War Britain', in M.

Higgonet *et al.* (eds) *Behind the Lines: Gender and the Two World Wars*, New Haven.

Hause, S. (1987) 'More Minerva than Mars: the French women's rights campaign and the First World War', in M. Higgonet *et al.* (eds) *Behind the Lines*, New Haven.

Hause, S. C. (1978) 'Women who rallied to the Tricolor: the effects of World War 1 on the French women's suffrage movement', *Proceedings of the Annual Meeting of the Western Society for French History* 6: 371–8.

Higgonet, M., Jensen, J., Michel, S. and Weitz, M. C. (eds) (1987) *Behind the Lines: Gender and the Two World Wars*, New Haven.

Horne, J. (1993) 'Social identity in war: France 1914–1918', in T. G. Fraser and A. Jeffery (eds) *Men, Women and War*, Dublin.

Layton, L. (1987) 'Vera Brittain's Testament(s)', in M. Higgonet *et al.* (eds) *Between the Lines: Gender and the Two World Wars*, New Haven.

Mosse, G. (1985) *Nationalism and Sexuality*, New York.

Sachsse, C. (1986) *Mutterlichreit alls Beruf*, Frankfurt am Main.

Showalter, E. (1987) 'Rivers and Sassoon: the inscription of male gender anxieties', in M. Higgonet *et al.* (eds) *Behind the Lines: Gender and the Two World Wars*, New Haven.

Thebaud, F. (1986) *La Femme au temps de la guerre de 14*, Paris.

Thebaud, F. (1994) 'The Great War and the triumph of sexual division', in F. Thebaud (ed.) *A History of Women in the West, Volume V: Toward a Cultural Identity in the Twentieth Century*, Cambridge, Mass.; London.

Wollacott, A. (1994) 'Khaki fever', *Journal of Contemporary History* **29**, 2: 325–47.

The new world order: reconstruction, revolution, counter-revolution?

Detragiache, D. (1983) 'Il fascismo femminile de San Sepolcro all'affare Matteotti (1919–25)', *Storia Contemporanea* **14**, 2: 211–51.

Kent, S. K. (1993) *Making Peace: The Reconstruction of Gender in inter-war Britain*, Princeton.

Miller, C. (1994) 'Geneva – the key to equality: inter-war feminists and the League of Nations', *Women's History Review* **3**, 2: 219–45.

Mosse, G. L. (1996) *The Image of Man: The Creation of Modern Masculinity*, New York.

Rupp, L. (1997) *Worlds of Women: The Making of an International Women's Movement*, Princeton.

Scott, J. W. (1996) *Only Paradoxes to Offer: French Feminists and the Rights of Man*, Cambridge, Mass.

Smith-Rosenberg, C. 'Discourses of sexuality and subjectivity: the new woman, 1870–1936', in M. Duberman *et al.* (eds) *Hidden from History: Reclaiming the Gay and Lesbian Past*, New York.

Sowerwine, C. (1987) 'The Socialist women's movement from 1850 to 1940', in R. Bridenthal, C. Koonz and S. Stuard (eds) *Becoming Visible: Women in European History*, Boston.

Theweleit, K. (1987) *Male Fantasies*, Minneapolis.

Tickner, L. (1989) *Spectacle of Women: The Imagery of the Suffrage Campaign, 1907–1917*, London.

Tylee, C. (1990) *The Great War and Women's Resistance to Militarism: Images of Militarism and Womanhood in Women's Writings, 1914–1964*, Basingstoke.

Bibliography

Primary sources

Achurch, J. (1889) 'On the difficulty of being Nora', in M. Egan (ed.) (1972) *Ibsen: The Critical Heritage*, London.

Addams, J., Balch, E. G. and Hamilton, A. (1972 [1915]) *Women at the Hague: The International Congress of Women and its Results*, intro. M. M. Randall, New York.

Aimé-Martin, L. (1834) *De l'Education des mères de famille, ou de la civilisation du genre humain par les femmes*, Paris.

Barbera, P. (1916) *Le Donne e la guerra*, Firenze.

Barbusse, H. (1918) *Le Feu. Journal d'une escouade*, Paris.

Bebel, A. (1891 [1879]) *Die Frau and der Sozialismus. Die Frau in der Vergangenheit, Gegenwart und Zukunft*, Stuttgart.

Belgiojoso, C. (1869) *Reflexions sur l'état actuel de l'Italie et sur son avenir*, Paris.

Bell, S. G. and Offen, K. (eds) (1983) *Women, the Family and Freedom: The Debate in Documents*, Stanford.

Betham-Edwards, M. (1905) *Home Life in France*, 2nd edn, London.

Brittain, V. (1978 [1933]) *Testament of Youth: An Autobiographical Study of the Years 1900–1925*, London.

Burke, E. (1965 [1790]) *Reflections on the Revolution in France and on the proceedings in certain societies in London related to that event*, New York.

Burney, F. (1814) *The Wanderer: or Female Difficulties*, London.

Butler, J. (1896) *Personal Reminiscences of a Great Crusade*, London.

Butler, J. (1900) *The Native Races and War*, London.

Butler, J. E. (1928 [1909]) *An Autobiographical Memoir*, ed. G. W. and L. A. Johnson, intro. J. Stuart, 3rd edn, Bristol.

Carlyle, T. (1874) 'Introduction', Goethe, *Wilhelm Meister's Lehrjahre*, trans. T. Carlyle, London.

Chamberlain, H. S. (1900) *Foundations of the Nineteenth Century* (Die grundragen des neunzehnten Jahrhunderts), Munchen.

Comte, A. (1875) *The Positive Philosophy of August Comte, Vol. 2*, trans. H. Martineau, London.

Crewe, Marquess of (1918) *Problems of Reconstruction: A Symposium*, London.

Cross, T. (1988) *The Lost Voices of World War I*, Bloomsbury.

Darwin, C. (1872 [1859]) *Origin of Species*, 6th edn, London.

De Beauvoir, S. (1958) *Memoires d'une jeune fille rangée*, Paris.

De Gouges, O. (1986 [1791]) *Declaration of the Rights of Woman and the Citizen*, in *Oeuvres*, Paris.

Deraismes, M. (1980) *Ce que veulent les femmes*, Articles et conferences de 1869 a 1891, Paris.

De Saint-Pierre, B. (1835 [1788]) *Paul et Virginie*, London.

De Staël, Mme G. (1813) *De l'Allemagne*, 1st edn, Paris.

De Staël, Mme G. (1966 [1821]) *Dix années d'exil*, Paris.

De Staël, Mme G. (1987 [1807]) *Corinne*, trans. Auriel M. Goldgerger, New Brunswick.

Donna, P. (n.d.) *La Funzione della Donna in tempo di Guerra*, Florence, Milan, Roma, Pisa, Naples, Bologna, Torino, Genova, Palermo, New York and Buenos Aires.

Drohojowska, Mme (1853) *Histoire des colonies françaises. Antilles, Ile Bourbon, Guyane Française*, Paris.

Durkheim, E. (1951 [1897]) *Suicide*, New York.

Ellis, H. (1903) *The Analysis of the Sexual Impulse: Studies in the Psychology of Sex, Vol. III*, Philadelphia.

Ellis, H. and Symonds, J. A. (1897) *Sexual Inversion*, London.

Engels, F. (1954 [1884]) *The Origin of the Family*, Moscow.

Engels, F. (1976 [1892]) *The Condition of the Working Class in England*, New York.

Fawcett, M. (1902) 'Report on the Concentration Camps in South Africa by the Committee of Ladies Appointed by the Secretary of State for War', London.

Fichte, J. G. (1968 [1807]) *Addresses to the German Nation*, New York.

Fourier, C. (1996 [1808]) *The Theory of the Four Movements*, ed. G. Stedman Jones and I. Patterson, Cambridge.

Freud, S. (1977 [1907]) *On Sexuality: Three Essays on the Theory of Sexuality and Other Works*, New York.

Gaffarel, P. (1899) *Les colonies françaises*, Paris.

Gaskell, E. (1985 [1848]) *Mary Barton: A Tale of Manchester Life*, London.

Geddes, P. and Thompson, J. A. (1889) *The Evolution of Sex*, New York.

Gobineau, Arthur Comte de (1967 [1853–5]) *Inequality of Human Races*, trans. A. Collins, New York.

Goethe, J. W. von. (1978 [1795]) *Wilhelm Meister's Years of Apprenticeship*, trans. H. M. Waidson, London.

Grand, S. (1898) *The Modern Man and Made*, London.

Grand, S. (1992 [1893]) *The Heavenly Twins*, Ann Arbor.

Graziani, G. (1914) *La Diana della Nuova Italia, Nazionalismo e political coloniale, L'Italia nel 1911*, Rome.

Haggard, R. (1886) *She*, London.

Hallowes, Mrs F. S. (1918) *Mothers of Men and Militarism*, London.

Hamilton, C. (1978 [1909]) *Marriage as a Trade*, London.

Hays, M. (1987 [1796]) *Memoirs of Emma Courtney*, London and New York.

Hippel, T. G. von (1979 [1792]) *On Improving the Status of Women*, trans. T. F. Sellner, Detroit.

Hobhouse, E. (1902) *Brunt of the War*, London.

Hobson, J. A. (1902) *Imperialism: A Study*, London.

Hobson, J. A. (1910) *A Modern Outlook: Studies of English and American Tendencies*, London.

Hobson, J. A. (1912) *Character and Life*, ed. P. L. Parker, London.

Hobson, J. A. (1917) *Democracy After the War*, London.

Hobson, J. A. (1921) *Problems of A New World*, London.

Huxley, T. H. (1902) 'Emancipation black and white', in T. H. Huxley, *Essays: Science and Education*, London.

Huysmans, J. K. (1959 [1884]) *Against Nature*, trans. R. Baldick, Middlesex.

Ibsen, H. (1935 [1889]) *The Doll's House*, London.

Ibsen, H. (1973 [1889]) *Ghosts*, trans. M. Meyer, London.

Labriola, T. (1919) *I problemi sociali della donna*, Firenze.

Le Bon, G. (1899) *The Psychology of Peoples*, London.

Le Bon, G. (1910 [1896]) *The Crowd: A Study of the Popular Mind*, 7th edn, London.

Le Roy Beaulieu, P. (1913) *La Question de la Population*, Paris.

Lewis, S. (1839) *Woman's Mission*, London.

Lombroso, G. (1921) *L'Anima della Donna: Riflessiona sulla vita*, 2nd edn, Bologna.

Marinetti, F. T. (1909) 'The founding and Manifesto of Futurism', in U. Apollonio (ed.) (1973) *Futurist Manifestoes*, New York.

Martineau, H. (1889) 'Female industry', *Edinburgh Review* **109**, 222 (April): 293–336.

Martineau, H. (1983 [1875]) *Autobiography*, London.

Mazzini, J. (1966 [1844–58]) *The Duties of Man and Other Essays*, London.

McLaren, B. (1917) *Women of the War*, London.

Michelet, J. (1973 [1845]) *The People*, trans. J. P. McKay, Urbana.

Michelet, J. (1985a [1854]) *Les Femmes de la Revolution*, in *Oeuvres Complètes*, ed. P. Viallaneix, vol. 16, Paris, pp. 353–570.

Michelet, J. (1985b [1858]) *L'Amour*, in *Oeuvres Complètes*, ed. P. Viallaneix, vol. 18, Paris, pp. 13–362.

Mill, J. S. (1869) *On the Subjection of Women*, London.

More, H. (1799) *Strictures on the Modern System of Female Education*, London.

Mozzoni, A. M. (1865) *La Donna in faccia al progetto del nuovo codice civile italiano*, Milano.

Mozzoni, A. M. (1871) 'La questione dell'emancipazione della donna in Italia', *La Roma del popolo*, 21 marzo.

Nordau, M. (1993 [1895]) *Degeneration*, trans. G. L. Mosse, Lincoln.

Paola, D. (n.d.) 'La donna della nuova Italia', *Documenti Del Contributo Femminile Alla Guerra* (Maggio 1915–Maggio 1917), Milano.

Proudhon, P. J. (1858) *De la Justice dans la revolution et dans l'Eglise*, Paris.

Reich, E. (1905) *Imperialism: its Prices, its Vocation*, London.

Rousseau, J. J. (1911 [1762]) *Émile*, New York.

Ruskin, J. (1865) 'Sesame and lilies', republished in *The Complete Works of John Ruskin* (1897), Boston.

Sand, G. (1848) *The French Republic! A Letter to the People of France*, London.

Sand, G. (1899) *Questions Politique et Sociale*, Paris.

Sand, G. (1970–1) *Histoire de ma Vie*, in *Oeuvres Autobiographiques*, ed. G. Lubin, Paris.

Sand, G. (1971) *Correspondence de George Sand, Juillet 1847–Dec 1848*, Paris.

Shelley, M. (1982 [1818]) *Frankenstein, or the Modern Prometheus*, Chicago.

Sighele, S. (1898) *La Donna Nova*, Rome.

Sighele, S. (1910) *Eva Moderna*, Milano.

Spencer, H. (1876) *Principles of Sociology*, London.

Stopes, M. (1919) *Married Love: A New Contribution to the Solution of Sex Difficulties*, London.

Stopes, M. (1920) *Wise Parenthood*, London.

Swanwick, H. (1916) *The War and its Effect Upon Women*, London.

Swanwick, H. (1935) *I Have Been Young*, London.

de Tocqueville, A. (1893) *Souvenirs de Alexis de Tocqueville*, Paris.

Von Suttner, B. (1894) *Lay Down Your Arms: The Autobiography of Martha von Tilling*, trans. T. Holmes, London.

Webb, B. (ed.) (November 1912) 'The awakening of women', *New Statesmen*, Special Supplement.

Weininger, O. (1903) *Geschlect und Charakterieine Prinzipelle Untersuchung*, Wein.

Werner, A. (1889) *Autobiography of G. Garibaldi*, trans. with a supplement by J. White Mario, London.

White, A. (1886) *The Problem of a Great City*, London.

White, A. H. (1973 [1901]) *Efficiency and Empire*, ed. and introduction by G. R. Searle, Brighton.

White Mario, J. (1897) *Le opere pie e l'infanticidio legale*, Rovigo.

White Mario, J. (1909) *The Birth of Modern Italy: Posthumous Papers of Jessie White Mario*, ed. Duke Litta-Visconti-Arese, London.

Wilde, O. (1908 [1891]) *Portrait of Dorian Gray*, Paris.

Wollstonecraft, M. (1960 [1790]) *Vindication of the Rights of Men*, Gainesville.

Wollstonecraft, M. (1975 [1796]) *Maria, or the Wrongs of Woman*, New York.

Wollstonecraft, M. (1988 [1792]) *Vindication of the Rights of Woman*, New York.

Zola, E. (1956 [1887]) *Germinal*, London.

Zola, E. (1995 [1883]) *The Ladies Paradise*, Oxford.

Secondary sources

Abelove, H. (1989) 'Some speculations on the history of sexual intercourse during the long eighteenth century in England', *Gender* 6: 125–30.

Accampo, E. A., Fuchs, R. G. and Stewart, M. L. (eds) (1995) *Gender and the Politics of Social Reform in France, 1870–1914*, Baltimore.

Adams, M. (1990) *The Great Adventure: Male Desire and the Coming of World War I*, Bloomington.

Aerts, M. (1986) 'Catholic constructions of femininity: three Dutch women's organisations in search of a politics of the personal, 1912–1940', in J. Friedlander, B. W. Cook, A. Hessler-Harris and C. Smith-Rosenburg (eds) *Women in Culture and Politics: A Century of Change*, Bloomington.

Alexander, S. (1983) *Women's Work in Nineteenth Century London: A Study of the Years 1820–1850*, London.

Alexander, S. (1988) *Fabian Women's Tracts*, London.

Alexander, S. (1994) *Becoming a Woman and Other Essays in the 19th and 20th Century*, London.

Allen, A. T. (1988) 'German radical feminism and eugenics, 1900–1908', *German Studies Review* 11, 1: 31–56.

Anderson, H. (1992) *Women's Movement in Fin-de-Siècle Vienna*, New Haven and London.

Angeleri, M. C. (1996) 'Dall'emancipazioniasmo all'interventismo democratico. Il primo movimento politico delle donne di Fronte Alla Grande Guerra', *Dimensioni e problemi della ricerca storica*, 1: 199–216.

Angerer, M. (1996) 'The discourse on female sexuality in nineteenth-century Austria', in D. F. Good, M. Gardner and M. J. Maynes (eds) *Austrian Women in the Nineteenth and Twentieth Centuries*, Oxford and Providence.

Applewhite, H. B. and Levy, D. G. (1987) 'Women and political revolution in Paris', in R. Bridenthal, C. Koonz and S. Stuard (eds) *Becoming Visible: Women in European History*, Boston.

Applewhite, H. B. and Levy, D. G. (eds) (1990) *Women and Politics in the Age of the Democratic Revolution*, Ann Arbor.

Applewhite H. B., Levy, D. G. and Durham Johnson, M. (eds) *Women in Revolutionary Paris, 1789–1795: Selected Documents*, Urbana.

Barry, D. (1996) *Women and Political Insurgency: France in the Mid-Nineteenth Century*, Basingstoke.

Battersby, C. (1990) *Gender and Genius: Towards a Feminist Aesthetic*, London.

Beer, G. (1983) *Darwin's Plots*, London.

Benjamin, M. (ed.) (1991) *Science and Sensibility: Gender and Scientific Enquiry, 1780–1945*, Oxford.

Berg, M. (1985) *The Age of Manufactures, 1700–1820: Industry, Innovation, and Work in Britain*, London.

Bezucha, R. (ed.) (1972) *Modern European Social History*, Lexington, Mass.

Bigaran, M. (1982) 'Mutamenti dell'emancipazionismo alla vigilia della grande guerra', *Memoria* 13, 2: 125–32.

Bigaran, M. (1985) 'Progetti e dibattiti parlamentari sul suffragio femminile. Da Peruzzi a Giolitti', *Rivista di storia contemporanea* 1 (gennaio): 50–82.

Bigaran, M. (1987) 'Il voto alle donne in Italia dal 1912 al fascismo', *Rivista di storia contemporanea* 2 (aprile): 240–65.

Black, N. (1984) 'The Mothers' International: The Women's Co-Operative Guild and Feminist Pacifism' *Women's Studies International Forum* 76, Oxford and New York.

Blakeley, B. (1981) 'Women and imperialism: the Colonial Office and female emigration to South Africa, 1901–1910', *Albion* 13, 2: 131–49.

Bland, L. (1995) *Banishing the Beast. English Feminism and Sexual Morality 1885–1914*, Harmondsworth.

Bland, L. and Mort, F. (1984) 'Look out for the good time girl: dangerous sexualities as threat to national health', in *Formations of Nation and People*, London.

Bloch, M. and J. H. (1980) 'Women and the dialectics of nature in 18th century French thought', in C. P. MacCormack and M. Strathern (eds) *Nature, Culture and Gender*, Cambridge.

Blom, I. (1980) 'The struggle for women's suffrage in Norway, 1885–1913', *Scandinavian Journal of History* 5, 1: 3–22.

Blom, I. (1993) 'Equality and the threat of war in Scandinavia, 1884–1905', in T. G. Fraser and K. Jeffery (eds) *Men, Women and War*, Dublin.

Bochachevsky-Chomiak, M. (1980) 'Socialism, feminism and nationalism: the first stages of women's organisations in the eastern part of the Austrian Empire', in T. Yedlin (ed.) *Women in Eastern Europe and the Soviet Union*, New York.

Bochachevsky-Chomiak, M. (1982) 'Natalia Kobrynska: a formulator of feminism', in A. Markovits and F. Sysyn (eds) *Nation Building and the Politics of Nationalism*, Cambridge, Mass.

Bock, G. (1989) 'Women's history and gender history: aspects of an international debate', *Gender and History* 1, 1: 7–30.

Bock, G. and James, S. (eds) (1992) *Beyond Equality and Difference*, London.

Bock, G. and Thane, P. (1991) *Maternity and Gender Policies: Women and the Rise of the European Welfare States 1880s–1950s*, London and New York.

Boetcher-Joeres, R. (1979) 'Louise Otto and her journals: a chapter in nineteenth-century German feminism', *Internationales Archiv fur Sozialgeschichte der Deutschen Literatur* 4: 100–29.

Boetcher-Joeres, R. and Burkhard, M. (eds) (1989) *Out of Line/Ausgefallen: The Paradox of Marginality in the Writings of Nineteenth Century German Women*, Amsterdam.

Bosworth, R. (1991) 'Mito e linguaggio nella politica estera italiana', in R. J. B. Bosworth and S. Romano (eds) *Politica Estera Italiana 1860–1985*, Bologna.

Bourke, J. (1996) *Dismembering the Male: Men's Bodies, Britain and the Great War*, London.

Bowlby, R. (1985) *Just Looking: Consumer Culture in Dreiser, Gissing and Zola*, New York.

Boxer, M. (1995) 'French women in revolutionary action and thought', *Journal of Women's History* 7, 4: 151–61.

Boxer, M. and Quaetert, J. (1987) *Connecting Spheres: Women in the Western World 1500 to the Present*, New York.

Bradford, S. (1982) *Disraeli*, London.

Brantlinger, P. (1988) *Rule of Darkness: British Literature and Imperialism, 1830–1914*, Ithaca.

Braybon, G. (1981) *Women Workers in the First World War: The British Experience*, London.

Braybon, G. and Summerfield, P. (1987) *Out of the Cage: Women's Experiences in Two World Wars*, London.

Brehmer, I., Jacobi-Dittrich, J., Kleinau, E. and Kuhn, A. (eds) (1983) *Frauen in der Geschichte IV. 'Wissen heist leben . . . ' Beitrage zur Bildungsgeschicte von Frauen im 18 und 19*, Dusseldorf.

Bridenthal, R., Koonz, C. and Stuard, S. (eds) (1987) *Becoming Visible: Women in European History*, Boston.

Bristow, J. (1991) *Empire Boys: Adventures in a Man's World*, London.

Brombert, B. A. (1977) *Cristina: Portraits of a Princess*, New York.

Burdett, C. (1994) 'A difficult vindication – Olive Schreiner's Wollstonecraft introduction', *History Workshop* 37: 177–88.

Burton, A. (1992) 'The white woman's burden: British feminists and "The Indian Woman", 1865–1915', in N. Chaudhuri and M. Strobel (eds), *Western Women and Imperialism: Complicity and Resistance*, Bloomington.

Burton, A. (1994) *Burdens of History*, Chapel Hill.

Burton, A. (1996) 'Recapturing Jane Eyre: reflections on historicizing the colonial encounter in Victorian Britain', *Radical History Review* 64 (Winter): 59–72.

Bussemer, H. (1985) *Frauenemanzipation und Bildungsburgertum. Sozialgeschichte der Frauenbewegung in der Reichgrundungszeit*, Weinheim und Basel.

Butler, M. (1981) *Romantics, Rebels, Reactionaries: English Literature and its Background, 1760–1830*, Oxford.

Buzard, J. (1993) 'Victorian women and the implications of Empire', *Victorian Studies* 36, 4: 443–53.

Caine, B. (1992) *Victorian Feminists*, Oxford.

Caine, B. (1997) *English Feminism, 1780–1980*, Oxford.

Candy, C. (1994) 'Relating feminisms, nationalisms and imperialisms: Ireland, India and Margaret Cousins's sexual politics', *Women's History Review* 3, 4: 581–94.

Canning, Kathleen (1992) 'Gender and the politics of class formation: rethinking German labor history', *American Historical Review* 97, 3: 736–68.

Cavallo, S. (1980) 'Assistenza femminile e tutela dell'onore nella Torino del XVIII secolo', *Annali della Fondazione Luigi Einaudi* **14**: 127–55.

Chandler, A. D. (1990) 'Fin de siècle: industrial transformation', in M. Teich and R. Porter (eds) *Fin de Siècle and its Legacy*, New York.

Chickering, R. (1975) *Imperial Germany and a World Without War: The Peace Movement and German Society 1893–1914*, Princeton.

Chickering, R. (1984) *We Men Who Feel Most German: A Cultural Study of the Pan-German League 1886–1914*, Cambridge, Mass.

Chickering, R. (1988) ' "Casting their gaze more broadly": women's patriotic activism in imperial Germany', *Past and Present* **118**: 156–85.

Christ, C. (1977) 'Victorian masculinity and the "angel in the house" ', in M. Vicinus (ed.) *A Widening Sphere: Changing Roles of Victorian Women*, Bloomington.

Clark, A. (1995) *Struggle for the Breeches*, Berkeley and London.

Clark, H. C. (1993) 'Women and humanity in Scottish enlightenment social thought: the case of Adam Smith', *Historical Reflections* **19**, 3: 335–62.

Clarke, N. 'Thomas Carlyle and the man of letters as hero', in M. Roper and J. Tosh (eds) *Manful Assertions: Masculinities in Britain since 1800*, London and New York.

Cole, J. H. (1996) 'There are only good mothers: the ideological work of women's fertility in France before World War 1', *French Historical Studies* **19**, 3: 639–72.

Conner, S. P. (1962) 'Les femmes militaires: women in the French Army 1792–1815', *France Institute on Napoleon and the French Revolution/Consortium on Revolutionary France*, Tallahasee.

Conway, J. (1972) 'Stereotypes of femininity in a theory of sexual evolution', in M. Vicinus (ed.) *Suffer and Be Still: Women in the Victorian Age*, Bloomington.

Cook, B. W. (1986) 'Feminism, socialism, and sexual freedom: women in culture and politics', in J. Friedlander, B. W. Cook, A. Kessler-Harris and C. Smith-Rosenburg (eds) *Women in Culture and Politics: A Century of Change*, Bloomington.

Cooper, F. and Stoler, A. L. (eds) (1997) *Tensions of Empire: Colonial Cultures in a Bourgeois World*, Berkeley.

Cooper, H., *et al.* (1989) *Arms and the Woman: War, Gender, and Literary Representation*, Chapel Hill.

Copley, A. (1989) *Sexual Moralities in France, 1780–1980: New Ideas on the Family, Divorce and Homosexuality*, London.

Corbin, A. (1992) 'A sex in mourning: the history of women in the nineteenth century', in M. Perrot (ed.) *Writing Women's History*, Oxford and Cambridge, Mass.

Cori, P. di (1979) 'Storia, sentimenti, solidarieta nelle organizazzione femminile dall'eta giolittiana al fascimo', *Nuova DWF* (January–June): 10–11.

Corrado Pope, B. (1987) 'The influence of Rousseau's ideology of domesticity', in M. J. Boxer and J. Quataert (eds) *Connecting Spheres: Women in the Western World, 1500 to the Present*, New York.

Costin, L. B. (1982) 'Feminism, pacifism, internationalism and the 1915 International Congress of Women', *Women's Studies International Forum* 5, 3/4:
301–15.

Cova, A. (1991) 'French feminism and maternity: theories and politicies 1890–1918',
in G. Bock and P. Thane (eds) *Maternity and Gender Policies: Women and the Rise
of the European Welfare States 1880s–1950s*, London and New York.

Crow, T. (1994) 'A male republic: bonds between men in the art and life of Jacques-
Louis David', in G. Perry and M. Rossington (eds) *Femininity and Masculinity in
Eighteenth Century Art and Culture*, Manchester.

Daniel, U. (ed.) (1989) *Arbeiterfrauen in der Kriegsgesellschaft. Beruf, Familie und
Politik im Ersten Weltkrieg*, Gottingen.

Daniels, E. A. (1972) *Jessie White Mario: Risorgimento Revolutionary*, Athens,
Georgia.

Davidoff, L. and Hall, C. (1987) *Family Fortunes, Men and Women of the English
Middle Class 1780–1850*, London.

Davin, A. (1997) 'Imperialism and motherhood,' in A. L. Stoler and F. Cooper (eds)
Tensions of Empire: Colonial Cultures in a Bourgeois World, Berkeley.

Dawson, G. (1991) 'The blond bedouin: Lawrence of Arabia, imperial adventure and
the imagining of English-British masculinity', in M. Roper and J. Tosh (eds)
Manful Assertions: Masculinities in Britain since 1800, London and New York.

Dawson, G. (1994) *Soldier Heroes: British Adventure, Empire and the Imagining of
Masculinities*, London.

Delamont, S. and Duffin, L. (1978) *The Nineteenth Century Woman: Her Cultural
and Physical World*, London.

Detragiache, D. (1983) 'Il fascismo femminile da San Sepolcro all'affare Matteotti
(1919–25)', *Storia Contemporanea* 14, 2: 211–51.

Djikstra, B. (1986) *Idols of Perversity: Fantasies of Feminine Evil at the Fin de Siècle*,
Oxford.

Donzelot, J. (1980) *The Policing of Families*, London.

Drewitz, I. (1983) *The German Women's Movement*, Bonn.

Duberman, M., Vicinus, M. and Chauncy, G. (eds) (1989) *Hidden from History:
Reclaiming the Gay and Lesbian Past*, New York.

Duffin, L. 'Prisoners of progress: women and evolution', in S. Delamont and L. Duffin
(eds) *The Nineteenth-Century Woman*, London.

Dyhouse, C. (1976) 'Social Darwinistic ideas and the development of women's
education in England, 1880–1920', *History of Education* 5, 1: 41–58.

Edmondson, L. (1984) *Feminism in Russia 1900–1917*, London.

Engel, B. A. (1992) 'Engendering Russia's history: women in post-emancipation
Russia and the Soviet Union', *Slavic Review* 51, 2: 309–21.

Engelhardt, U. (1985) 'Noch im "Dunkel der Geschichte"? Neuere Bücher zu einigen
Voraussetzungen und Manifestationen der fruhen Frauenbewegung in Deutsch-
land', *Archiv für Sozialgeschichte* 25: 554–87.

Engelstein, L. (1994) *The Keys to Happiness: Sex and the Search for Modernity in fin-de-siécle Russia*, Ithaca.

Evans, R. (1976a) 'Feminism and female emancipation in Germany', *Central European History* 9: 323–52.

Evans, R. (1976b) 'Prostitution, state and society in imperial Germany', *Past and Present* 70: 106–29.

Evans, R. (1979) *The Feminists: Women's Emancipation Movements in Europe, America and Australasia 1840–1920*, London.

Evans, R. (ed.) (1981) *The German Family: Essays on the Social History of the Family in Nineteenth and Twentieth-Century Germany*, London.

Evans, R. J. (1980) 'German Social Democracy and women's suffrage 1891–1918', *Journal of Contemporary History* 15, 3: 533–57.

Evans, R. J. (1987) *Comrades and Sisters: Feminism, Socialism and Pacifism in Europe 1870–1945*, Brighton.

Faderman, L. and Eriksson, B. (eds) (1990) *Lesbians in Germany: 1890s–1920s*, Tallahassee.

Faure, C. (1986) 'The Utopia of the New Woman in the Work of Alexandra Kollontai and its Impact on the French Feminist and Communist Press' in J. Friedlander *et al.* (eds) *Women in Culture and Politics: A Century of Change*, Bloomington.

Faure, C. (1991) *Democracy Without Women: Feminism and the Rise of Liberal Individualism in France*, Bloomington.

Faure, C. (1992) 'Les Constituants de 1789 avaient-ils la volonté deliberée d'evincer les femmes de la vie politique?', *History of European Ideas* 15, 4–6: 537–42.

Fee, E. (1974) 'The sexual politics of Victorian social anthropology', in M. Hartman and L. Banner (eds) *Clio's Consciousness Raised: New Perspectives on the History of Women*, New York.

Frevert, U. (1988) *Burgerinnen und Burger. Geschlechterverhaltnisse im 19. Jahrhundert*, Gottingen.

Findlay, L. M. (1986) '"Maternity must forth": the poetics and politics of gender in Carlyle's French Revolution', *Dalhousie Review* 66 1/2: 130–54.

Finzi, S. V. (1992) 'Female identity between sexuality and maternity', in G. Bock and S. James (eds) *Beyond Equality and Difference*, London.

Foldy, M. S. (1997) *The Trials of Oscar Wilde: Deviance, Morality and Late Victorian Society*, New Haven.

Fout, J. (ed.) (1984) *German Women in the Nineteenth Century: A Social History*, New York.

Frader, L. L. (1987) 'Women in the industrial economy', in R. Bridenthal, C. Koonz and S. Stuard (eds) *Becoming Visible: Women in European History*, 2nd edn, Boston.

Frader, L. L. and Rose, S. O. (eds) (1996) *Gender and Class in Modern Europe*, Ithaca and London.

Fraisse, G. (1986) 'Natural law and the origins of nineteenth century feminist thought in

France', in J. Friedlander, B. Wiesen Cook, A. Kessler-Harris and C. Smith-Rosenburg (eds) *Women in Culture and Politics: A Century of Change*, Bloomington.

Fraisse, C. (1993) 'A philosophical history of sexual difference', in G. Duby and M. Perrot (eds) *A History of Women in the West*, vol. 4, Cambridge, Mass.

Franchini, S. (1986) 'L'istruzione femminile in Italia dopo l'Unità. Percorsi di una ricerca sugli educandati pubblici di elite', *Passato e presente* 10: 53–94.

Franchini, S. (1988) 'L'educazione delle donne all'indomani dell Unità', *Passato e presente* 17: 11–36.

Fraser, N. (1987) 'What's critical about critical theory? The case of Habermas and gender', in S. Benhabib and D. Cornell (eds) *Feminism as Critique: On the Politics of Gender*, Minneapolis.

Fraser, T. G. and Jeffery, K. (eds) (1993) *Men, Women and War*, Dublin.

Freis, P. (1970) *L'opinion publique et les élite face au suffrage feminin en Suisse*, Geneve.

Frevert, U. (1989) *Women in German History: From Bourgeois Emancipation to Sexual Liberation*, trans. S. McKinnon Evans with T. Bond and B. Norden, Oxford and New York.

Friedlander, J., Wiesen Cook, B., Kessler-Harris, A. and Smith-Rosenburg, C. (eds) (1986) *Women in Culture and Politics: A Century of Change*, Bloomington.

Fuchs, R. G. (1995) 'France in a comparative perspective', in E. A. Accampo, R. G. Fuchs and M. L. Stewart (eds) *Gender and the Politics of Social Reform in France, 1870–1914*, Baltimore.

Fuchs, R. G. (1996) 'Population and the state in the Third Republic', *French Historical Studies* 19, 3: 633–40.

Gaffin, J. and Thoms, D. (1983) *Caring and Sharing: The Centenary History of the Co-operative Women's Guild*, Manchester.

Gardiner, J. (ed.) (1993) *The New Woman*, London.

Gatens, M. (1996) *Imaginary Bodies: Ethics, Power and Corporeality*, London.

Gelblum, A. (1992) 'Feminism and pacifism: the case of Anita Augspurg and Lida Gustava Heymann', *Tel Aviver Jahrbuch fur deutsche Geschichte* 21: 207–25.

Gemie, S. (1992) 'Politics, morality and the bourgeoisie: the work of Paul Leroy-Beaulieu (1843–1916)', *Journal of Contemporary History* 27: 345–62.

Gerhard, U. (1978) *Verhaltnisse und Verhinderungen Frauenarbeit, Familie und Rechte der Frauen im 19. Jahrhundert Mit Dokumenten*, Frankfurt am Main.

Gibson, M. (1986) *Prostitution and the State in Italy 1860–1915*, New Brunswick, New Jersey.

Gibson, M. (1990) 'On the insensitivity of women: science and the woman question in liberal Italy, 1890–1910', *Journal of Women's History* 2, 2: 11–41.

Gilbert, S. (1987) 'Soldier's heart: literary men, literary women and the Great War', in M. Higgonet, J. Jenson, S. Michel and M. Weitz (eds) *Behind the Lines: Gender and the Two World Wars*, New Haven.

Gilman, S. (1993) *The Case of Sigmund Freud: Medicine and Identity at the Fin-de-siècle*, Baltimore.

Gilman, S. L. (1985) *Difference and Pathology: Stereotypes of Sexuality, Race, and Madness*, Ithaca and London.

Gilman, S. L. (1993) *Freud, Race, and Gender*, Princeton.

Glickman, R. (1984) *Russian Factory Women: Workplace and Society, 1880–1914*, Berkeley.

Godineau, D. (1990) 'Masculine and feminine political practice during the French Revolution, 1793–Year III', in H. B. Applewhite and D. G. Levy (eds) *Women and Politics in the Age of the Democratic Revolution*, Ann Arbor.

Good, D. F., Gradner, M. and Maynes, M. J. (eds) (1996) *Austrian Women in the Nineteenth and Twentieth Centuries: Cross Disciplinary Perspectives*, Providence.

Goodman, D. (1994) *The Republic of Letters: A Cultural History of the French Enlightenment*, Ithaca.

Goodman, K. (1982) 'Poesis and praxis in Rahel Varnhagen's letters', *New German Critique* 27.

Gordon, F. (1990) *The Integral Feminist: Madeleine Pelletier, 1874–1939*, Cambridge.

Gordon, F. (1992) 'Reproductive rights: the early 20th century European debate', *Gender and History* 4, 3: 387–99.

Gould, J. (1987) 'Women's military services in First World War Britain', in M. Higgonet, J. Jenson, S. Michel and M. C. Weitz (eds) *Behind the Lines: Gender and the Two World Wars*, New Haven.

Gould, S. J. (1981) *The Mismeasure of Man*, New York.

Gray, M. (1987) 'Prescriptions for productive female domesticity in a transitional era: Germany's Hausmutterliteratur, 1780–1840', *History of European Ideas* 8, 4/5: 413–26.

Gray, M. (1990) 'From the household economy to rational agriculture: the establishment of liberal ideals in German agricultural thought', in K. Jarausch and L. Jones (eds) *In Search of a Liberal Germany: Studies in the History of German Liberalism from 1789 to the Present*, New York.

Gray, R. (1993) 'Factory legislation and the gendering of jobs in Britain, 1830–1860', *Gender and History* 5: 56–80.

Groenewegen, P. (ed.) (1994) *Feminism and Political Economy in Victorian England*, London.

Grogan, S. (1992) *French Socialism and Sexual Difference: Women and the New Society, 1803–1844*, London.

Grogan, S. (1998) *Flora Tristan*, London and New York.

Gubar, S. (1987) ' "This is my rifle. This is my gun": World War II and the Blitz on women', in M. Higgonet, J. Jenson, S. Michel and M. C. Weitz (eds) *Behind the Lines: Gender and the Two World Wars*, New Haven.

Gullickson, G. (1992) 'The unruly woman of the Paris Commune', in D. O. Helly and

S. M. Reverby (eds) *Gendered Domains: Rethinking Public and Private in Women's History*, New York.

Gutwirth, M. (1992) *The Twilight of the Goddesses: Women and Representation in the French Revolutionary Era*, New Bruswick.

Habermas, J. (1987) *Theory of Communicative Action*, Cambridge.

Hackett, A. (1972) 'The German women's movement and suffrage, 1890–1914: a study of national feminism', in R. J. Bezucha (ed.) *Modern European Social History*, Lexington, Massachusetts, Toronto and London.

Hall, C. (1985) 'Private persons versus public someones: class, gender and politics in England, 1780–1850', in C. Steedman, C. Urwin and V. Walkerdine (eds) *Language, Gender and Childhood*, London.

Hall, C. (1992) *White Male and Middle-Class: Explorations in Feminism and History*, Cambridge.

Hall, L. A. (1996) 'Impotent ghosts from no man's land, flappers' boyfriends, or crypto-patriarchs? Men, sex and social change in 1920s Britain', *Social History* 21, 1: 54–70.

Hanley, S. (1989) 'Engendering the state: family formation and state building in early modern France', *French Historical Studies* 16, 1: 4–27.

Hargreaves, A. (1981) *The Colonial Experience in French Fiction*, London.

Hartman, M. S. and Banner, L. (eds) (1974) *Clio's Consciousness Raised: New Perspectives on the History of Women*, London.

Hause, S. (1987) 'More Minerva than Mars: the French women's rights campaign and the First World War', in M. Higgonet, J. Jenson, S. Michel and M. C. Weitz (eds) *Behind the Lines: Gender and the Two World Wars*, New Haven.

Hause, S. (1978) 'Women who rallied to the Tricolor: the effects of World War 1 on the French women's suffrage movement', *Proceedings of the Annual Meeting of the Western Society for French History* 6: 371–8.

Hause, S. and Kenney, A. R. (1981) 'The limits of suffragist behaviour: legalism and militancy in France, 1876–1922', *American Historical Review* 85, 4: 781–806.

Hemingway, A. (1993) 'Gender, genius and progress: Benthamism and the arts in the 1820s', *Art History* 16, 4: 619–46.

Hertz, D. (1978) 'Salonières and literary women', *New German Critique* 14: 97–108.

Herzog, D. (1990) 'Liberalism, religious dissent and women's rights: Louise Dittmar's writings from the 1840s', in K. Jarausch and L. Jones (eds) *In Search of a Liberal Germany: Studies in the History of German Liberalism from 1789 to the Present*, New York.

Herzog, D. (1996) *Intimacy and Exclusion: Religious Politics in Pre-Revolutionary Baden*, Princeton.

Hesse, C. (1989) 'Female authorship and revolutionary law', *Eighteenth Century Studies* 3: 469–87.

Higgonet, M., Jenson, J., Michel, S. and Weitz, M. C. (eds) (1987) *Behind the Lines: Gender and the Two World Wars*, New Haven.

Hill, B. (1987) *Eighteenth Century Women*, London.

Hitchcock, T. (1996) 'Redefining sex in eighteenth-century England', *History Workshop Journal* **41**: 73–92.

Hobsbawm, E. J. (1962) *The Age of Revolution, 1789–1848*, New York.

Hobsbawm, E. J. (1987) *The Age of Empire 1870–1914*, London.

Holt, R. (1991) 'Women, men and sport in France, c. 1870–1914: an introductory survey', *Journal of Sport History* **18**, 1: 121–34.

Horn, D. G. (1994) *Social Bodies: Science Reproduction and Italian Modernity*, Princeton.

Horne, J. (1993) 'Social identity in war: France 1914–1918', in T. G. Fraser and K. Jeffery (eds) *Men, Women and War*, Dublin.

Howard, J. (1978) 'The woman question in Italy 1861–1880', Ph.D. thesis, Ann Arbor.

Howard, J. (1980) 'Patriot mothers in the post-Risorgimento: women after the Italian revolution', in C. R. Berkin and C. M. Lovett (eds) *Women War and Revolution*, New York.

Hufton, O. (1992) *Women and the Limits of Citizenship in the French Revolution*, Toronto.

Hufton, O. (1995) *The Prospect Before Her: A History of Women in Western Europe*, London.

Hull, I. (1996) *Sexuality, State, and Civil Society in Germany, 1700–1815*, Ithaca.

Hunt, L. (1983) 'Hercules and the radical image in the French Revolution', *Representations* **2** (Spring): 95–117.

Hunt, L. (1984) *Politics, Culture and Class in the French Revolution*, Berkeley.

Hunt, L. (1992) *The Family Romance of the French Revolution*, Berkeley.

Hurwitz, E. F. (1977) 'The international sisterhood', in R. Bridenthal, C. Koonz and S. Stuard (eds) *Becoming Visible: Women in European History*, Boston.

Jackson, M. (1994) *The Real Facts of Life: Feminism and the Politics of Sexuality, c. 1850–1940*, London.

Jacobus, M. I. (1992) 'Incorruptible milk: breast-feeding and the French revolution', in S. E. Melzer and L. W. Rabine (eds) *Rebel Daughters: Women and the French Revolution*, New York.

Jalland, P. and Hooper, J. (eds) (1986) *Woman from Life to Death: The Female Life Cycle in Britain, 1780–1914*, Brighton.

Joeres, R. B. and Maynes, M. J. (eds) (1986) *German Women in the 18th and 19th Centuries: A Social and Literary History*, Bloomington.

John, A. V. (1986) *Unequal Opportunities: Women's Employment in England 1800–1918*, Oxford.

Johnson, C. (1995) *Equivocal Beings: Politics, Gender, and Sentimentality in the 1790s*, Chicago.

Jolly, M. (1993) 'Colonizing women: the maternal body and empire', in S. Gunew and A. Yeatman (eds) *Feminism and the Politics of Difference*, Sydney.

Jones, M. G. (1952) *Hannah More*, London.

Jordanova, L. (1990) *Sexual Visions: Images of Gender in Science and Medicine Between the Eighteenth and Twentieth Centuries*, London.

Jordanova, L. (1992) 'Body images', *Art History* 15, 4: 537–41.

Kahn-Hut, R., Kaplan Daniels, A. and Colvard, R. (1982) *Women and Work: Problems and Perspectives*, New York.

Kaplan, M. (1982) 'Tradition and transition', in L. Baeck (ed.) *Institute Yearbook* 27: 3–36.

Kelikian, A. (1996) 'Science, gender and moral ascendancy in liberal Italy', *Journal of Modern Italian Studies* 1, 3: 377–89.

Kennedy, R. E. (1973) *Irish Emigration Marriage and Fertility*, Berkeley.

Kent, S. K. (1993) *Making Peace: the Reconstruction of Gender in inter-war Britain*, Princeton.

Kern, S. (1983) *The Culture of Time and Space 1880–1918*, Cambridge, Mass.

Kirkham, M. (1983) *Jane Austen: Feminism and Fiction*, Brighton.

Klaus, A. (1993) 'Depopulation and race suicide: materialism and pronatalist ideologies in France and the United States', in S. Koven and S. Michel (eds) *Mothers of a New World*, London and New York.

Koos, C. A. (1996) 'Gender, anti-individualism, and nationalism: the Alliance Nationale and the pronatalist backlash against the femme moderne', *French Historical Studies* 19, 3: 699–723.

Korppi-Tommola, A. (1990) 'Fighting together for freedom: nationalism, socialism, feminism, and women's suffrage in Finland 1906', *Scandinavian Journal of History* 15, 3: 181–91.

Koven, S. and Michel, S. (1990) 'Womanly duties: maternalist politics and the origins of the welfare state in France, Germany, Great Britain and the U.S. 1880–1920', *American Historical Review* 95, 4: 1076–1108.

Koven, S. and Michel, S. (eds) (1993) *Mothers of a New World: Maternalist Politics and the Origins of Welfare States*, New York.

Kowaleski-Wallace, E. (1991) *Their Father's Daughters: Hannah More, Maria Edgeworth, and Patriarchal Complicity*, New York.

Landes, J. (1988) *Women and the Public Sphere in the Age of the French Revolution*, Ithaca.

Landes, J. (1992) 'Representing the body politic: the paradox of gender in the graphic politics of the French revolution', in S. E. Meizer and L. W. Rabine (eds) *Rebel Daughters: Women and the French Revolution*, New York and Oxford.

Laqueur, T. (1990) *Making Sex: Body and Gender from the Greeks to Freud*, Cambridge, Mass.

Laqueur, T. (1992) 'Sexual desire and the market economy during the industrial revolution', in D. C. Stanton (ed.) *Discourses of Sexuality from Aristotle to AIDS*, Ann Arbor.

La Vigna, C. (1987) 'The Marxist ambivalence toward women: between socialism and feminism in the Italian Socialist Party', in M. Boxer and J. H. Quataert (eds) *Socialist Women*, New York.

Layton, L. (1987) 'Vera Brittain's Testament(s)', in M. Higgonet, J. Jenson, S. Michel and M. C. Weitz (eds) *Behind the Lines: Gender and the Two World Wars*, New Haven.

Lee, R. (1981) 'The German family: a critical survey of the current state of historical research on the German family', in R. J. Evans and W. R. Lee (eds) *Essays on the Social History of the Family in Nineteenth- and Twentieth-Century Germany*, London.

Lloyd, G. (1984) *The 'Man of Reason': Male and Female in Western Philosophy*, Sydney.

Lorence-Kot, B. (1987) 'Klementya Tanska Hoffmanowa cultural nationalism and a new formula for Polish womanhood', *History of European Ideas* 8, 4/5: 435–50.

Lougee, C. C. (1976) *Le Paradis des Femmes: Women, Salons, and Stratification in Seventeenth Century France*, Princeton.

Lown, J. (1990) *Women and Industrialization: Gender at Work in Nineteenth-Century England*, Cambridge.

McBride, T. (1976) *The Domestic Revolution: The Modernization of Household Service in England and France, 1820–1920*, New York.

Mackenzie, J. (1987) 'The imperial pioneer and hunter and the British masculine stereotype', in J. A. Mangan (ed.) *Manliness and Morality*, New York.

McLaren, A. (1978) 'Abortion in France: women and the regulation of family size 1800–1914', *French Historical Studies* 10, 3: 461–85.

McLelland, K. (1989) 'Some thoughts on masculinity and the "representative artisan" in Britain, 1850–1880', *Gender and History* 1, 2: 164–77.

McMillan, J. (1988) 'Women, religion and politics: the Ligue Patriotique des Francaises', *Western Society for French History* 15: 355–64.

McPhee, P. (1997) 'Towards a sesquicentennial: the gendered body politic and the French revolution of 1848', unpublished ms, University of Melbourne.

Mangan, J. A. (1986) *The Games Ethic and Imperialism: Aspects of the Diffusion of an Ideal*, Harmondsworth.

Mangan, J. A. (1992) 'Men, masculinity, and sexuality: some recent literature', *Journal of the History of Sexuality* 3, 2: 303–13.

Mangan, J. A. (1996) 'Duty unto death: English masculinity and militarism in the age of new imperialism', in J. A. Mangan (ed.) *Tribal Identities: Nationalism, Europe, Sport*, London.

Marshall, B. L. (1994) *Engendering Modernity: Feminism, Social Theory and Social Change*, Cambridge.

Matarelli, S. (1991) 'Idées d'empire en Italie pendant la grande guerre', *Guerres Mondiales et Conflits Contemporains* **41**, 161: 21–30.

Maugue, A. 'The New Eve and the Old Adam', in C. Fraisse and M. Perrot (eds) *A History of Women*, vol. 4, Cambridge, Mass.

Mayer, A. J. (1981) *The Persistence of the Old Regime: Europe to the Great War*, New York.

Meinander, H. (1992) 'Towards a bourgeois manhood: Nordic views and visions of physical education for boys, 1860–1930', *International Journal of the History of Sport* **9**, 3: 337–55.

Mellor, A. K. (ed.) (1988) *Romanticism and Feminism*, Bloomington.

Mellor, A. K. (1993) *Romanticism and Gender*, New York and London.

Melzer, S. E. and Rabine, L. W. (eds) (1992) *Rebel Daughters: Women and the French Revolution*, New York and Oxford.

Miller, C. (1994) 'Geneva – the key to equality: inter-war feminists and the League of Nations', *Women's History Review* **3**, 2: 219–45.

Miller, M. B. (1981) *The Bon Marché: Bourgeois Culture and the Department Store, 1869–1920*, Princeton.

Mohrmann, R. (1977) *Die Andere Frau*, Stuttgart.

Moon, J. S. (1978) 'Feminism and socialism: the Utopian synthesis of Flora Tristan', in M. Boxer and J. Quaetert (eds), *Socialist Women: European Socialist Feminism in the Nineteenth and Twentieth Centuries*, New York.

Mosedale, S. (1978) 'Science corrupted: Victorian biologists consider the woman question', *Journal of History of Biology* **11**, 1: 1–55.

Moses, C. (1982) 'Saint-Simonian men/Saint-Simonian women: the transformation of feminist thought in 1830s France', *Journal of Modern History* **54**, 1: 240–67.

Moses, C. (1984) *French Feminism in the Nineteenth Century*, Albany, New York.

Moses, C. and Rabine, L. (1993) *Feminism, Socialism and French Romanticism*, Bloomington.

Mosse, G. (1964) *The Crisis of German Ideology: Intellectual Origins of the Third Reich*, New York.

Mosse, G. (1980) *Masses and Man: Nationalist and Fascist Perceptions of Reality*, New York.

Mosse, G. (1985) *Nationalism and Sexuality: Respectability and Abnormal Sexuality in Modern Europe*, New York.

Mosse, G. (1996) *The Image of Man: The Creation of Modern Masculinity*, New York.

Nava, M. (1996) 'Women, the city and the department store', in A. O'Shea (ed.) *Modern Times: A Century of English Modernity*, London.

Nelson, C. and Sumner Holmes, A. (eds) (1997) *Maternal Instincts: Visions of Motherhood and Sexuality in Britain, 1875–1925*, London.

Neubauer, J. (1991) *The Fin-de-Siècle Culture of Adolescence*, New Haven.

Nicholson, L. (1986) *Gender and History: The Limits of Social Theory in the Age of the Family*, New York.

Nolte, C. E. (1993) ' "Every Czech a sokol!": feminism and nationalism in the Czech Sokol Movement', *Austrian History Yearbook* 21: 79–100.

Nye, R. (1975) *Origins of Crowd Psychology: Gustave Le Bon and the Crisis of Mass Democracy in the Third Republic*, London.

Nye, R. (1984) *Crime Madness and Modern Politics in France: The Medical Concept of a National Decline*, Princeton.

Nye, R. (1993) *Masculinity and Male Codes of Honor in Modern France*, Oxford.

Offen, K. (1984) 'Depopulation, nationalism, and feminism in fin-de-siècle France', *American Historical Review* 89: 648-76.

Offen, K. (1986) 'Ernest Legouve and the doctrine of equality in difference for women: a case study of male feminism in 19th century French thought', *Journal of Modern History* 58: 452–82.

Offen, K. (1987a) 'A nineteenth-century French feminist rediscovered: Jenny P. de Hericourt, 1809–1875', *Signs* 13, 1: 144–58.

Offen, K. (1987b) 'Liberty, equality, and justice for women: the theory and practice of feminism in nineteenth-century Europe', in R. Bridenthal, C. Koonz and S. Stuard (eds) *Becoming Visible: Women in European History*, Boston.

Oppenheim, J. (1994) 'Victorian and Edwardian women: the halves of modern English social history', *Journal of Modern History* 66, 1: 79–91.

Osterud, N. G. (1991) 'Gender and industrialisation', *Gender and History* 3, 1: 97–103.

Osterud, N. G. (1986) 'Gender division and the organization of work in the Leicester hosiery industry', in A. John (ed.) *Unequal Opportunities: Women's Employment in England 1800–1918*, Oxford.

Ottaviano, C. (1982) 'Antonio Labriola e il problema dell'espansione coloniale', *Annali della Fondazione Luigi Einuadi* 16: 305–28.

Outram, D. (1989) *The Body and the French Revolution: Sex, Class and Political Culture*, New Haven.

Pateman, C. (1989) *The Disorder of Women*, Oxford.

Paulsell, P. (1976) 'The relationship of "Young Germany" to questions of women's rights', Ph.D. thesis, University of Michigan.

Pedersen, J. E. (1996) 'Regulating abortion and birth control: gender, medicine, and Republican politics in France, 1870–1920', *French Historical Studies* 19, 3: 673–98.

Pedersen, S. (1991) 'National bodies, unspeakable acts: the sexual politics of colonial policy-making', *Journal of Modern History* 63: 647–80.

Perrot, M. and G. Fraisse (eds) (1989) *History of Private Life: IV*, trans. A. Goldhammer, Cambridge, Mass.

Perrot, M. (1993) *A History of Women in the West Vol. 4: Emerging Feminism from Revolution to World War*, Cambridge, Mass.

Perry, R. (1991) 'Colonizing the breast: sexuality and maternity in eighteenth-century England', *Journal of the History of Sexuality* 2, 2: 204–34.

Phillips, A. and Taylor, B. (1980) 'Sex and skill: notes towards a feminist economics', *Feminist Review* 6.

Pick, D. (1989) *Faces of Degeneration: A European Disorder, c.1848–c.1918*, New York.

Picq, F. (1986) 'Bourgeois feminism in France', in J. Friedlander, B. Weisen Cook, A. Kessler-Harris and C. Smith-Rosenburg (eds) *Women in Culture and Politics: A Century of Change*, Bloomington.

Pierard, R. V. (1971) 'The transportation of white women to German Southwest Africa 1898–1914', *Race* 7, 3: 317–22.

Pieroni Bortolotti, F. (1975) *Alle origine del movimento femminile in Italia 1848–1892*, Torino.

Pilbeam, P. (1990) *The Middle Classes in Europe 1789–1914: France, Germany, Italy and Russia*, London.

Pinchbeck, I. (1981 [1930]) *Women Workers and the Industrial Revolution*, London.

Polasky, J. L. (1986) 'Women in revolutionary Belgium: from stone throwers to hearth tenders', *History Workshop* 21: 87–104.

Poovey, M. (1989) *Uneven Developments: The Ideological Work of Gender in mid-Victorian England*, London.

Poovey, M. (1993) 'Exploring masculinities', *Victorian Studies* 36, 2: 223–6.

Poovey, M. (1995) *Making a Social Body: British Cultural Formation, 1830–1864*, Chicago.

Pope, B. C. (1994) 'Female troubles and troubled men in eighteenth- and nineteenth-century France', *Journal of Women's History* 6, 3: 126–31.

Portemer, J. (1959) 'Le statut de la femme en France, depuis la reformation des coutumes jusqu'à la redaction du code civil', *Recueils de la Société Jean Bodin pour l'histoire comparative des institutions* 12: 447–97.

Porter, R. and Hall, L. (1995) *The Facts of Life: The Creation of Sexual Knowledge in Britain, 1650–1950*, New Haven and London.

Prasch, T. J. (1995) 'Orientalism's other, other orientalisms: women in the scheme of the Empire', *Journal of Women's History* 7, 4: 175–88.

Proctor, C. E. (1990) *Women, Equality, and the French Revolution*, New York.

Pugh, E. (1982) 'Florence Nightingale and J. S. Mill debate women's rights', *Journal of British Studies* 21, 2: 118–38.

Quataert, J. H. (*c.* 1978) 'Unequal partners in an uneasy alliance: women and the working class in Imperial Germany', in M. J. Boxer and J. H. Quataert (eds) *Socialist Women*, New York.

Quataert, J. H. and Boxer, M. J. (eds) (1987) *Connecting Spheres: Women in the Western World, 1500 to the Present*, New York.

Quine, M. S. (1996) *Population Politics in Twentieth Century Europe: Fascist Dictatorships and Liberal Democracies*, London and New York.

Ramusack, B. N. (1992) 'Cultural missionaries, maternal imperialists, feminist allies', in N. Chaudhuri and M. Strobel (eds) *Western Women and Imperialism: Complicity and Resistance*, Bloomington.

Reagin, N. R. A. (1995) *German Women's Movement: Class and Gender in Hanover 1880–1933*, Chapel Hill.

Reggiani, A. H. (1996) 'Procreating France: the politics of demography, 1919–1945', *French Historical Studies* 19, 3: 725–54.

Rendall, J. (1985) *The Origins of Modern Feminism: Women in Britain, France and the United States*, Basingstoke.

Reynolds, K. and Hume, N. (1993) *Victorian Heroines: Representations of Femininity in Nineteenth-Century Literature and Art*, New York.

Reynolds, S. (1986) 'Marianne's citizens? Women, the republic and universal suffrage in France', in S. Reynolds (ed.) *Women, State and Revolution*, Brighton.

Riley, D. (1988) *Am I That Name? Feminism and the Category 'Woman' in History*, Minnesota.

Rizzo, T. (1988) 'Sexual violence in the enlightenment: the state, the bourgeoisie, and the cult of the victimized woman', *Western Society for French History* 15: 122–9.

Rochat, G. (1974) *Il colonialismo Italiano*, Torino.

Rodin Pucci, S. (1990) 'The discrete charms of the exotic: fictions of the harem in 18th century France', in R. Porter and M. Teich (eds) *Exoticism in the Enlightenment*, Manchester and New York.

Rohents, W. (1989) *Prophet in Exile: Joseph Mazzini in England, 1837–1868*, New York.

Roper, M. and Tosh, J. (eds) (1991) *Manful Assertions: Masculinities in Britain since 1800*, London.

Rose, S. O. (1992) *Limited Livelihoods, Gender and Class in Nineteenth Century England*, Berkeley.

Rose, S. O. (1993) 'Gender and labor history: the nineteenth century legacy', *International Review of Social History* 38, 1: 145–62.

Ross, E. (1993) *Love and Toil: Motherhood in Outcast London, 1870–1918*, New York.

Rupp, L. (1997) *Worlds of Women: The Making of an International Women's Movement*, Princeton.

Ryan, J. (1994) 'Women, modernity and the city', *Theory, Culture and Society* 11: 35–68.

Sachsse, C. (1986) *Mutterlichkeit alls Beruf. Sozialreform und Frauenbewegung 1871–1929*, Franfkfurt am Main.

Saurer, E. (1993) 'Frauengeschichte in Osterreich', *Homme* 4, 2: 37–63.

Scaraffia, L. (1991) *Donna o cosa. I movimenti femminili dal risorgimento a oggi*, Torino.

Scheibinger, L. (1989) *The Mind Has No Sex? Women in the Origins of Modern Science*, Cambridge, Mass.

Schmidt-Linsenhoff, V. (ed.) (1989) *Sklavin oder Burgerin? Franzosische Revolution und Neue Weiblichkeit 1760–1830*, Frankfurt am Main.

Schreiner, O. (1994) 'Introduction to the life of Mary Wollstonecraft and the rights of women', *History Workshop* 37: 189–93.

Schulkind, E. (1950) 'Le role des femmes dans la commune de 1871–1848', *Revue des Revolutions Contemporaines* 42: 15–29.

Schwarz, Gudrun (1986) ' "Viragos" in male theory in nineteenth-century Germany', in J. Friedlander, B. Wiesen Cook, A. Kessler-Harris and C. Smith-Rosenburg (eds) *Women in Culture and Politics: A Century of Change*, Bloomington.

Scott, J. and Tilly, L. (1975) 'Women's work and the family in nineteenth-century Europe', *Comparative Studies in Society and History* 17: 36–64.

Scott, J .W. (1995) 'Universalism and the history of feminism', *Differences* 7, 1: 1–14.

Scott, J. W. (1988) *Gender and the Politics of History*, New York.

Scott, J. W. (1989) 'French feminists and the Rights of "Man": Olympe de Gouges's Declarations', *History Workshop Journal* 28: 1–21.

Scott, J. W. (1993) 'The woman worker', in M. Perrot (ed.) *History of Women in the West: Emerging Feminism from Revolution to World War*, Cambridge, Mass.

Scott, J. W. (ed.) (1996a) *Feminism and History*, Oxford.

Scott, J. W. (1996b) *Only Paradoxes to Offer: French Feminists and the Rights of Man*, Cambridge, Mass.

Searle, G. R. (1976) *Eugenics and Politics in Britain, 1900–1914*, Leyden.

Secci, L. (1984) 'German women writers and the revolution of 1848', in J. C. Fout (ed.) *German Women in the Nineteenth Century: A Social History*, New York.

Sewell, W. (1988) 'Le citoyen/la citoyenne: activity, passivity, and the revolutionary concept of citizenship', in C. Lucas (ed.) *The French Revolution and the Creation of Modern Political Culture, Vol. 2: The Political Culture of the French Revolution*, Oxford.

Shapiro, A. (1996) *Breaking the Codes: Female Criminality in Fin-de-Siècle Paris*, Stanford.

Sherrick, R. (1982) 'Towards universal sisterhood', *Women's Studies International Forum*, 5, 6: 655–61.

Shires, L. (1994) 'Of maenads, mothers and feminized males: Victorian readings of the French Revolution', in L. Shires (ed.) *Rewriting the Victorians: Theory, History and the Politics of Gender*, New York.

Shorter, E. (1973) 'Female emancipation, birth control, and fertility in European history', *American Historical Review* 78, 3: 605–40.

Shorter, E. (1976) *The Making of the Modern Family*, London.

Showalter, E. (1987) 'Rivers and Sassoon: the inscription of male gender anxieties', in

M. Higonnet, J. Jenson, S. Michel and M. C. Weitz (eds) *Behind the Lines: Gender and the Two World Wars*, New Haven.

Showalter, E. (1991) *Sexual Anarchy. Gender and Culture at the Fin-de-Siècle*, London.

Sinha, M. (1995) *Colonial Masculinity: The 'Manly Englishman' and the 'Effeminate Bengali' in the Late Nineteenth Century*, Manchester and New York.

Smith, B. G. (1981) *Ladies of the Leisure Class: The Bourgeoises of Northern France in the Nineteenth Century*, Princeton.

Smith, P. (1996) *Feminism and the Third Republic: Women's Political and Civil Rights in France, 1918–1945*, Oxford.

Smith-Rosenberg, C. (1989) 'Discourses of sexuality and subjectivity: the new woman, 1870–1936', in M. Duberman, M. Vicinus and C. Chauncy (eds) *Hidden from History: Reclaiming the Gay and Lesbian Past*, New York.

Sohn, A. (1986) 'Catholic women and political affairs: the case of the patriotic league of French women', in J. Friedlander, B. Weisen Cook, A. Kessler-Harris and C. Smith-Rosenburg (eds) *Women in Culture and Politics: A Century of Change*, Bloomington.

Soloway, R. (1990) *Demography and Degeneration: Eugenics and the Declining Birthrate in Twentieth-Century Britain*, Chapel Hill.

Sowerwine, C. (1987) 'The socialist women's movement from 1850 to 1940', in R. Bridenthal, C. Koonz and S. Stuard (eds) *Becoming Visible: Women in European History*, Boston.

Spencer, S. I. (ed.) (1984) *French Women and the Age of Enlightenment*, Bloomington.

Sperber, J. (1994) *The European Revolutions, 1848–1851*, Cambridge.

Stargardt, N. (1994) *The German Idea of Militarism*, Cambridge.

Stark, G. D. (1981) 'Pornography, society and the law in Imperial Germany', *Central European History* 14: 200–29.

Starr Guilloton, D. (1987) 'Toward a new freedom: Rahel Varnhagen and the German women writers before 1848', in A. Goldberger (ed.) *Woman as Mediatrix*, New York.

Steinbrugge, L. (1995) *The Moral Sex: Women's Nature in the French Enlightenment*, trans. P. Selwyn, New York.

Stewart, M. L. (1989) *Women, Work and the French State: Labour, Protection and Social Patriarchy*, Montreal.

Stites, R. (1978) *The Women's Liberation Movement in Russia: Feminism, Nihilism and Bolshevism 1860–1930*, Princeton.

Stoehr, I. (1991) 'Housework and motherhood: debates and policies in the women's movement in Imperial and Weimar Germany', in G. Bock and P. Thane (eds) *Maternity and Gender Policies: Women and the Rise of the European Welfare States 1880–1950s*, London and New York.

Stoler, A. L. (1997) 'Sexual affronts and racial frontiers: European identities and the cultural politics of exclusion in colonial Southeast Asia', in F. Cooper and A. L. Stoler (eds) *Tensions of Empire: Colonial Cultures in a Bourgeois World*, Berkeley.

Stone, J. (1995) 'The Republican brotherhood: gender and ideology', in E. A. Accampo, R. G. Fuchs and M. L. Stewart (eds) *Gender and the Politics of Social Reform in France, 1870–1914*, Baltimore.

Strobel, M. (1991) *European Women and the Second British Empire*, Bloomington.

Strumingher, L. (1987) 'The Vesuviennes: images of women warriors in 1848 and their significance for French history', *History of European Ideas* 8, 4/5: 451–88.

Strumingher, L. (1989) 'The struggle for unity among Parisian women: the Voix des Femmes, March–June 1848', *History of European Ideas* 11: 273–88.

Taricone, F. (1991) 'L'associazionismo femminile italiano. Il consiglio nazionale della donne italiane', *Bolletino della domus mazziniana* 37, 2: 195–215.

Taricone, F. (1994) *Teresa Labriola. Biographica politica di un'intellettuala tra Ottocento e Novecento*, Milano.

Taylor, B. (1983) *Eve and the New Jerusalem: Socialism and Feminism in the Nineteenth Century*, London.

Taylor, B. (1992) 'Mary Wollstonecraft and the wild wish of early feminism', *History Workshop Journal* 33: 197–219.

Teich, M. and Porter, R. (eds) (1990) *Fin de Siècle and its Legacy*, Cambridge.

Thalman, R. (1990) *Entre Emancipation et Nationalisme, la Presse Feminine D'Europe 1914–1945*, Paris.

Thebaud, F. (1986) *La Femme au temps de la guerre de 14*, Paris.

Thebaud, F. (1994) 'The Great War and the triumph of sexual division', in F. Thebaud, (ed.) *A History of Women in the West, Volume V: Toward a Cultural Identity in the Twentieth Century*, Cambridge, Mass.; London.

Theweleit, K. (*c.* 1987–8) *Male Fantasies, Vols I and II* Minneapolis.

Thompson, D. (1987) 'Woman, work and politics in nineteenth-century England: the problem of authority', in J. Rendall (ed.) *Equal or Different. Women's Politics 1800–1914*, Oxford.

Tickner, L. (1989) *Spectacle of Women: The Imagery of the Suffrage Campaign, 1907–1917*, London.

Tilly, L. and Scott, J. (1978) *Women, Work and Family*, New York.

Tomaselli, S. (1995) 'Responses to the French Revolution', *Gender and History* 7, 2: 315–20.

Tosh, J. (1991) 'Domesticity and manliness in the Victorian middle class: the family of Edward White Benson', in M. Roper and J. Tosh (eds) *Manful Assertions: Masculinities in Britain since 1800*, London.

Tosh, J. (1994) 'What should historians do with masculinity? Reflections on 19th century Britain', *History Workshop* 38: 179–202.

Townsend, C. (1993) 'I am the woman for spirit: a working woman's gender transgression in Victorian London', *Victorian Studies* 36, 3: 293–314.

Tylee, C. (1990) *The Great War and Women's Resistance to Militarism: Images of Militarism and Womanhood in Women's Writings, 1914–1964*, Basingstoke.

Veauvy, C. and Pisano, L. (eds) (1997) *Paroles Oubliées. Les femmes et la construction de l'Etat-nation en France et en Italie 1789–1860*, Paris.

Vidler, A. (1994) 'Psychopathologies of modern space: metropolitan fear from agoraphobia to estrangement', in M. S. Roth (ed.) *Recovering History: Culture, Politics and the Psyche*, Stanford.

Waelti-Walters, J. (1987) 'New women in the novels of Belle Epoque France', *History of European Ideas* 8, 4/5: 537–48.

Walkowitz, J. R. (1980) *Prostitution and Victorian Society: Women, Class and the State*, Cambridge.

Walkowitz, J. R. (1992) *City of Dreadful Delight: Narrative of Sexual Danger in Late Victorian England*, London.

Wambaugh, S. (1933) *Plebiscites since the World War: With a Collection of Official Documents, vol. 1*, Washington.

Ware, V. (1992) *Beyond the Pale: White Women, Racism and History*, London and New York.

Weber, E. (1986) *France: Fin de Siècle*, Cambridge, Mass.

Weeks, J. (1977) *Coming Out: Homosexual Politics in Britain from the Nineteenth Century to the Present*, London.

Weeks, J. (1989) *Sex, Politics and Society: The Regulation of Sexuality since 1800*, London.

Wertheim, M. (1995) *Pythagoras' Trousers: God, Physics, and the Gender Wars*, New York.

Wildenthal, L. (1993) ' "She is the victor": bourgeois women, nationalist identities and the ideal of the independent woman farmer in German Southwest Africa', *Social Analysis* 33: 68–88.

Wildenthal, L. (1997) 'Race, gender, and citizenship in the German Colonial Empire', in A. L. Stoler and F. Cooper (eds) *Tensions of Empire: Colonial Cultures in a Bourgeois World*, Berkeley.

Williams, R. H. (1982) *Dream Worlds: Mass Consumption in Late Nineteenth Century France*, Berkeley.

Wilson, E. (1991) *The Sphinx in the City: Urban Life, the Control of Disorder, and Women*, Berkeley.

Wiltsher, A. (1985) *Most Dangerous Women Feminist Peace Campaigners of the Great War*, London.

Wishnia, J. (1989) 'Women and the anti-war movement in World War 1', *Western Society for French History* 16: 339–44.

Wolff, J. (1989) 'The invisible *flâneuse*: woman and the literature of modernity', in A. Benjamin (ed.) *The Problems of Modernity*, London.

Wollacott, A. (1994a) 'Khaki fever', *Journal of Contemporary History* **29**, 2: 325–47.

Wollacott, A. (1994b) *On Her Their Lives Depend: Munition Workers in the Great War*, Berkeley.

Worsnop, J. (1990) 'A reevaluation of "The problem of surplus women" in 19th-century England', *Women's Studies International Forum* **13**, 1/2: 21–31.

Yaeger, P. S. and Kowalski-Wallace, B. (1990) *Refiguring the Father: New Feminist Readings of Patriarchy*, Carbondale.

Yates, G. G. (ed.) (1985) *Harriet Martineau on Women*, New Brunswick.

Zantop, S. (1997) *Colonial Fantasies: Conquest, Family, and Nation in Precolonial Germany, 1770–1870*, Durham.

Zevaes, A. (1931) 'Une candidature feministe en 1849', *La revolution de 1848 et les revolutions du XIXe siècle, 1830, 1848, 1870*, Paris.

Zucker, S. (1991) *Kathinka Zitz-Halein and Female Civic Activism in Mid-Nineteenth-Century Germany*, Carbondale and Edwardsville.

Index